ACTIVITIES AND ASSIGNMENTS: *Balance the Traditional and More Interactive*

- Teacher presents material ▶ Students read, write, and talk every day ▶ Students actively experience concepts
- Whole-class teaching ▶ Small-group instruction ▶ Wide variety of activities, balancing individual work, small groups, and whole-class activities
- Uniform curriculum for all ▶ Jigsawed curriculum (different but related topics according to kids' needs or choices)
- Light coverage of wide range of subjects ▶ Intensive, deep study of selected topics
- Short-term lessons, one day at a time ▶ Extended activities; multiday, multistep projects
- Isolated subject lessons ▶ Integrated, thematic, cross-disciplinary inquiries
- Focus on memorization and recall of facts ▶ Focus on applying knowledge and problem solving
- Short responses, fill-in-the-blank exercises ▶ Complex responses, evaluations, writing, performances, artwork
- Identical assignments for all ▶ Differentiated curriculum for all styles and abilities

STUDENT WORK AND ASSESSMENT: *Inform Teachers, Students, Parents*

- Products created for teachers and grading ▶ Products created for real events and audiences
- Classroom/hallway displays: No student work posted ▶ "A" papers only ▶ All students represented
- Identical, imitative products displayed ▶ Varied and original products displayed
- Teacher feedback via scores and grades ▶ Teacher feedback and conferences are substantive and formative
- Products are seen and rated only by teachers ▶ Public exhibitions and performances are common
- Data kept private in teacher gradebook ▶ Work kept in student-maintained portfolios
- All assessment by teachers ▶ Student self-assessment an official element ▶ Parents are involved
- Standards set during grading ▶ Standards available in advance ▶ Standards codeveloped with students

TEACHER ATTITUDE AND OUTLOOK: *Take Professional Initiative*

Relationship with students is:

- Distant, impersonal, fearful ▶ Positive, warm, respectful, encouraging
- Judging ▶ Understanding, empathizing, inquiring, and guiding
- Directive ▶ Consultative

Attitude toward self is:

- Powerless worker ▶ Risk taker/experimenter ▶ Creative, active professional
- Solitary adult ▶ Member of team with other adults in school ▶ Member of networks beyond school
- Staff development recipient ▶ Director of own professional growth

View of role is:

- Expert, presenter, gatekeeper ▶ Coach, mentor, model, guide

The *Seven Structures* of
Best Practice Teaching

All of these seven teaching structures are simple, effective, and time-tested. While they can profoundly shift the classroom balance from teacher-directed to student-centered learning, many of them are actually quite easy to implement; they are easy to begin, easy to slot into the existing teaching day, easy to experiment with incrementally. Indeed, far from requiring teachers to master a huge inventory of technical instructional methods, **Best Practice** largely means returning to some fundamental, perhaps mistakenly discarded approaches, and fine-tuning them until they work. These straightforward and replicable structures are very powerful: they can effectively take the teacher offstage, decentralize the classroom, and transfer responsibility for active learning to the students in any subject, at any grade level.

1. **Gradual release of responsibility**

2. **Classroom workshop**

3. **Strategic thinking**

4. **Collaborative activities**

5. **Integrative units**

6. **Representing to learn**

7. **Formative-reflective assessment**

FOURTH EDITION

Best Practice

Bringing Standards to Life in America's Classrooms

Steven Zemelman
Harvey "Smokey" Daniels
Arthur Hyde

Heinemann
Portsmouth, NH

Heinemann
361 Hanover Street
Portsmouth, NH 03801–3912
www.heinemann.com

Offices and agents throughout the world

The authors and publisher wish to thank those who have generously given permission to reprint borrowed material in this book:

Figure 2.2: "Optimal Learning Model" from *Regie Routman in Residence: Transforming Our Teaching*, DVD-based literacy series by Regie Routman. Copyright © 2008 by Regie Routman. Published by Heinemann, Portsmouth, NH. Reprinted by permission of the author.

(credits continue on page xvi)

Library of Congress Cataloging-in-Publication Data
Zemelman, Steven.
    Best practice : bringing standards to life in America's classrooms / Steven Zemelman, Harvey "Smokey" Daniels, and Arthur Hyde.—4th ed.
        p. cm.
    Includes bibliographical references and index.
    ISBN 978-0-325-04354-8
    ISBN 0-325-04354-X
1. Teaching—United States—Case studies. 2. Direct instruction—United States—Case studies. 3. Active learning—United States—Case studies. 4. Teaching—Standards—United States. 5. Education—Curricula—Standards—United States. 6. Educational change—United States. I. Daniels, Harvey. II. Hyde, Arthur A. III. Title.
    LB1025.3.Z46 2012
    371.102—dc23   2011047860

Acquisitions Editor: Tina Miller
Production Editor: Patricia Adams
Cover and Interior Design: Lisa Fowler
Typesetter: Kim Arney
Manufacturing: Steve Bernier

Printed in the United States of America on acid-free paper
16 15 14 13 12 VP 1 2 3 4 5

Contents

PART 2 *Best Practice Across the Curriculum*

▶ **The *Best Practice Video Companion*—Coming Fall 2012**

The *Best Practice Video Companion* will include short, lively video clips of students and teachers at work in outstanding classrooms for authentic illustrations of each key strategy described in the book. For education courses, PLCs, teacher book clubs, and communities of practice, it will provide brief and specific looks at the learning activities discussed in *Best Practice*, Fourth Edition. This resource will make concrete what is involved in great teaching and learning. Watch Heinemann.com for more information.

Welcome, Colleagues

This is a book about excellent teaching and powerful learning. Its principles come from authoritative and reliable sources—the major professional organizations, research centers, and subject-matter groups in American education. Its recommendations draw upon scientific research of rigorous design, both experimental and qualitative. The classroom stories woven through the book come from some of the country's most accomplished teachers. And the practices endorsed here have proven effective with students from kindergarten through high school, across the curriculum, and among learners of diverse languages, abilities, backgrounds, and learning styles.

This book is for everyone in education—for young teachers just entering their training; for principals, administrators, instructional coaches, parents, and school board members; for researchers and policy makers and politicians; and even for old-timers like us three coauthors—each with more than forty years of teaching under our belts. The work of this volume is to get us all on the same page, speaking the same language about kids and learning. Here, we gather to find the consensus, the core, the fundamental understandings that bind us together in the service of students, no matter what role we take in their growth and development. When we educators read and discuss this rich and powerful information—as veterans, as newbies, as faculties, as teams—we define for ourselves what "best practice" means, and how we can embody it in our work with young people.

Lately, the education profession has been living through a tumultuous time. Nearly everyone in the society has gotten into the act of "reforming" schools: politicians, business titans, think tanks, taxpayers, commentators, pundits, journalists, and researchers. Education-oriented cover stories, blue-ribbon commissions, government reports, exposés, recommendations, talk shows, documentaries, conferences, jokes, gossip, and legislation abound. Indeed, we are writing this book during the reign of yet another "education president," in a state with a self-declared "education governor," and in Chicago, a city famed for its high profile school reform projects.

While heartfelt public concern about education is certainly useful, very little of this sudden interest has been admiring, pleasant, or even civil. Our national reappraisal of education began with widespread anger about urban dropout rates, worry about low test scores, and fears about the perceived slippage in American workers' global competitiveness. These concerns are constantly stirred by a drumbeat of downbeat headlines, such as this morning's offering: "Shocking News: 82% of U.S. Schools Failing." Not surprisingly, much of this school reform energy has been spent on blaming and finger-pointing: responsibility for our nation's educational disappointments has been enthusiastically and variously apportioned among TV, video games, single-parent families, teacher unions, urban gangs, bad textbooks, sexual permissiveness, drugs, schools of education, and dozens of other causes.

But now, after almost three decades of recriminations and reform efforts, we finally have a new national momentum, a fresh set of common standards, and a mandate from both the federal government and the public at large to make big changes in the way we educate this country's young people.

Yet, notwithstanding the grand politics and stirring headlines, teaching at its core remains a very personal, one-to-one enterprise. With all the research that's flown by in recent years, one of the most prominent findings has been just how much the quality of teaching matters. Give a child a good teacher for three years in a row, and that kid's achievement scores will be 50 percent higher than with ineffective teachers during that same span (Zuckerman 2011). Put students in classrooms where teachers get to know kids personally and invite their interaction, and test scores rise (Newmann 2001). Explicitly teach kids the social skills of collaboration, and both achievement test scores and grades rise 11 percent (Durlak 2011). Indeed, the single most powerful variable in student achievement—more than socioeconomic status or school funding—is the quality of the teaching learners receive. But what does *quality* mean?

How do good teachers create those gains, minute by minute, day by day? Standards and curricula and mandates may explain *what* students should learn—but where's the *how*? *How* do those world-class, kids'-life-changing teachers do it? What do they say and do, in what order, and with what shadings and tones? How do they organize space and allocate time? How do they open up their heads and demonstrate skillful thinking in math, science, reading, history? How do they create sequences of activities that lead learners to deep understanding? How do they build conceptual knowledge that lasts beyond Friday's test? How do they find and use the most powerful materials, the most engaging texts? How do they keep each child in the zone between the known and the unknown, between the easy-peasy and the too-damn-hard? How do they shape growth, give feedback, offer encouragement, and provide challenge?

We seek to answer those questions here, in stories from classrooms, in research findings, in exemplary lessons and rich units of study.

Teaching is a unique profession. No matter what happens on the macro-national-political level, the real work always comes down to a group of young people and one grown-up, a teacher. Once that classroom door is closed, everything depends on the knowledge, planning, artistry, and heart of that special adult. When teachers bring Best Practice to life, kids find their curiosity fanned, their questions honored, their work ethic stimulated, their craftsmanship and pride rewarded. A hunger for knowledge becomes the most natural and delightful appetite of all. No matter how much shouting and static may be happening in the world outside the school, the classroom can still be a sacred space, one where spirits coalesce, lives change, and futures are forged. This book seeks to define and describe that space.

Works Cited

Durlak, Joseph, et al. 2011. The Impact of Enhancing Students' Social and Emotional Learning: A Meta-Analysis of School-Based Universal Interventions. *Child Development* 82(1): 405–432.

Newmann, Fred, et al. 2001. *Authentic Intellectual Work and Standardized Tests: Conflict or Co-Existence?* Chicago, IL: Chicago Consortium on School Research.

Zuckerman, Mortimer. January 14, 2011. Best and Brightest Teachers Key to Solving U.S. Education Crisis. *U.S. News.*

Acknowledgments

As we've written our twenty-odd books, we have thanked many people who have enriched our lives and our work, and without whom we couldn't have accomplished very much—colleagues, friends, editors, family. This time we want to honor two groups of people who have been especially important for whatever we've managed to achieve—our personal mentors and the schools where we have most profoundly developed our thinking. Both sets of mentors have helped us learn the essentials we needed to understand, and built the framework for our writing, and especially for *Best Practice*, Fourth Edition.

▶ Steve's Mentors

Ted Baird—who, in his acerbic way at Amherst College, helped us young teachers realize that writing meant thinking deeply about things that mattered.

Janet Emig—in whose office I sat one day long ago at Rutgers University, a young teacher realizing all the good help I hadn't known was out there, as I struggled to help students write.

Marty Gliserman—with whom I team taught at Livingston College, Rutgers, and from whom I learned that teaching and learning could be an interactive inquiry adventure.

Annabelle Leviton—my piano teacher who showed me how to repeat my mistakes so I could study them closely and find creative exercises that dissolved them.

Donald Graves—who opened up a whole world of thinking, observing, and doing in teaching, and who remained a warm support throughout my career.

▶ Steve's Mentor Schools

Central Park East Schools, New York—providing us with the model that led to many years of work on small schools in Chicago.

Best Practice High School, Chicago—where a courageous faculty collaborated to create learning activities that truly embodied what we believed in, educationally—and that worked.

Clissold School, Chicago—where I watched Debra Henderson and her seventh-grade students find sheer joy in learning.

Hendricks Academy, Chicago—a caring and talented faculty and principal turning a school into a real place of opportunity in a struggling neighborhood.

Washington Irving School, Chicago—one of the first schools where I saw a determined principal, Madeleine Maraldi, and her staff reinvigorate themselves to create a great school.

Deerfield High School, Deerfield, Illinois—a place where the teachers I know work together, share ideas, and learn with their students.

▶ Smokey's Mentors

Doug Holcomb—my Latin teacher and theater director at Blake School, who smoked in class, demonstrating that memorable teachers often break the rules.

Rae Moses—professor of sociolinguistics at Northwestern University, who made me her apprentice in teaching, writing, research, and publishing.

Yolanda Simmons, Pat Bearden, Barbara Morris, and Toni Murff—who helped me understand the African-American experience in Chicago.

Donald Graves—(me too, Steve)—for so many reasons, but above all, his unfailing graciousness and generosity toward every reader, teacher, and fan he ever met.

Neil Postman—the NYU author, educator, and media literacy theorist. In one handwritten letter, he advised: "Try to be famous. It can be quite delightful."

▶ Smokey's Mentor Schools

Salazar School, Santa Fe, New Mexico—where I taught a wonderful bunch of sixth graders, pursuing complex small-group inquiry projects.

Federal Hocking High School, Stewart, Ohio—an astonishing faculty and Superintendent George Wood have created a national demonstration site for content-area literacy and teacher-powered staff development.

Ka Waihona o ka Na`auao School, West Oahu, Hawaii—where I was powerfully reminded that culture, not "data," must drive the curriculum.

Baker Demonstration School, Evanston, Illinois—my own children were brilliantly educated in this holdout/hideout of progressive education.

Burley School, Chicago—one of the top schools in the United States for consistent Best Practice teaching, room to room, day to day, kid to kid. The formula? Unwavering focus, dedicated work, and rampant curiosity.

▶ Art's Mentors

Allan Glatthorn—who taught me how to synthesize a dozen books into a set of coherent ideas.

Don Moore—who taught me more about the politics of education than any course could possibly have done.

Ethel Migra—who explained the principles of group dynamics through the cases with which I was working.

Paul Trafton—who helped me learn the lexicon of mathematics education.

Judi Zawojewski—who shared her love of mathematics and her knowledge of problem solving.

Becky Barr—who graciously shared her insights into literacy.

▶ Art's Mentor Schools and Districts

Elementary School District 97—Oak Park, Illinois

Public Schools District 90—River Forest, Illinois

Community Unit School District 200—Wheaton Warrenville, Illinois

Community Unit School District 203—Naperville, Illinois

Community Consolidated School District 181—Hinsdale, Illinois

School District 67—Lake Forest, Illinois

School District 13—Bloomingdale, Illinois

School District 62—Des Plaines, Illinois

School District 112—North Shore, Illinois

School District 37—Avoca, Illinois

All, in their own special ways, have helped kids learn math deeply and effectively.

Figure 2.3: "Text Codes" chart from *Texts and Lessons for Content-Area Reading* by Harvey Daniels and Nancy Steineke. Copyright © 2011 by Harvey Daniels and Nancy Steineke. Published by Heinemann, Portsmouth, NH. Reprinted by permission of the publisher.

Standards for the English Language Arts by the International Reading Association and the National Council of Teachers of English. Copyright © 1996 by the International Reading Association and the National Council of Teachers of English. Reprinted with permission.

Excerpts from the *Common Core State Standards* © Copyright 2010. National Governors Association Center for Best Practices and Council of Chief State School Officers. All rights reserved.

Front cover photograph: © Digital Vision/Getty Images/HIP
Smaller cover photographs (*left to right*): © Photodisc/Getty Images/HIP; © Jupiterimages/Brand X Photos/Getty Images/HIP; © Houghton Mifflin Harcourt/HIP; © Comstock/Getty Images/HIP; © Creatas/Jupiterimages/Getty Images/HIP

Additional cover and interior photographs: Unless otherwise noted, photographs © Sherry Day

Figures 2.4, 3.1, and 3.4: © Harvey Daniels

Critical Issues Features:
Technology: © Ariel Skelley/Blend Images/Getty Images/HIP; ELL: © PNC/Brand X Pictures/Getty Images/HIP; The Arts: © Photodisc/Getty Images/HIP; School Leaders: © Harcourt School Publishers/HIP

More/Less Chart: © Comstock/Getty Images/HIP

Chapter Openers:
Chapter 1: © Digital Vision/Getty Images/HIP; Chapter 2: © Artville/Getty Images/HIP; Chapter 3: © Photodisc/Getty Images/HIP; Chapter 4: © Photodisc/Getty Images/HIP; Chapter 5: © Artville/Getty Images/HIP; Chapter 6: © Corbis/HIP; Chapter 7: © Photodisc/Getty Images/HIP; Chapter 8: © Photodisc/Getty Images/HIP

Chapter 1

What Do We Mean *by*

Best Practice?

The expression "best practice" was originally borrowed from the professions of medicine, law, and architecture, where "good practice" and "best practice" are everyday phrases used to describe solid, reputable, state-of-the-art work in a field. If a professional is following best practice standards, he or she is aware of current research and consistently offers clients the full benefits of the latest knowledge, technology, and procedures. If a doctor, for example, does not follow contemporary standards of medicine and a case turns out badly, peers may criticize his decisions and treatments by saying something like, "That was simply not best practice."

Until recently, we haven't had an everyday term for state-of-the-art work in education. In fact, some veteran teachers would even *deny* the need for a current, research-based standard of instruction. "I just give 'em the basics," such teachers say. "It's worked just fine for thirty years, and I don't go for any of this newfangled mumbo-jumbo." One wonders how long such self-satisfied teachers would continue going to a doctor who says: "I practice medicine exactly the same way today that I did thirty years ago. I haven't changed a thing. I don't pay any attention to all that newfangled mumbo-jumbo—MRIs, vaccines, antibiotics, and such."

Some people insist that education as a field does not enjoy the clear-cut evolution of medicine, law, or architecture. But still, if educators are people who take ideas seriously, who believe in inquiry, and who subscribe to the possibility of human progress, then our professional language must label and respect practice that is at the leading edge of the field. So that's why we have imported (and capitalized) the term *Best Practice*—as a shorthand emblem of serious, thoughtful, informed, responsible, state-of-the-art teaching.

As you'll learn in the following pages, there is a strong consensus among the seemingly disparate subject-matter fields about how kids learn best. Virtually all the authoritative voices and documents in every teaching field are calling for schools that are more student-centered, active, experiential, authentic, democratic, collaborative, rigorous, and challenging. That's a short definition of Best Practice teaching; the rest of the book will deepen that description.

But since this book began its life in 1993, the term *Best Practice* itself has suffered from "terminology drift," a process by which useful educational ideas become overly popular, are carelessly used, and come unmoored from their original meanings. When we see "Best Practice worksheets" being sold at professional conferences, and tucked into free "Best Practice" tote bags, we get worried. So in just a moment, we will begin defining more precisely what we mean by Best Practice.

This book is about the really big ideas in education, the ones with depth and staying power.

This book is about the really big ideas in education, the ones with depth and staying power. You'll soon be visiting classrooms and schools where these enduring ideas are honored and their distinctive activities are enacted. And while *Best Practice* deals mostly in facts, it also has a strong, unabashed, and partisan vision: we believe (and we hope we are about to prove) that progressive educational principles can and should govern classroom practice in American schools. While some people belittle the earlier cycles of progressive innovation during the 1930s and 1960s as transient fads, this book shows how the current wave of curriculum-based reform connects and culminates those past eras, and offers hope of creating the strongest and most enduring school improvements this country has ever seen.

THE COMMON CORE STATE STANDARDS

Since 1993, each successive edition of *Best Practice* has drawn upon authoritative and current sources to define "best practice teaching." For us, this has meant looking for consensus among scores of reports from subject-matter organizations, research centers, and professional groups. Back in the 1980s and 1990s, more than a dozen curricular organizations, including the National Council of Teachers of Mathematics, the International Reading Association, the American Association for the Advancement of Science, and the National Council of Teachers of English, issued standards documents that are still in force today, many having been revised and updated in the interim. Organizations like the National Board for Professional Teaching Standards have created and maintained clear specifications of what constitutes excellent teaching. So, in this book, we happily undertake the correlation of all these sources once again.

But now, with this fourth edition, we have a major new resource to draw upon—the Common Core State Standards (CCSS), as developed by the Council of Chief State School Officers and the National Governors Association. As we go to press, forty-five states have signed on to the CCSS Standards for English Language Arts and Mathematics, thus agreeing to have their own standards, developed mostly in the 1990s and 2000s, replaced by their national counterparts. Many agencies, state departments of education, and commercial publishers have begun offering curricula matched to these standards. Also coming soon are new national assessments designed to stimulate and measure student progress on the new standards.

These are landmark developments. Since America's founding, the work of educating children has mainly been left to local communities. Indeed, some have said that our public schools are the last vestige of local governance left in our democracy. Now, with the Common Core and all its ancillary mandates, America for the first time moves toward a truly national educational system. Some, but not all, of the most educationally effective countries in the world have taken this approach. Now we are going to see how it works for America.

The CCSS really "raise the bar." Many math teachers say that the standards make mathematics two years tougher; work that used to be done in fifth grade is now pushed down to third, while formerly third-grade work is now required in first. The English language arts standards are less consistent, but their key word is *complexity*; the standards writers insist that all students should be reading books that are on grade level, with neither teacher nor textual support. Clearly the theme is "tough love."

Our own plaintive cry is, can we please have the *rigor* without the *mortis*? Here's what we see as some opportunities and some difficulties with the Common Core Standards.

▶ Strengths of the Common Core State Standards

- Expectations for students and teachers are general but clear.
- Rich and challenging curriculum and materials are endorsed.
- Content consistency across grade levels and subjects is valuable in a mobile society.
- The call for more nonfiction reading and writing redresses an old curricular imbalance.

- More active classrooms are recommended, with higher levels of student engagement, collaboration, and responsibility.
- The need for scaffolding is recognized, for gradual learning ladders that allow students to reach higher goals.
- The standards leave pedagogy to teachers. "Teachers are free to provide students with whatever tools and knowledge their professional judgment and experience identify as most helpful in meeting the goals set out in the Standards" (CCSS, ELA, 4).

▶ *Challenges in the Common Core State Standards*

- Authorship did not include teachers, eroding trust among potential users.
- Grade-level standards are sometimes inconsistent: some targets are far too low, many are impossibly high.
- The omission of science and social studies, except as they include literacy skills, as well as the arts and languages means these subjects will receive less time and teaching in schools.
- Recommended readings stress very old and "classic" texts, implicitly repudiating contemporary children's, young adult, and multicultural literature.
- Most educated adults in our communities could not meet the CCSS.
- The full standards documents are overwhelming, covering 356 pages.
- Standards leave teachers wondering: "What do I *do*?"

One further note: the ultimate impact of the CCSS on classrooms will be determined by the tests used to measure student achievement—and teacher performance. The tests now being developed will, at least at first, look very much like the high-stakes standardized tests we already administer in most states. It will take several more years to create the computer-based, multiple, largely formative assessments envisioned by the two consortia currently developing the tests. Under the worrisome headline "Technological-Capacity Questions Dog Assessment Consortia," an *Education Week* story details all the difficulties with instituting national tests in a school system that is still highly decentralized, diverse, and, in fact, may not even be able to meet the electricity demands of a national computerized test (Gewertz 2011).

The establishment of the CCSS offers educators an array of opportunities—and some problems as well. But one thing is for sure: these standards do not show teachers how to teach. Indeed, the framers of the standards explicitly foreswore the realm of pedagogy:

> The best understanding of what works in the classroom comes from the teachers who are in them. That's why these standards will establish *what* students need to learn, but they will not dictate *how* teachers should teach. Instead, schools and teachers will decide how best to help students reach the standards. (CCSS ELA, 3)

It is that vital missing link—effective, skillful, powerful teaching—that we explicitly address in this book. There's one final thing we can predict with complete confidence: as always, students who have been taught well, who have actively explored a rich and challenging curriculum, will score very well on *whatever* tests are designed and given in any year.

THE CONSENSUS ON BEST PRACTICE

The more/less chart on pages 6–7 gives an overview of Best Practice teaching—what it looks like, and what it doesn't. Obviously, there is more afoot here than the congruence of teaching recommendations from traditionally separate fields of the American school curriculum. A more general educational paradigm has developed across content boundaries and grade levels. This coherent philosophy and spirit reaches across the curriculum and up through the grades. Whether it is called Best Practice, inquiry learning, interdisciplinary studies, project-based learning, or authentic instruction, or some other name or no name at all, this evolving paradigm is broad and deep and enduring.

SOURCES OF CONSENSUS To outsiders, education must sometimes look like a pretty fractious field. And there's no doubt, we do have our hot-button issues. When school people get into debates about phonics or classroom management or which founding fathers to revere most, things can get heated. But these occasional dustups, often superhyped by the media, are truly the exception. Much as in medicine or architecture or law, there are widely, deeply held agreements—best practices—that bind the profession together. Educators enjoy a vast web of underlying agreements about what effective teaching and learning look like. These ideas have developed over many decades of research, study, experimentation, analysis, and documentation. Despite differing perspectives and opinions, the major stakeholders in education have agreed upon a family of practices, a broad instructional consensus, that informs this book—and which we have represented in the more/less chart. Complete references may be found at the end of this chapter, but here we list the key organizations, reports, and other works from which we have principally drawn.

- American Association for the Advancement of Science 2007
- Carnegie Corporation 2006, 2010
- Center for the Improvement of Early Reading Achievement 2008
- Center for the Study of Mathematics Curriculum 2010
- Common Core State Standards 2010
- Daniels 2011
- Darling-Hammond 2008, 2010
- Farstrup and Samuels 2002
- Graham and Perin 2007
- Harste 1989
- Herczog 2010
- Hillocks 1986
- Kamil, Pearson, Moje, and Afflerbach 2011
- National Association for the Education of Young Children 2009

- National Board for Professional Teaching Standards 2003, 2008
- National Center for History in the Schools 1996
- National Council for the Social Studies 1994, 1997, 2010
- National Council of Teachers of English and the International Reading Association 1996, 2009
- National Council of Teachers of Mathematics 1991, 1995, 2000, 2006
- National Institute of Education 1985
- National Reading Panel 2000
- National Research Council 1996, 2000, 2007, 2009, 2011
- National Staff Development Council 2011
- Partnership for 21st Century Skills 2011
- Sierra-Perry 1996
- Smagorinsky 1996
- Wilhelm 1996

Common Recommendations of National Curriculum Reports

This chart represents the consensus definition of Best Practice as two sets of bullet points: things to reduce in the classroom, and things to increase. Or, to put it more succinctly, what should teachers do less and what should they do more?

 ## LESS

- *LESS* whole-class, teacher-directed instruction (e.g., lecturing)
- *LESS* student passivity: sitting, listening, receiving, and absorbing information
- *LESS* solitude and working alone
- *LESS* presentational, one-way transmission of information from teacher to student
- *LESS* rigidity in classroom seating arrangements
- *LESS* prizing of silence in the classroom
- *LESS* classroom time devoted to fill-in-the-blank worksheets, dittos, workbooks, and other "seatwork"
- *LESS* student time spent reading textbooks and basal readers
- *LESS* focus on "covering" large amounts of material in every subject area
- *LESS* rote memorization of facts and details
- *LESS* reliance on shaping behavior through punishments and rewards
- *LESS* tracking or leveling of students into "ability groups"
- *LESS* use of pull-out special programs
- *LESS* emphasis on competition and grades in school
- *LESS* time given to standardized test preparation
- *LESS* use of and reliance on standardized tests

MORE

- *MORE* experiential, hands-on learning
- *MORE* active learning, with all the attendant noise and movement of students doing and talking
- *MORE* student-student interaction
- *MORE* flexible seating and working areas in the classroom
- *MORE* diverse roles for teachers, including coaching, demonstrating, and modeling
- *MORE* emphasis on higher-order thinking, on learning a field's key concepts and principles
- *MORE* deep study of a smaller number of topics, so that students internalize the field's way of inquiry
- *MORE* development of students' curiosity and intrinsic motivation to drive learning
- *MORE* reading of real texts: whole books, primary sources, and nonfiction materials
- *MORE* responsibility transferred to students for their work: goal setting, record keeping, monitoring, sharing, exhibiting, and evaluating
- *MORE* choice for students (e.g., choosing their own books, writing topics, team partners, and research projects)
- *MORE* enacting and modeling of the principles of democracy in school
- *MORE* attention to affective needs and varying cognitive styles of individual students
- *MORE* cooperative, collaborative activity; developing the classroom as an interdependent community
- *MORE* heterogeneous classrooms where individual needs are met through individualized activities, not segregation of bodies
- *MORE* delivery of special help to students in regular classrooms
- *MORE* varied and cooperative roles for teachers, parents, and administrators
- *MORE* use of formative assessments to guide student learning
- *MORE* reliance on descriptive evaluations of student growth, including observational/anecdotal records, conference notes, and performance assessment rubrics

▶ Clusters of Best Practice Principles

What is the nature of this new/old instructional model? What assumptions and theories about learning inform this approach? If we study the more/less list systematically, we can identify fourteen interlocking principles, assumptions, or theories that characterize this model of education. These principles are deeply interrelated, each influencing the others. And the list of principles, as you'll see, can be grouped into three main clusters: student-centered, cognitive, and interactive.

For almost any chunk of required subject matter, we can find "a way in" that can activate kids' intrinsic motivation.

STUDENT-CENTERED

The best starting point for schooling is young people's questions and interests; all across the curriculum, beginning with students' own questions should take precedence over the recounting of arbitrarily and distantly selected information. For almost any chunk of required subject matter, we can find "a way in"—a subtopic, a puzzle, an angle, an implication—that can activate kids' intrinsic motivation.

Authentic: Real, rich, complex ideas and materials are at the heart of the curriculum. Lessons or textbooks that water down, control, or oversimplify content ultimately disempower students.

Holistic: Young people learn best when they encounter whole ideas, events, and materials in purposeful contexts, not by studying subparts isolated from actual use.

Experiential: Active, hands-on, concrete experience is the most powerful and natural form of learning. Students should be immersed in the most direct experience possible for the content of every subject.

Challenging: Students learn best when faced with genuine challenges, choices, and responsibility in their own learning. We need to provide "content ladders" that move kids steadily upward in complexity and challenge, as school years and school careers proceed toward college and career readiness.

COGNITIVE

The most powerful learning comes when children develop true understanding of concepts through higher-order thinking associated with various fields of inquiry and through self-monitoring of their thinking. This means teachers must explicitly model the characteristic thinking processes and strategies of each subject area, apprenticing their students to the field's ways of knowing.

Developmental: Children grow through a series of definable but not rigid stages, and schooling should fit its activities to the developmental level of students.

Constructivist: Children do not just receive content; in a very real sense, they re-create and reinvent every cognitive system they encounter, including language, literacy, and mathematics. Students' work in school should be building knowledge through inquiry, not simply listening to someone else mention information.

Expressive: To fully engage with ideas, construct meaning, and remember information, students must regularly employ the whole range of communicative media—speech, writing, drawing, poetry, dance, drama, music, movement, and visual arts.

Reflective: Balancing the immersion in experience must be opportunities for learners to reflect, debrief, and abstract from their experiences what they have thought and learned. Putting that reflection to work, students set goals for themselves, monitor their progress, and take responsibility for their own growth.

INTERACTIVE

Powerful learning happens in classrooms where there is lively conversation, discussion, and debate. Teachers tap the power of young peoples' social energy to advance their thinking.

Sociable: Learning happens most efficiently in an atmosphere of friendliness and mutual support, and teachers take steps to create safe, comfortable, and energizing classroom communities.

Collaborative: Small-group learning activities draw upon the social power of learning better than individualistic, competitive approaches. In school, as in life, people must learn to work effectively in small groups—with partners, teams, and longer-term inquiry groups of all types.

Democratic: The classroom is a model community; students learn what they live as members of that community. In school, we are not just training "consumers"; we are nurturing citizens—our future neighbors, coworkers, and fellow voters.

We can represent these three clusters of principles graphically, as shown in Figure 1.1.

Figure 1.1
*Three clusters of
principles*

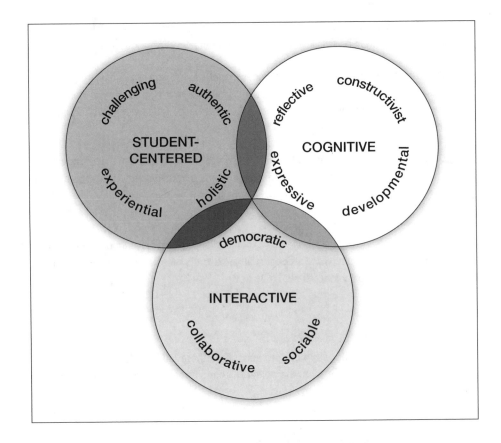

THE IMPORTANCE OF
BEST PRACTICE PRINCIPLES

The remainder of this book, as we discuss each subject in the school curriculum, spells out what these key principles really mean in practice. However, to explain why these ideas are so important, we elaborate briefly on them here.

Schooling should be STUDENT-CENTERED, taking its cues from young people's interests, concerns, and questions. Making school student-centered involves building on the natural curiosity children bring with them and asking kids what they want to learn. Teachers help students list their own questions, puzzles, and goals, and then structure for them widening circles of experience and investigation of those topics. Teachers infuse into such kid-driven curricula all the skills, knowledge, and concepts that society mandates—or that the state curriculum guide requires—though always in original sequences and combinations.

But student-centered schooling does not mean passive teachers who respond only to students' explicit cues. Teachers also draw on their deep understanding of children's developmental needs and enthusiasms to design experiences that lead students into areas they might not choose, but that they will enjoy and engage in deeply. Teachers also bring their own interests into the classroom to share, at an age-appropriate level, demonstrating how a learner gets involved with ideas. Thus, student-centered education begins by cordially inviting children's whole, real lives into the classroom; it solicits and listens to their questions; and it provides a balance between activities that follow children's lead and ones that lead children. And it places the teacher very firmly in the roles of model and coach, as the most experienced learner in the room.

Learning activities need to be AUTHENTIC. Kids want to know how the world works and how they fit in. Sometimes we adults err by offering simplified materials and activities so children are not overwhelmed with complexity. But too often we underestimate children and oversimplify things, creating materials or situations that are so synthetic as to be unlifelike—and, ironically, educationally worthless. The most notorious examples of this are the linguistically deprived stories appearing in some basal reading texts. We now understand that children routinely handle phenomenal complexity in their own daily lives—indeed, learning the thousands of abstract rules underlying spoken language is proof of kids' ability to sort out the complex tangle of data the real world inevitably presents.

What does authenticity mean in the curriculum? In reading, it means that the rich, artful, and complex vocabulary of Grimm's fairy tales is far more educational than the dumbed-down "decodable" versions in some commercial reading programs. In math, it means that children investigate ways of dividing a pizza or a cake, rather than working the odd-numbered fractions problems at the end of the chapter. Authenticity also means that children are reading and writing and calculating and investigating for purposes that they have chosen, not just because the teacher gave an assignment or because a task appears in a textbook. Yes, teachers can and should sometimes give assignments that a whole class works on, to share and compare the resulting ideas they've generated. But if teachers don't also take steps to turn schoolwork into something the children truly own, then the results will be mechanical, more an exercise in dutifully following directions than in real valuing of thought and knowledge.

Learning in all subjects needs to be HOLISTIC. In the conventional American curriculum, information and ideas are presented to children in small "building blocks." While the teacher may find these subparts meaningful and may know they add up to an eventual understanding of a subject, their purpose and significance aren't always apparent to children. This part-to-whole approach undercuts motivation for learning because learners don't perceive why they are doing the work. It disconnects skills from thinking and analyzing. It also deprives students of an essential condition for learning—encountering material in its full, lifelike context. When the "big picture" is put off until later, "later" often never comes. We know that children do, in fact, need to acquire skills and abilities such as spelling and multiplying and evaluating good evidence for written arguments. But holistic learning means that children gain these abilities most effectively by going from whole to part—when kids read whole books, write whole stories, and carry out whole investigations of natural phenomena, and in the process practice specific basic skills. Brief lessons on the use of quotation marks are learned fastest and remembered longest when the class writes personal narratives enhanced with dialogue. And, meanwhile, the focus on a rich whole text or inquiry ensures that children are simultaneously making far more mental connections—albeit often unconscious ones—than the teacher ever has time to directly teach within the one or two or three "skills" that she has time to cover.

As often as possible, schools should feature learning that is EXPERIENTIAL. Like all humans, students learn most powerfully from *doing,* not just listening. This simple psychological fact has different implications in different subjects. In writing and reading, it means that students grow more by composing and reading whole, real texts, rather than doing worksheets and exercises. With mathematics, it means working with objects—sorting, counting, and building patterns of number and shape—and carrying out real-world projects that involve collecting data, estimating, calculating, drawing conclusions, and making decisions. In science, it means conducting experiments and taking field trips to investigate natural settings, pollution problems, and labs at nearby factories, universities, or hospitals. For social studies, students can conduct opinion surveys, prepare group reports that teach the rest of the class, and role-play famous events, conflicts, and political debates. In all school subjects, the key is to help students think more deeply, to discover the detailed implications of ideas through direct or simulated immersion in them.

Following all these principles means that school is CHALLENGING. While some people think that experiential, authentic, holistic tasks are "easier" for students, teachers using state-of-the-art practices know that the opposite is true. Requiring students to choose and develop their own topics for writing, for example, makes their task harder, not easier. If the teacher simply commands: "Imagine you are a butterfly. Write one paragraph with lots of adjectives telling how it feels to land on a flower," the author's job is basically fill-in-the-blanks. The really challenging work is for young writers to find their own topics every day—pursuing the promising ones as far as they will go, discarding the clunk-

Like all humans, students learn most powerfully from doing, not just listening.

ers, then revising or starting over. This idea of getting students off cognitive welfare and into taking responsibility for their own learning is an earmark of Best Practice. As the Common Core Standards remind us, students should be steadily working their way up to more complex tasks, taking increasing responsibility for their own learning.

Powerful learning comes from COGNITIVE experiences. Many teachers have moved well beyond believing that memorized definitions constitute real understanding and are reorganizing their classrooms to facilitate higher-order, conceptual learning. Full comprehension and appreciation for concepts such as *tangent, democracy, metaphor,* and *photosynthesis* come from complex, varied experiences that gradually build deep understanding that is increasingly abstract, general, and powerful.

Teachers must help students develop the specific types of thinking that our civilization values, such as analytical reasoning, interpretation, metaphorical thinking, creative design, categorization, hypothesizing, drawing inferences, and synthesis. Students need to experience these kinds of thinking for themselves, with appropriate modeling and facilitation from their teachers and others. When they do, language, thinking, and conceptual understanding are intertwined as students *construct* ideas, systems, and processes for themselves.

The National Research Council (2000, 2007, 2009) has shown how the principles and findings on cognition can be used to guide students' understanding in school. Three major implications for teaching emerge:

1. *The importance of activating prior understandings.* New understandings are necessarily constructed on a foundation of existing understandings and experiences.

2. *The essential role of factual knowledge and conceptual frameworks in understanding.* Factual knowledge must be placed in a conceptual framework to be well understood. Concepts are given meaning by multiple representations that are rich in factual detail.

3. *The importance of self-monitoring.* Often called "metacognition," appropriate self-monitoring and reflection can support learning with understanding. Helping students to become effective learners means enabling them to take control of their own learning, consciously define learning goals, and monitor their own progress.

Children's learning must be approached as DEVELOPMENTAL. This is one of the most carelessly used words in educational parlance, used to support all sorts of contradictory ideas. To us, *developmental* does not mean labeling or teaching students according to their purported level on a fixed hierarchy of cognitive stages. Nor does it mean lockstep instruction according to some textbook

As the Common Core Standards remind us, students should be steadily working their way up to more complex tasks, taking increasing responsibility for their own learning.

company's scope and sequence chart. Instead, *developmental* means that teachers approach classroom groups and individual students with a respect for their emerging capabilities. We recognize that kids grow in common patterns but at different rates that usually cannot be accelerated by adult pressure or input. Developmentally oriented teachers know that variance in the school performance of different children often results from differences in general growth. Such variations in the speed but not the direction or the ultimate degree of development should not be grounds for splitting up groups, but rather are diversities to be welcomed and melded into the richness of the classroom.

In developmental schooling, we help children by recognizing and encouraging beginning steps when they occur—whether on schedule or not. We study the research on how children actually advance in math or spelling and build programs around this knowledge, rather than marching through arbitrary word lists or problems. In complex areas like writing, we chart children's progress in many ingredients of composing and understand how some abilities will appear to regress as children challenge themselves with other, more difficult rhetorical tasks. In math, along with review and exploration of this week's topic, we include challenging, enjoyable activities that go beyond the textbook unit so that we find out what various kids are really ready for.

Children's learning involves their CONSTRUCTING ideas and systems. Studies of early language acquisition, science learning in school, reading processes, mathematical cognition, and many other areas show that human beings never just take in and memorize material. Even when staring at clouds or smoke or trash in an empty lot, we are constantly trying to find meaning in what we see. In a very real sense, people reinvent whatever they encounter, by constantly making and revising mental models of the world. That's exactly how we learn complex systems like mathematics, language, anthropology, or anything else. For example, when two-year-olds invent and use words like *feets* or *goed,* words that they have never heard from any adult, they are demonstrating constructivism. Children don't just imitate the language around them; they use it as raw material to generate hypotheses, to reinvent the language itself. Along the way, they create original, temporary forms that serve until new hypotheses generate new structures. Kids don't merely learn to speak; every one of them, in a profound sense, rebuilds his or her native language.

Best Practice teachers recognize that all children can reinvent math, reading, and writing, no matter how "disadvantaged" their backgrounds, and they are eager to tap into the thinking abilities children bring to school. They know that the keys are experience, immersion, and engagement in a safe, interactive community. Kids need much time to practice reading, writing, doing mathematics, and experimenting. They need encouragement to reflect, to share their emerging ideas and hypotheses with others, to have their errors and temporary understandings respected. Constructivist teachers cheerfully embrace the understanding that their most helpful role isn't one of direct telling and teaching. Indeed, given the fundamentally internal nature of this deep learning, presenting rules, skills, or facts plays only a limited role in students' growth. Instead, teachers model their own thinking, and create conditions in which children can steadily construct their own understandings.

Students need to learn and practice many forms of EXPRESSION to deeply engage ideas. Traditional school has been reception-based; that is, students sit quietly and listen while the teacher talks, mentions, presents, tells, opines, and explains—supposedly "filling them up" with the curriculum. We now understand that learning doesn't work this way, and we recognize the sad irony of schools in which teachers do all the expressing. Recent brain research shows that to understand, own, and remember ideas, students need not just to receive, but also to *act upon them* (Steineke 2008). Expressing ideas can mean something as simple as talking in pairs or peer groups or having a written conversation with a partner, or as sophisticated as preparing and presenting a formal public report or creating an artifact that embodies the concepts under study. When a learner can successfully translate an idea from one medium to another—for example, expressing the Sixth Amendment to the U.S. Constitution in a dramatic skit or a sonnet—we realize that she possesses the information in a solid and flexible way. And, aside from the cognitive benefits of such rich instruction, expression taps into many children's love of performing. Indeed, it is a natural human tendency to find a friendly audience and exercise your strongest medium of expression. A progressive curriculum stresses exhibitions and performances, inviting students to express ideas through the widest possible array of media.

Effective learning is balanced with opportunities for REFLECTION. Too often, school is a process of stimulus-response. The work cycle is: do it, turn it in, get your grade, forget it, and move on. But learning is greatly strengthened when children have time to look back on what they've learned, to digest and debrief, to recognize broader principles, to appreciate their accomplishments and understand how they overcame obstacles. It is hard to think reflectively in the middle of doing an experiment or revising a draft, but afterward students can review what happened and apply what they learned to future efforts.

Is this reflective thinking process foreign to kids? No—we find evidence of it in their play and family interactions all the time. But kids need school time set aside for reflection, and they need to become consciously aware of its power and their ability to use it. Adding reflective thinking to school learning can be a simple instructional innovation. When kids finish a small-group project, they pause to review what social skills they used, and list the ones that need improvement next time around. The addition of a student learning log for each subject, with time regularly set aside for responding to well-structured teacher prompts, builds reflection into the day and moves students to a new level of thinking. Inviting students to create yearlong work portfolios is an even broader way to make reflection part of the routine work of school, as students collect and comment upon their best pieces of work, perhaps sharing them with parents or peers.

Reflective thinking applies to teachers, too. It is not enough to assess kids through quizzes and tests, compiling points that yield numerical or letter grades. Instead, the aim of most classroom assessments should be to guide student learning and inform upcoming teaching. This means teachers carefully observe learners, using guides or rubrics to structure their observations. They hold regular one-to-one student conferences and engage in written exchanges with students. They collect and study student work—not just to red-mark errors, but to find evidence of learning in progress and then determine the most appropriate next steps for each learner.

The aim of most classroom assessments should be to guide student learning and inform upcoming teaching.

INTERACTIVE: *In interactive classrooms, teachers tap into the primal power of social relations to promote learning.* Search the term *classroom* on Google Images, and what do you mostly find? Pictures of children arranged in straight rows looking forward toward a teacher. Or search *teacher*, and you get countless images of an adult holding forth in a room of silent, passive listeners. How deeply this image is ingrained our psyches! And yet how contrary to the kind of learning that engages kids' interest. Most people find that working with others brings energy to learning, and decades of research backs up this assumption: kids benefit when they learn, talk, think, write, research, debate, and perform together. But young people are not necessarily born (or raised) to work together efficiently in an interdependent community. That means teachers have to build those relationships intentionally and explicitly, early in the year, and work to maintain them throughout.

Classrooms should be SOCIABLE work environments. Friendliness and support characterize the atmosphere of high-functioning classrooms (or workplaces, or families). People enjoy learning together, they feel safe, and disputes or put-downs are rare. To create this low-risk climate, Best Practice teachers understand that they are in the friendship-building business. Their standard is "everyone works with everyone in this classroom." That means nobody can say, "I won't work with her [him/them]."

But, of course, not all students arrive in a classroom knowing or liking each other, and unless acquaintance is built early and solidly among all class members, then stereotypes, suppositions, prejudices, or rumors can come to rule relationships. What works in our favor is that *people like people they know*. If kids get to know each other, more often than not they will like each other. So, thoughtful teachers infuse acquaintance-building activities in the opening weeks of school, making sure that every student repeatedly works with every other student in the room. This friendship-building business especially applies to high school kids, even if a teacher has six classes a day. The time spent building interpersonal relationships and group esprit pays off big-time as the year unfolds. Imagine a secondary classroom where put-downs have been systematically ruled out of the game: the chances of kids engaging with the work and taking risks as learners increase exponentially.

Some of the most efficient learning activities are COLLABORATIVE. When we think of the social side of learning, we most readily envision group discussions, kids listening to one another's ideas, carrying out projects and writing letters and stories *for* one another. Collaborative learning also promotes children's learning *with and from* one another. The American workplace requires extensive collaboration and group problem solving, not just competitiveness and isolation. Collaborative small-group activity has proven an especially effective mode for school learning—and solid achievement gains have been documented across the curriculum by Darling-Hammond et al. (2008), Johnson and Johnson (1998), Sharan (1999), and others.

Collaborative work allows learners to receive much more extensive support and feedback than they can ever get from a single teacher who must spread his time among all students. Of course, group work requires training students and carefully designing meaningful, authentic activities—otherwise, the result can be inefficient and shallow. But cooperation works very well when teachers employ the training techniques that have been refined in recent years. And habitual cooperation pays off both in time better used in the classroom and, later on, as a valuable skill in life. As a recent study showed, people who develop good collaboration skills before leaving school go on to make more money than their classmates—and one's "collaboration IQ" is a better predictor of lifetime earnings than any standardized test score (ScienceDaily 2008)!

As a recent study showed . . . one's "collaboration IQ" is a better predictor of lifetime earnings than any standardized test score!

Classrooms can become more effective and productive when procedures are DEMOCRATIC. It is a classic bit of American hypocrisy that we claim to be a democracy and yet send our children off to profoundly authoritarian schools. But even if we don't choose to democratize schools as a matter of principle, there are instructional reasons for doing so. Democratic processes can make learning more efficient, more widely spread throughout the classroom, and more likely to have lifelong effects. First and most important, children need to exercise *choice*—choice in books they read, topics they write about, and activities they focus on during some parts of the day. This means that teachers must help children learn how to make intelligent choices, not just arbitrary ones or choices of avoidance. When children learn to make good choices, not only are they more committed to their work, they also acquire habits that make them lifelong readers, writers, and learners of math, science, and social issues—and, not inconsequentially, active, critical, involved citizens.

But democracy is not just freedom to choose. In a genuinely democratic classroom, children learn to negotiate conflicts so they work together more effectively and appreciate one another's differences. They learn that they are part of a larger community, and just as they can gain from it, they must also sometimes give to it. They hear about differences in one another's cultures, religions, regional backgrounds, and personal beliefs. Too often, this valuing of community within difference is missing in both rich and poor neighborhoods, and its absence undercuts education in countless ways, leaving us with discipline problems, bullying, vandalism, hostility toward school, and low self-esteem among students. Democracy in the classroom is not just a frill or an isolated social studies unit, but an educational necessity.

Even with young children, Best Practice teachers are careful not to inculcate daylong dependency on teacher instructions, directions, and decisions. They see their overriding goal as nurturing children's capacity to run their own brains, conduct their own inquiries, track and evaluate their own efforts. So they expect students to take considerable responsibility—to establish learning goals, monitor their own learning, apply the abilities they've acquired, keep their own records, and select new projects when they're finished with something, rather than just fill in an extra ditto sheet. As students gradually assume more responsibilities, the teacher provides a safe space for experimenting with newer and more difficult tasks, adding challenges as kids are ready for them. In the rigorous classes where these approaches abound, kids rise to the challenge.

The Balanced Classroom

Throughout the coming chapters you will find vignettes from many real teachers and real classrooms. It is tempting, as one reads any book about good instruction, to be excessively impressed by innovative, highly wrought, teacher-designed activities, implicitly assuming that increased student learning comes mainly from increased teacher doing. But it's not that simple. There must always be a balance in the classroom between teacher-organized activity and children's own initiative and self-directed work. It is during kids' self-sponsored activities that much of the most powerful learning occurs and the effects of good teaching get a chance to bloom. During the buzz and talk that goes on while small groups work, during the jotting and quiet of journal time, during the children's play with math manipulatives or puzzles, while kids sketch out ideas on a piece of butcher paper—so much learning is happening that even when there's a bit of digressing and fooling around, an observer gets dizzy watching it.

As another way of making clear this special kind of artful, balanced teaching, we have created the chart "Indicators of Best Practice," which also appears on the inside front cover. This graphic delineates eight areas—physical facilities, classroom climate/management, student voice and responsibility, language and communication, activities and assignments, student work and assessment, teacher attitude and outlook—that directly affect the teacher-student dynamic. The elements within these areas are not either/or practices. They are on a continuum that represents how, as teachers move toward the kind of instruction described in this book, the characteristics of their teaching will change and develop in many dimensions.

Whatever your purpose as a reader, we urge you to view the recommendations and classroom stories in this book as elements of a process of professional growth and not as examples of perfection. School districts or individual teachers rarely advance in one single, straight-line jump. None of the teachers whose classrooms are described here consider themselves paragons; all talk about being somewhere in the middle of a long, complex journey. Indeed, it is a defining characteristic of good teachers that they are learners themselves, constantly observing to see what enriches children's experience—and what makes teaching more invigorating and rewarding. Thoughtful readers will find many ways to improve upon and extend the activities described here. In fact, as we've talked with these teachers, we've usually ended up brainstorming additional options and variations that bring even more principles of Best Practice into play. We certainly invite our readers to join in this process of extending and fine-tuning.

So What's New?

This family of ideas, the model we now call Best Practice teaching, will be quite familiar to anyone who worked in American schools during the late 1960s and early 1970s—someone raised on the ideas of Jean Piaget, Lev Vygotsky, James Britton, James Moffett, Jerome Bruner, Erik Erikson, Carl Rogers, Jerome Harste, John Holt, Herbert Kohl, Neil Postman, and Charles Weingartner. But then this list doesn't exactly hold any surprises for people who lived through the progressive era of the 1930s or who have studied the work of John Dewey. Yes, today's "new" integrated and holistic educational paradigm can fairly be called a continuation of progressive thinking.

However, while it is harmonious with and descended from past progressive eras, Best Practice is not identical to "whole language" in the 1980s, or to the "open classrooms" of the 1960s, or to the Deweyian schools of the 1930s. Though still rooted in the view of children as fundamentally good, self-regulating, and trustworthy, today's movement is driven by more than an optimistic conception of children's nature. This time around, the philosophical orientation is better balanced with pedagogical pragmatism and insight about cognition. We are blending a positive view of young people with our commitment to meaningful curriculum content and our improved understanding of how learning works. In earlier times, some progressive innovations failed because they were backed with more passion than practical, well-thought-out procedures for implementing them. Now, we return to the same basic theories, with the same beliefs about kids' capabilities, but equipped with much better ideas about how adult helpers can make them work.

So, yes, many of the ideas in this book are old and familiar. Best Practice is the furthest thing from a fad. Throughout America's history, there have always been parents and educators who wanted schools to be engaging, lifelike, animated places where kids' curiosity was respected. In the 1830s, Horace Mann, often honored as the "father of American education," advocated for free public education for all children, with equal schooling for boys and girls; a curriculum that stressed practical, real-life subjects; and a pedagogy built upon kids' curiosity rather than the harsh discipline typical at that time. Indeed, progressive education in the United States has been just as "traditional" as having kids silently do seatwork or take machine-scored tests. There's a dynamic in our culture, an ongoing debate about how best to educate the young. Whatever the era, some people always seem to think that tight control of students and the transmission of content are the correct path. Others recognize the powerful abilities children bring to the classroom, and want to build curriculum around experience, collaboration, and active doing. This latter model, which we now call Best Practice, has been competing for acceptance in American culture for many generations.

Now this model of teaching appears again, this time in a stronger, more coherent form. Perhaps the current cycle of Best Practice innovation will have an even deeper impact on education than the innovations of the 1960s and 1980s, or even the era of John Dewey. While the authors of this book have no doubt that cyclical variations will continue into future generations, we also believe in progress. With each cycle, some things change that never change back, and some cycles leave a stronger heritage than others. We believe that today's is potentially the most important, powerful, and enduring phase of educational renewal ever to occur in American schools.

> *Throughout America's history, there have always been parents and educators who wanted schools to be engaging, lifelike, animated places where kids' curiosity was respected.*

THE BIGGER PICTURE

This book is definitely concerned with improving the teaching and learning in American schools, which we think is urgently important. But we do not agree with today's screaming headlines and shrill pundits, who relentlessly promote the idea that this country's educational system is in catastrophic decline. Much of the data that feeds this sky-is-falling mentality comes from international test score comparisons in which U.S. schools fare poorly. But contrary to what you may have read, there is another side to the story.

Sure, poor teachers do exist in this country, and there are schools and districts that shortchange their students. But most of our schools compare favorably to the highest-scoring countries in the world. On the benchmark Program for International Student Assessment (PISA) tests, U.S. fifteen-year-olds score 14th of 65 in reading. That places American kids above the students in England, Germany, Sweden, Israel, and may other developed nations. But still, wait a minute. Only 14th of 65? This is America—aren't we supposed to be number one? The United States should be leading the pack, not stuck in the middle, right?

Well, if you view these international test scores in light of the general welfare of children in different countries, the results look somewhat different. For example, on a list of thirty-four developed nations, the United States had the highest infant mortality, the greatest income inequality, and highest unemployment. Further, the United States is first in the proportion of children living in poverty, first for children living with hunger, and first in the proportion of people in the penal system. Overall, the U.S. ranks 29th in the world in the care, support, and opportunity it provides to young people (Blow 2011).

And yet in spite of these challenges, somehow, American kids still rank 14th of 65 in reading. You might even call that *outperforming*. Most of the countries that outscore the United States on the PISA tests have universal child care and development services that focus intensely on children's health and development from birth onward, with special assistance devoted to immigrant families or to children speaking non-native languages. The United States, on the other hand, is a country that seems content to live with a large underclass of poor, underserved, and ill-cared-for children.

Now here is some PISA test data that's especially illuminating.

- Of all the nations participating in the PISA assessment, the United States has the largest number of students living in poverty—21.7 percent. The next closest nations are the United Kingdom and New Zealand, which have poverty rates that are 75 percent of ours.

- In U.S. schools where 10 percent or less of the pupils live in poverty, students scored *number two in the world*, behind the disaggregated Chinese province of Shanghai.

- Even in U.S. schools where between 10 and 25 percent of young people live in poverty, those kids still scored *third in the world*, behind Korea and Finland.
- American schools with a 25 to 50 percent poverty rate scored *tenth in the world*.
- Only in U.S. schools where 75 percent or more of the students live in poverty, do they score at the bottom of the rankings. (McCabe 2010)

Clearly, the United States does not have a "mediocre" educational system—but a tragically *bipolar* one. About 75 percent of our schools do quite well by international standards, while the other quarter of schools, where concentrations of poor children are gathered, struggle perennially. Only when you average these two disparate pools of test scores can you get a number that can be misread (or misrepresented) as "mediocrity." A recent U.S. Department of Education Report elaborated on this phenomenon, explaining that the notorious "achievement gap" in U.S. schools is caused by an "opportunity gap" that inexplicably still exists for poor children and children of color in America's schools (Shah 2011).

We are not talking about a cultural gap or a racial gap—but a background knowledge gap.

Let us be clear: we are no apologists for poor teaching or ineffective schools. With our combined 130 years of teaching, nothing makes our blood boil faster than observing a teacher who doesn't care, or visiting a school that doesn't try. We get very nervous when we see students failing to acquire knowledge, doing mindless worksheets, or practicing superficial test-gaming strategies. But, to be honest, we see this very rarely. Last year, between us, we worked with kids and teachers in twenty-five states, and almost invariably we encountered sincere and dedicated educators doing their level best for the kids in their care.

Nor do we believe that children who happen to come from poor families or communities cannot learn powerfully and well. But the simple reality is that these kids' experiences do not match the curricular domains and expectations of school as well as those of middle class students. We are not talking about a cultural gap or a racial gap—but a *background knowledge gap.* This, of course, can be made up over time by skillful and dedicated teachers. But unfortunately, students in America's poorest schools are twice as likely to be taught by novice or ineffective teachers (Sanders and Rivers 1996).

So, forget the hyperventilated headlines: America's schools are not failing wholesale. Every day, the great majority of our three-million-member teacher corps are reaching and engaging students, helping them to build knowledge and love learning. But the system still shortchanges far too many kids. There's ample evidence that students in lower-performing schools are far more likely to be offered a passive, dumbed-down, skill-and-drill curriculum. So, in addition to addressing the issues of poverty, which underlie poor performance in so many cases, we have to start *today* to ensure Best Practice teaching for every single student in every American school.

Works Cited

American Association for the Advancement of Science 2007. Atlas of Science Literacy, Vols. 1 and 2. Washington, DC. AAAS.

Anderson, Richard, et al. 1985. *Becoming a National of Readers: Report of the Commission on Reading* Washingon, DC: National Institute of Education.

Blow, Charles M. February 11, 2011. Empire at the End of Decadence. *New York Times.*

Center for the Improvement of Early Reading Achievement. *Teaching Every Child to Read: Frequently Asked Questions.* 2008. Ann Arbor, MI: CIERA.

Center for the Study of Mathematics Curriculum. *Curriculum Design, Development, and Implementation in an Era of Common Core State Standards.* 2010. Symposium Proceedings. Arlington, VA: Center for the Study of Mathematics Curriculum. http://mathcurriculumcenter.org/conferences/ccss/index.php/.

Common Core State Standards for English Language Arts and Literacy in History/Social Studies, Science, and Technical Subjects. 2010. National Governors Association and Council of Chief State School Officers.

Common Core State Standards for Mathematics. 2010. National Governors Association and Council of Chief State School Officers.

Copple, Carol, and Sue Bredekamp, eds. 2009. *Developmentally Appropriate Practice in Early Childhood Programs Serving Children from Birth Through Age 8.* Washington, DC: National Association for the Education of Young Children.

Daniels, Harvey. 2011. *Comprehension Going Forward; Where We Are, What's Next.* Portsmouth, NH: Heinemann.

Darling-Hammond, Linda. 2010. *The Flat World and Education.* New York: Teachers College Press.

Darling-Hammond, Linda, et al. 2008. *Powerful Learning: What We Know About Teaching for Understanding.* San Francisco: Jossey-Bass.

Farstrup, Alan E., and S. Jay Samuels, eds. 2002. *What Research Has to Say About Reading Instruction.* Newark, DE: International Reading Association.

Gewertz, Catherine. April 14, 2011. Common Assessments a Test for Schools' Technology. *Education Week.*

Graham, Steve, and Dolores Perin. 2007. *Writing Next: Effective Strategies to Improve Writing of Adolescents in Middle and High Schools.* New York: Carnegie Corporation.

Graham, Steve, and Michael Hebert. 2010. *Writing to Read: Evidence for How Writing Can Improve Reading.* New York: Carnegie Corporation.

Harste, Jerome C. 1989. *New Policy Guidelines for Reading: Connecting Research and Practice.* Urbana, IL: National Council of Teachers of English.

Herczog, Michelle. September 2010. Using the NCSS National Curriculum Standards for Social Studies: A Framework for Teaching, Learning, and Assessment to Meet State Social Studies Standards. *Social Education.*

Hillocks, George. 1986. *Research on Written Composition: New Directions for Teaching.* Urbana, IL: National Council of Teachers of English.

International Reading Association and the National Council of Teachers of English. 1996. *Standards for the English Language Arts.* Newark, DE, and Urbana, IL: IRA and NCTE.

International Reading Association and the National Council of Teachers of English. 2009. *Standards for the Assessment of Reading and Writing.* Newark, DE, and Urbana, IL: IRA and NCTE.

Johnson, David, and Roger Johnson. 1998. *Learning Together and Alone: Cooperative, Competitive and Individualistic Learning* (5th edition). New York: Allyn and Bacon.

Kamil, Michael L., P. David Pearson, Elizabeth Birr Moje, and Peter P. Afflerbach, eds. 2011. *Handbook of Reading Research, Volume IV*. New York: Routledge.

Kilpatrick, J., Jane Swafford, and Bradford Findell, eds. 2001. *Adding It Up: Helping Children Learn Mathematics*. Washington, DC: National Research Council, National Academies Press.

McCabe, Cynthia. December 9, 2010. The Economics Behind International Education Rankings. *NEA Today*.

National Board for Professional Teaching Standards. 2003. *Standards for Generalist/Early Childhood*. Arlington, VA: NBPTS.

———. 2003. *Standards for Generalist/Middle Childhood*. Arlington, VA: NBPTS.

———. 2003. *Standards for Generalist/Adolescence*. Arlington, VA: NBPTS.

———. 2008. *Measuring What Matters in Advancing 21st Century Teaching and Learning*. Arlington, VA: NBPTS.

National Center for History in the Schools. 1996. *National Standards for History Basic Edition* (revised). Los Angeles: National Center for History in the Schools.

National Council for the Social Studies. 1994. *Expectations of Excellence: Curriculum Standards for Social Studies*. Washington, DC: National Council for the Social Studies.

———. 1997. *National Standards for Social Studies Teachers*. Washington, DC: National Commission on Social Studies in the Schools.

———. 2010. *National Curriculum Standards for Social Studies: A Framework for Teaching, Learning, and Assessment* (revised edition). Washington, DC: National Council for the Social Studies.

National Council of Teachers of Mathematics. 1989. *Curriculum and Evaluation Standards for School Mathematics*. Reston, VA: National Council of Teachers of Mathematics.

———. 1991. *Professional Standards for Teaching Mathematics*. Reston, VA: National Council of Teachers of Mathematics.

———. 1995. *Assessment Standards for School Mathematics*. Reston, VA: National Council of Teachers of Mathematics.

———. 2000. *Principles and Standards for School Mathematics*. Reston, VA: National Council of Teachers of Mathematics.

———. 2006. *Curriculum Focal Points for Prekindergarten Through Grade 8 Mathematics*. Reston, VA: National Council of Teachers of Mathematics.

National Reading Panel. 2000. *Report of the National Reading Panel: Teaching Children to Read*. Washington, DC: National Institute for Child Health and Human Development, Department of Health and Human Services.

National Research Council. 1996. *National Science Education Standards*. Washington, DC: National Academies Press.

———. 2000. *Inquiry and the National Science Education Standards: A Guide for Teaching and Learning*. Washington, DC: National Academies Press.

———. 2007. *Taking Science to School: Learning and Teaching Science K–8*. Washington, DC: National Academies Press.

———. 2009. *Surrounded by Science: Learning Science in Informal Environments*. Washington, DC: National Academies Press.

———. 2011. *A Framework for K–12 Science Education*. Washington, DC: National Academies Press.

National Staff Development Council. 2011. *Learning Forward: Standards for Professional Learning*. Oxford, OH: NSDC.

Newmann, Fred, et al. 2001. *Authentic Intellectual Work and Standardized Tests: Conflict or Co-Existence?* Chicago, IL: Chicago Consortium on School Research.

Partnership for 21st Century Skills. 2011. P21 Framework Definitions. www.p21.org.

Sanders, W. L., and Rivers, J. C. 1996. Cumulative and Residual Effects of Teachers on Future Student Academic Achievement. Knoxville, TN: University of Tennessee Value-Added Research and Assessment Center.

ScienceDaily. October 16, 2008. 10 Years On, High-School Social Skills Predict Better Earnings Than Test Scores.

Shah, Nervi. July 1, 2011. Federal Data Shed Light on Education Disparities. *Education Week*.

Sharan, Shlomo. 1999. *Handbook of Cooperative Learning Methods*. New York: Praeger.

Sierra-Perry, Martha. 1996. *Standards in Practice: Grades 3–5*. Urbana, IL: National Council of Teachers of English.

Smagorinsky, Peter. 1996. *Standards in Practice: Grades 9–12*. Urbana, IL: National Council of Teachers of English.

Steineke, Nancy. 2008. *Assessment Live*. Portsmouth, NH: Heinemann.

Wilhelm, Jeffrey D. 1996. *Standards in Practice: Grades 6–8*. Urbana, IL: National Council of Teachers of English.

Zuckerman, Mortimer. January 14, 2011. Best and Brightest Teachers Key to Solving U.S. Education Crisis. *U.S. News*.

Indicators of Best Practice

This chart illustrates movement from a teacher-directed to a student-centered classroom. Growth along this continuum does not mean complete abandonment of established instructional approaches. Instead, teachers add new alternatives to a widening repertoire of choices, allowing them to move among a richer array of activities, creating a more diverse and complex balance.

CLASSROOM SETUP: *Promotes Student Collaboration*

- *Setup for teacher-centered instruction (separate desks)* ▶ *Student-centered arrangement (tables)*
- *Rows of desks* ▶ *Varied learning spaces for whole-class, small-group, and independent work*
- *Bare, unadorned space* ▶ *Commercial decorations* ▶ *Student-made artwork, products, displays of work*
- *Few materials* ▶ *Textbooks and handouts* ▶ *Varied resources (books, magazines, artifacts, manipulatives, etc.)*

CLASSROOM CLIMATE: *Actively Involves Students*

- *Management by consequences and rewards* ▶ *Order maintained by engagement and community*
- *Teacher creates and enforces rules* ▶ *Students help set and enforce norms*
- *Students are quiet, motionless, passive, controlled* ▶ *Students are responsive, active, purposeful, autonomous*
- *Fixed student grouping based on ability* ▶ *Flexible grouping based on tasks and choice*
- *Consistent, unvarying schedule* ▶ *Predictable but flexible time usage based on activities*

VOICE AND RESPONSIBILITY: *Are Balanced Between Teacher- and Student-Directed*

- *Teacher relies solely on an established curriculum* ▶ *Some themes and inquiries are built from students' own questions ("negotiated curriculum")*
- *Teacher chooses all activities* ▶ *Students often select inquiry topics, books, writing topics, audiences, etc.*
- *Teacher directs all assignments* ▶ *Students assume responsibility, take roles in decision making, help run classroom life*
- *Whole-class reading and writing assignments* ▶ *Independent reading (SSR, reading workshop, or book clubs) and independent writing (journals, writing workshop)*
- *Teacher assesses, grades, and keeps all records* ▶ *Students maintain their own records, set own goals, self-assess*

LANGUAGE AND COMMUNICATION: *Deepen Learning*

- *Silence* ▶ *Purposeful noise and conversation*
- *Short responses* ▶ *Elaborated discussion* ▶ *Students' own questions and evaluations*
- *Teacher talk* ▶ *Student–teacher talk* ▶ *Student–student talk plus teacher conferring with students*
- *Talk and writing focus on: Facts* ▶ *Skills* ▶ *Concepts* ▶ *Synthesis and reflection*

ACTIVITIES AND ASSIGNMENTS: *Balance the Traditional and More Interactive*

- Teacher presents material ▶ Students read, write, and talk every day ▶ Students actively experience concepts
- Whole-class teaching ▶ Small-group instruction ▶ Wide variety of activities, balancing individual work, small groups, and whole-class activities
- Uniform curriculum for all ▶ Jigsawed curriculum (different but related topics according to kids' needs or choices)
- Light coverage of wide range of subjects ▶ Intensive, deep study of selected topics
- Short-term lessons, one day at a time ▶ Extended activities; multiday, multistep projects
- Isolated subject lessons ▶ Integrated, thematic, cross-disciplinary inquiries
- Focus on memorization and recall of facts ▶ Focus on applying knowledge and problem solving
- Short responses, fill-in-the-blank exercises ▶ Complex responses, evaluations, writing, performances, artwork
- Identical assignments for all ▶ Differentiated curriculum for all styles and abilities

STUDENT WORK AND ASSESSMENT: *Inform Teachers, Students, Parents*

- Products created for teachers and grading ▶ Products created for real events and audiences
- Classroom/hallway displays: No student work posted ▶ "A" papers only ▶ All students represented
- Identical, imitative products displayed ▶ Varied and original products displayed
- Teacher feedback via scores and grades ▶ Teacher feedback and conferences are substantive and formative
- Products are seen and rated only by teachers ▶ Public exhibitions and performances are common
- Data kept private in teacher gradebook ▶ Work kept in student-maintained portfolios
- All assessment by teachers ▶ Student self-assessment an official element ▶ Parents are involved
- Standards set during grading ▶ Standards available in advance ▶ Standards codeveloped with students

TEACHER ATTITUDE AND OUTLOOK: *Take Professional Initiative*

Relationship with students is:

- Distant, impersonal, fearful ▶ Positive, warm, respectful, encouraging
- Judging ▶ Understanding, empathizing, inquiring, and guiding
- Directive ▶ Consultative

Attitude toward self is:

- Powerless worker ▶ Risk taker/experimenter ▶ Creative, active professional
- Solitary adult ▶ Member of team with other adults in school ▶ Member of networks beyond school
- Staff development recipient ▶ Director of own professional growth

View of role is:

- Expert, presenter, gatekeeper ▶ Coach, mentor, model, guide

Chapter 2

The Seven Structures *of*

Best Practice Teaching

We've already shown that Best Practice is a set of harmonious and interlocking *principles of teaching* and *learning*. In the rest of this book, we'll visit twenty different teachers from all around America. Each of them enacts a coherent model of teaching that is student-centered, experiential, expressive, reflective, authentic, holistic, interactive, sociable, collaborative, democratic, cognitive, developmental, constructivist, and challenging. But what do these Best Practice teachers do differently from other educators? How do they implement and live out these principles, this paradigm? Do they drive to school with national curriculum standards on their laps, deciding at the last stoplight which methods to use today?

To begin, let's spend three days in one Best Practice classroom—Katie Muhtaris' fifth grade at Burley School in Chicago. Burley is a public neighborhood school on Chicago's north side where kids come from white, Hispanic, African American, and multiracial backgrounds. Katie is a National Board Certified teacher who has been working with young people for ten years. Outside the classroom, she's an amateur photographer, writes an educational blog, takes Greek classes, and owns a "very handsome" golden retriever named Rex. Katie is a voracious reader, a great storyteller, and always seems to have a smile on her face.

As we arrive at Room 302, Katie's students are just finishing up a round of literature circles, small peer-led book clubs that quite resemble the reading groups often enjoyed by adult book lovers. The students are tucked together in six groups of four or five, sitting "eye to eye, knee to knee," as Katie calls it, having intense conversations about the final chapters of their chosen books. To support and cue their discussion, group members frequently refer to Post-it notes they've made while reading, which peek conveniently out of the edges of their books.

Visitors to the room are often surprised to see that these eleven-year-olds can sustain literary conversations for twenty to thirty minutes at a stretch without teacher-fed questions, prompts, or even much oversight. Just like adult readers gathered in a friend's living room, they share questions, offer interpretations, laugh, pose questions, debate and dispute, digress, and make personal connections between the book and their own lives.

Ike, Brianna, Jose, David, and Elliot have just finished *Bud, Not Buddy*, Christopher Paul Curtis' Newbery Award–winning novel about a lost African American boy set during the Great Depression. Let's listen in as the kids talk about a section late in the book where Mr. Calloway learns for the first time that his daughter, who ran away after he mistreated her, died many years ago.

Ike: One of my questions was, I want to know if Mr. Calloway was happy that he knew that his daughter died, because I think it would have been . . . I think he might appreciate knowing where she is now. And is Mr. C. happy that he knows that Buddy is his grandson?

> Collaborative Activity

David: I would be a little shocked if I was him. That was in one of my Post-its . . . like, to find out that your daughter's dead and to find out that you had a grandson that you had never seen before in your life. That would be a shock.

Brianna: *(Looking at a note in her book.)* It seemed like . . .

Jose: He appeared out of nowhere in a car . . .

Brianna: It was kind of sad, because he was crying in his room. So Ike, going back to where you said you think he'd be happy to know where she is and how she's dead . . . he was *not* happy!

Elliot: Well, I think he was both happy and sad. He was sad about her death, but at least now he knows where she ended up.

Ike: Yeah, I agree because I think the way that he was happy is that she ran away and he didn't know where she was and now he might be relieved because he finally found out where she is and that she's dead. So at least he knows, so he actually knows now where his daughter is.

Jose: Yeah, because he finally found out that she's dead. But you know, he's pretty sad and happy at the same time knowing where she ended up. But he still probably takes it back being mean to her. You can understand that he wanted his daughter to stay in school, but I bet if he had a second chance, he wouldn't have been so mean to her like that.

The kids' conversation shows a lot. Clearly, they have read the book with care and are grappling with the big life-and-death ideas in the story. Also, they are using a set of specific social skills for peer discussion, including taking turns, building on others' ideas, disagreeing respectfully (but sometimes emphatically), supporting their interpretations with evidence from the text, and more. Katie is not on stage talking and telling. Instead, these children are taking major responsibility for their own learning—choosing and reading a book, making prediscussion notes, coming to meetings, and sustaining productive conversations for twenty minutes or more. But make no mistake, there's tons of teaching behind these literature circles. What we are witnessing here is the payoff of many Best Practice lessons, during which Katie has prepared the kids to be active, responsible, self-challenging learners. Let's go back and see how this started—and where it goes from here.

KATIE EXPLAINS ▶

When I selected this set of books, I made sure they had literary merit and were aligned with the Chicago Public Schools' social studies curriculum. But I also considered the vertical curriculum, taking into account the concepts students will study in later grades or during the year. In this way, my students are able to build rich and layered background knowledge that supports them in reading increasingly complex text.

KATIE EXPLAINS ▶

I model building a reading calendar with whatever book I'm currently reading in my own neighborhood book club. Students will usually break up pages mathematically without taking into account their schedules. So I use a think-aloud to show how I plan my reading time. For example, sometimes I plan my weekly reading in a few larger chunks, which I feel help me to enjoy the story more—and fit my reading around other activities in my life.

Two weeks ago, kids formed their literature circles, based not on their official reading level, but on their own choice from among seven historical novels. Katie included both easier and harder options, so that every child could find a book he or she could read, and wanted to read. (This means Katie needed at least four to six copies of each title to make a set.) After a structured preview of the choices, kids submitted a written ballot listing their top three picks. Katie then reviewed these, thinking about each student's reading skills and topic interests, and also envisioned the social groupings that would result if everyone got their first-choice books. For a couple of students who selected books that seemed way too hard for them, Katie held quick one-to-one conferences to help each student understand the support they'd need to push through a tough book. This might mean quick conferences with the teacher every other day, or a buddy to discuss questions that arise along the way.

Upon receiving the book they chose (still mostly first or second choices, even after Katie's engineering), each group sits down to make a schedule of three face-to-face meetings to occur on their way through the book—after one third, after two thirds, and at the end. Accordingly, they must divide up the pages to be read in rough thirds, to match each of the planned meeting dates on a calendar Katie has provided.

Having created these written plans, you might think kids were ready for three meetings during which they would mostly operate independently, with occasional conferences with the teacher. But Katie wants to be sure. Too many small-group projects run aground when some people dominate and others slack off, conversations veer off topic, time is wasted, and morale sags. So, as a final preparation, each group prepares a list of "ground rules" to ensure smooth operation and good discussions (see an example in Figure 2.1). This is a lesson that Katie has taught several times this year, so kids go right to work figuring out what guidelines they will need to work with this particular combination of people.

After Katie leads some whole-class listing of good group cooperation guidelines, each literature circle makes its own set of rules. One team—Gretchen, LaTanya, Tom, Joyce, and Ralph, who have worked together before and know each other's strengths and foibles well—created this list of ground rules:

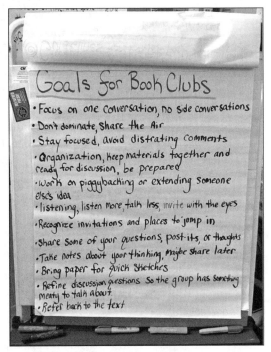

Figure 2.1 *Anchor chart of book club conversation rules*

- ✓ Do the reading on time.
- ✓ Bring your book and your notes every day.
- ✓ Try really hard to concentrate.
- ✓ Look at the person you are talking to.
- ✓ Share the air and include everyone.
- ✓ Don't bring anything to the meeting that can distract you.
- ✓ Keep your hands to yourself.
- ✓ Realize when you're off topic so you can stop.
- ✓ Don't look for weird things on the laptops.
- ✓ Make someone leave if they are distracting you.
- ✓ No going to other groups.

Katie has kids sign and hand in their group ground rules for her approval. It's by creating and following their own collaboration rules that kids are able to have sustained conversations, not just in book clubs, but across the curriculum, all year long. Katie adds: "As the year continues, students will begin to offer more rules that they know they need. For example, Sam had difficulty remembering to bring his book on discussion day, so he offered a rule that said to bring your things for discussion a day early so that you wouldn't forget."

So now, as today's end-of-book discussions come to a close, Katie gathers the class together once again and prepares them to take the next step. Though literature circles have been a staple of American classrooms for almost twenty years, often the culminating experience for book clubs has been some kind of "project": creating a missing scene from the book, putting on a skit, or making dioramas of events in the story. But teachers like Katie realize that this kind of activity can be shallow and unchallenging. She wants kids to go deeper, thinking back over the wonderings and curiosities that are left in the wake of any deep reading experience. So, in this next stage of fifth-grade book clubs, kids will graduate from analyzing a single novel to a far-ranging cross-disciplinary inquiry, conducting research in an array of nonfiction texts and genres.

Gradual Release/ Modeling Strategic Thinking ▷

Katie: Whenever we finish a good book, we usually have even more questions than we did when we started. We wonder about the people, places, ideas, and conflicts embedded in the book, right? We've explored that as a class before. Remember when we read *The Composition* and so many of you wondered about government dictatorship? Have you had that experience in any of your books? Can someone share?

KATIE EXPLAINS ▶

I usually start planting the seeds for this kind of thinking early in the year by using a shared read-aloud such as a picture book or nonfiction article. Once students have had several experiences engaging in this kind of thinking as a class, they begin to generate questions that go beyond the scope of the book. I've noticed that this modeling and support helps them to notice questions that they would normally ignore or pass by in favor of a "skinnier," plot-based question.

Julia: I just finished *Stargirl* and I was really wondering about why people are always picking on other people for being different. Like, why would they do that and how could we make them stop?

Katie: That's a really powerful question, Julia, and one that affects everyone in this room. You just reminded me of a book I read recently called *Words in the Dust*. Remember last week I did a book talk on it? Well, I finished it over the weekend. It was amazing! And when I was done, I realized that I had all these things I was still wondering about, so I wrote my lingering questions in my notebook.

- *Where did the author get the idea and information for this book?*

- *Are there other books that are similar to this that I can read? I'm really interested in life in the Middle East.*

- *Why don't they fix cleft palates in some countries? What happens to those children? Do they have lives like the main character in the book?*

This last question really stuck with me. I was so sad and angry for the main character and I just kept thinking, "Is this happening in the world right now?" I was so curious about this question that I looked up some information about it on the Internet right away. And one thing I found was that there are some great organizations that give children surgeries to fix their mouths. Isn't that wonderful? I found a couple websites that I'm going to use to find more information.

Bailey: I think I heard about that on a show I was watching. They have doctors who volunteer.

Katie: Yes, I think you're right, I'll let you know more when I find out. I am so interested in this topic and I'm just getting started—and I have a lot more I want to read.

Julio: Does the girl get her lip fixed in the story?

Katie: You know, Julio, I think you might just have to read the book; I don't want to give too much away.

Julio: *(smiling)* Maybe I will.

Katie: Friends, did you notice that my questions aren't all just about stuff within the book? I really let my curiosity go and started coming up with all kinds of questions. Some of them might be answered by the author, but to answer others, I have to do research outside the book.

It seems like you guys are really ready to try this out with your lit circle books, so now I'm going to give you about ten minutes to get back in your groups and start listing your lingering questions about the books you have just finished. Talk about the things you are still curious about, still wonder about, now that the book is over.

(She begins handing out one lap-sized whiteboard to each group.)

Make sure that some of those lingering questions are big, global, beyond-the-book topics. OK, so you have your whiteboards and you have your marker. Pick a recorder, and have a good conversation.

As the *Bud, Not Buddy* group gathers in a circle on the rug, plenty of researchable questions pop up, and Jose, the group's recorder, has his hands full getting down everyone's ideas.

Ike: Well, one of my questions was . . . Did people in the Great Depression . . . did they feel that President Hoover was a bad person? What were the bad qualities about President Hoover and what were the good qualities?

David: In the book, the author said that there's a ton of orphans that would just be packed into these orphanages, so I thought, why were there so many orphans and how did it happen? Is it because people couldn't afford them or something like that?

Elliot: Oh, and to build on that question . . . What happened to them? What happened to the orphans after the Depression?

Brianna: My question is . . . what happened on the other side of this story . . . what was Hoover's point of view? How did he think of it? Did he feel unhappy about the way people thought of him? Did he have any doubts? Did he really care what was happening to the people?

Ike: So me and Brianna's questions kind of connect as well as David and Elliot's.

Jose: And there's another one . . . were there people that couldn't support a family? And what did they do when they were jobless and homeless? Like what would they do if they can't support their family anymore?

Brianna: Like . . . would they steal and stuff?

Jose: Yeah, what would they do then?

Ike: Well, I think that they would try to do what Bud did. I think that's why all those people were trying to board the trains, because they needed to get food, they needed to get jobs to support their family.

Integrative Units/
Collaborative
Activities ▷ As time runs out, each kid volunteers to take on one of the questions now listed on their whiteboard. Katie explains that they need to be working on two things: individual written notes on each kid's learning, and a small-group performance to be shared with the whole class in two days. Now, the class shifts smoothly into an inquiry workshop. Kids jump on the computers and into bins of books that Katie has provided, anticipating many of the questions that would emerge from this particular set of books.

Students will do much of their written reporting in the "inquiry" section of their multipurpose reader's notebooks. Katie models using her notebook with all types of texts and shows ways she follows up with her own questions. Knowing they'll have more research time tomorrow, kids work for another fifteen minutes, bookmarking promising websites, making notes, and putting Post-it notes on key passages of resource books. Today, several groups are using Edmodo, a website where kids share information and work together. But now it's 11:45, time for lunch, and everyone packs up and heads down the hall.

The next day, Katie allows kids another forty-five minutes of research time. Students work, sometimes side by side, sometimes independently. Because Ike and Brianna's questions about President Hoover overlap, the two begin working together. But soon, Brianna's investigation takes a U-turn. While looking into Hoover's attitudes toward the public, she bumps into another Depression topic that's even more interesting, and she changes her focus on the fly. No problem for Ike; he carries on alone. As kids work, Katie circulates around the room, offering help to groups or individuals. Sometimes she helps them to sharpen a too-broad question—or to expand a skinny one that merely requires factual information to answer. She's in the role of coach and facilitator, as the master researcher in the room. Her job is not to answer every question a kid might pose, but to show them how to *find* those answers skillfully, using the many tools at hand.

She stops by as Ike has just started searching on one of the classroom's wireless laptops.

Katie: What are you up to?

Ike: I'm gonna look for information on the question I picked, about the Hoovervilles.

Katie: What search engine have you got running there?

Ike: Um . . . I just used Net Trekker, but I think I am going to use Ask.

Katie: OK . . . Ask . . . and what keywords are you going to use to search?

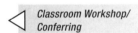

Classroom Workshop/ Conferring

Keith: Yeah, well, first I am going to use the Great Depression.

Katie: The Great Depression? *(Katie smiles.)* You might get about fifty million hits with that. Could you narrow it a bit? What specifically are you looking for? What about the Hoovervilles were you trying to find out?

Ike: Well, I want to find out what they really looked like, the towns. I can't quite picture them in my head.

Katie: OK, so what search terms would help you find some pictures of Hoovervilles without getting a ton of other Depression stuff?

Ike: Maybe just search "Hooverville pictures"?

Katie: Sounds good. And what search engine might work for this?

Ike: Google Images?

Katie: OK, let's try that and see what happens.

Ike: *(Typing.)* OK. *(Waits for the page to load.)* Whoa! Wow, look at all of these, there're tons of 'em. *(They both peer at the screen as Ike scrolls down to reveal hundreds of black-and-white photos.)*

Katie: Are you noticing what I'm noticing?

Ike: I don't think these pictures are all of Hoovervilles. Like this is just a guy hopping a train and this is what, just a dump filled with old tires.

Katie: Right, it's kind of weird how this happens—you search a very specific term, and still they give you lots of pictures that aren't what you asked for.

Ike: Yeah . . .

Katie: Here is another way to go at this. Go to the class website and use the custom Google search form there. *(Ike is already typing the address.)* I have already filtered some of the websites out for you. I kinda thought ahead about some topics that might come up from your reading *Bud, Not Buddy*.

Ike: Cool. *(Nods; he is completely absorbed in the screen.)*

Katie: I'll come back in a few minutes and see how you are doing.

Formative-Reflective
Assessment ▷

Kids continue to work as Katie visits, assists, and observes. She is also assessing their learning as she goes. She carries with her a clipboard with a simple form she uses to jot quick notes about each student's efforts. It is divided into several columns, representing the things Katie is looking for.

Preparation: Is the student arriving with all materials, ready to work? Is she researching, taking notes, and planning what she wants to share?

Participation: Is the student asking questions, making comments, and contributing to the team inquiry?

Memorable quotes: What has the student said that shows what he has learned? Has he said something particularly insightful?

Thinking strategies: What specific thinking strategies is the student using?

Social skills: How is the student relating to his small group? The larger group?

Thoughts for future teaching: What do I need to do to lift this student to the next level?

Later, she will sit down with her notes and transfer the most relevant observations into her personal notebook where she collects ideas for which lessons students might need next. She uses this information to identify any students who would benefit from further small-group instruction or who may need additional scaffolding during the inquiry process.

She also takes this time to reflect on what went well in the lesson, whether students demonstrated the kind of thinking and inquiry she was looking for, and what she might have done differently.

Representing
to Learn ▷

As time winds down for today's session, Katie brings kids together for a brief conversation about how they can "show what they know" after their ambitious research efforts. After a half-year in Katie's classroom, kids know that written reports are not the only way to share what they have learned. They enjoy a range of choices: tableaux, podcasts, essays, videos, sketches, talk shows, debates, and more. The *Bud, Not Buddy* group decides they want to share their findings about the Great Depression through a symposium, sitting around a table with Katie as moderator and their classmates as an audience. In their allocated five minutes, they can't hope to recount everything they have learned, so they'll feature the highlights, some of the most illuminating and provocative information they found in their research.

Before the symposium begins, Katie reminds the other class members how to be an attentive audience, asking them to make "two-column notes" by dividing a blank sheet of paper in half vertically. On the left side of the paper, listeners are to write down any new or interesting information they hear, not word for word, but in quick key words or phrases. On the right side of the page, they are to jot down any questions they have, so they can ask them of the presenters later on. Then the symposium convenes.

Katie: OK . . . so you guys read *Bud, Not Buddy*. Tell me what your overall lingering question was again.

Brianna: Our lingering question was . . . What were the hardships people had to go through in the Great Depression? And one of the things that we learned was that children in the Great Depression, African American children, were protesting that their African American teachers should get paid the same amount that white people get paid, even though the white people were getting paid badly, too.

Katie: Wow. I never heard about that. Has anyone ever heard about those protests? Brianna, you did some really deep research to find that out!

Jose: We also learned that people lost their jobs and money, so they couldn't pay the mortgages, so they were forced to go to Hoovervilles. And that was a place where everybody went if they didn't have a home and didn't have any money.

David: They named Hoovervilles after President Herbert Hoover and they did this because they were saying . . . like . . . look at what you did to our country. You promised us better, but now it's worse.

Elliot: Another thing is that kids and other people would try to jump freight trains to get free rides to places where there were supposed to be better jobs.

Katie: Wow, that sounds dangerous.

Elliot: Yeah! And when he ran for president—President Hoover—he promised "a triumph over poverty" and "a chicken in every pot," when it would quickly become . . . when it would quickly become impossible for him to keep these promises.

Ike: *(Holding up a wireless laptop to share an image.)* This is one of the Hoovervilles in Sacramento and the houses aren't . . . are not in good shape. They're beat up because people have no money and nobody was there to help them build houses. And here is a big close-up of one of the houses that people lived in. This was one of the houses. They have beat-up fences and the houses were the size of a shack, and that's what they had to live in.

Reflective Assessment ▷

Katie: Wow, that's really impressive. It sounds like you guys learned a lot. But do you still have questions?

All: *(Kids nod.)* Yeah.

Katie: Yeah, so does this inquiry process ever stop for us?

All: No.

Katie: It kind of seems like it doesn't. The more answers we find, the more questions we come up with.

Brianna: It's kind of hard to get all the questions down, because, as you said, first we have a question that we want to answer, and then . . . it's like you're opening presents. You open one present, ooh, there's another present inside. *(She gestures untying a bow and looking excitedly inside a gift box.)* You open that present . . . there's another inside! Open another . . . another . . . another! It's like you can't find the end of all the questions.

Sometimes when we observe a Best Practice teacher like Katie at work, we feel that we are witnessing a kind of magic. The students are engaged and lively; the room hums with purposeful activity and accountable talk. The quality of the kids' thinking, writing, and conversations exceeds grade-level expectations by far. There are no "discipline problems." The students' test scores are beyond "proficient." Indeed, in the year Katie taught this lesson, Burley School had the second highest achievement score gains among all of Chicago's 670 schools. And yet, the kids are genuinely enjoying the work and savoring their learning. Visitors often ask: "How did you get these kids so far?"

It goes without saying that most effective teachers happen to be fine human beings: kind, empathic, and hardworking. Katie fits this description, and then some. But admirable personal traits are not sufficient conditions for Best Practice teaching. Beneath any great teacher's personality and seemingly "magic" spells, there's much more at work. Best Practice teachers utilize specific structures—sturdy, replicable, and nonidiosyncratic structures—patterns that any teacher can adopt if they choose to.

*B*est Practice teachers utilize specific structures— patterns that any teacher can adopt if they choose to.

Under the surface of Katie's three hours of inquiry circles are just a few recurrent structures, some basic ways of organizing kids, time, materials, space, and help. Like other master teachers, Katie actually draws from a surprisingly *small* repertoire of basic, recurrent arrangements and structures. These are the ones you saw labeled throughout Katie's story.

1. Gradual Release of Responsibility
2. Classroom Workshop

3. Strategic Thinking

4. Collaborative Activities

5. Integrative Units

6. Representing to Learn

7. Formative-Reflective Assessment

All of these seven teaching structures are simple, effective, and time-tested. While they can profoundly shift the classroom balance from teacher-directed to student-centered learning, many of them are actually quite easy to implement; they are easy to begin, easy to slot into the existing teaching day, easy to experiment with incrementally. Indeed, far from requiring teachers to master a huge inventory of technical instructional methods, Best Practice largely means returning to some fundamental, perhaps mistakenly discarded approaches, and fine-tuning them until they work. These straightforward and replicable structures are very powerful: they can effectively take the teacher off stage, decentralize the classroom, and transfer responsibility for active learning to the students in any subject, at any grade level.

Each of these key structures has its own robust literature of how-to's and implementation guides: in fact, several contain within their very design the management features necessary to make them work. But many of them do require careful training of students—happily, of course, the learning and social skills acquired during this training are valuable in themselves. Many of these key structures are the subject of recent articles or books that explain in detail how they can be adapted for different subjects and grade levels. Harvey and our colleague Marilyn Bizar have added to that literature with *Teaching the Best Practice Way: Methods That Matter, K–12* (2004), a book-length treatment of these seven building blocks of excellent pedagogy. In the next few pages, we offer a brief description and a few examples of each major structure, along with recommended readings that can provide more detailed information and guidance about each of these seven "methods that matter."

 # GRADUAL RELEASE OF RESPONSIBILITY

One of the key deep structures of Best Practice teaching is the Gradual Release of Responsibility (GRR) model, developed in 1983 by the pioneer reading researchers P. David Pearson and Meg Gallagher. The idea of gradual release is actually quite simple: in the most effective lessons, there is a stepwise transfer of responsibility from the teacher to the students. Our colleague Regie Routman has mapped gradual release as shown in Figure 2.2.

Let's look at the steps.

Optimal Learning Model

TO LEARNERS	WITH LEARNERS		BY LEARNERS

I DO IT	WE DO IT	→	WE DO IT	YOU DO IT
Demonstration	Shared Demonstration		Guided Practice	Independent Practice
TEACHER shows how to do it	**TEACHER** leads, negotiates, suggests		**STUDENT** takes charge, approximates, practices	**STUDENT** intiates, self-directs, self-evaluates
STUDENT listens, observes, minimally participates	**STUDENT** questions, collaborates, responds, reading/writing	HANDOVER OF RESPONSIBILITY	**TEACHER** encourages, clarifies, confirms	**TEACHER** affirms, coaches
INSTRUCTIONAL CONTEXT explanation, reading/writing aloud	**INSTRUCTIONAL CONTEXT** shared reading/writing	→	**INSTRUCTIONAL CONTEXT** guided reading/writing	**INSTRUCTIONAL CONTEXT** independent reading/writing

DEPENDENCE   **INDEPENDENCE** ➤

Figure 2.2

Optimal Learning Model from Regie Routman in Residence: Transforming Our Teaching, *DVD-based literacy series, 2008, 2009. Heinemann: Portsmouth, NH.*

IN KATIE'S LESSON ▶

Several cycles of gradual release teaching are evident in these lessons. Notice that we begin toward the end of one cycle, with students independently practicing book club discussions. Katie pulls them back together to model noticing your lingering questions, then invites kids to share with her in doing it out loud. Next she releases kids to practice with her close guidance. In one-to-one and small-group conferences, she directly models research skills. Then kids go independent once again, evaluating their research and creating performances.

Modeling. "I do it, you watch." A classic gradual release lesson often begins with the teacher demonstrating or sharing some kind of thinking, while the whole class attends carefully. This puts the teacher in a familiar role, at the center of attention, acting as an expert and an informer. But this initial teacher presentation differs from traditional lecturing in two ways. First of all, it is *short* (often called a focus lesson or mini-lesson, taking no more than fifteen minutes) and is quickly followed by student activity, engaging with the ideas or demonstration the teacher has just provided. Second, this teacher-centered segment focuses not so much on transmitting information but on showing, modeling, demonstrating, or evoking curiosity. In these kinds of lessons, we hear teachers say things like:

"Listen while I read this paragraph aloud and pay attention to . . ."

"Notice what happens when I combine these two powders . . ."

"Now I am going to show you how to . . ."

"I read the most interesting article yesterday . . ."

"Watch what I do and make notes about what you notice."

Shared practice. "We do it together." For this section of the lesson, the teacher and the kids co-create experiences around the curricular topic. If the teacher has begun by reading a book aloud and modeling her own thinking and reactions, now she might shift into a *shared reading* where kids are invited to chip in their own thoughts and reactions, and to discuss them with each other. In a math lesson, the teacher might shift from doing problems himself to having students call out the next steps, or come to the board with their own solutions. In both cases, the teacher is still holding the book or the chalk, and orchestrating the conversation—but the kids are now sharing in the work and the thinking.

Guided practice. "You do it, I help." Now, the kids are released to practice the thinking, the process, or the activity that was demonstrated in the first two stages—but under careful supervision of the teacher. Often this means that kids go off into small groups to work, some convened and actively taught by the teacher (as in Fountas and Pinnell's *Guided Reading*, 2001) while others carry on their practice with occasional teacher visits and support. Imagine a science room where kids have shifted from watching the teacher do an experiment to discussing it with the teacher, and now are moving to their partner stations to conduct the experiment themselves. The teacher circulates, monitors, and confers intently as students work.

Independent practice. "You do it on your own, I watch." The last phase of the gradual release cycle is when kids take full responsibility for their work, choosing and pursuing relevant materials and experiences that build their knowledge—and their fluency, stamina, and interest in the topic. Of course, teachers have to give kids a safe and predictable structure within which to undertake this independent practice. Free voluntary reading can take place within structures like sustained silent reading, reading workshop, or literature circles—in each, students read any book they choose. The writing structures in both *In the Middle* (Atwell 1998) and *Writing Circles* (Vopat 2009) allow students to choose and develop their own pieces. Some great models for independent practice in math are detailed in Arthur Hyde's *Comprehending Math* (2006). Sad to say, while math classes are often strong on the early phases of gradual release (featuring good teacher modeling, whole-class interaction, and guided practice), kids almost never get a chance to work with—dare we say play with—mathematical ideas, solving puzzles of their own choice, or investigating math topics about the financial world, how people lie with statistics, or how modern astronomers use math to search for other earthlike planets. For other subjects, inquiry circles (Harvey and Daniels 2009) offer structures that allow kids pursue answers to their own subject-area questions.

Yes, but . . . *where do we find the time for all this practice?*

Sometimes teachers worry that this last step, independent practice, is a luxury that cannot be afforded amid the press of standards and assessments. But time for practice may be the most critical missing link of all in kids' educational experience. Did you know that the average American primary grade student spends only about twelve minutes of the school day actually reading (Hiebert et al. 2007)? How could anyone possibly get better at this key activity without much, much more practice? If you need more convincing, think of how so many of today's greatest companies operate. At Google, employees are encouraged to take 20 percent of their work time to develop their own independent, unassigned "pet projects." Allowing staff members one full day a week for free exploration has resulted in 50 percent of all Google's new products to date, including Gmail (Hayes 2008).

Sharing. "We come together to reflect." Though it is not part of the formal GRR model, many teachers add a fifth step to the cycle. Following the first four phases, the whole class gathers once again to review, respond, and react to the day's learning. Sometimes a student or group will have a performance to offer, a piece of writing to share, or some research to recount. Teachers make sure that all kids are engaged as active audience members, listening thoughtfully and interacting with the presenters, and not enjoying a mini-nap as other students report.

▲　▲　▲

Even if you had never heard of the GRR model before, we'll bet it doesn't sound very exotic now. Many of its elements are ones that skillful teachers have tapped into for generations, either intentionally or unconsciously: hook the kids, show don't tell, keep the pace crisp, vary the activities and social groupings, get up close and personal to provide small-group and individualized help. When fully implemented, GRR radically changes our time allocations. Before, too much time was devoted to teachers talking, and not nearly enough time to helping kids practice enough to actually get good at math, or writing, or doing research. And GRR requires teachers to take on a variety of roles throughout the day: modeling, coaching, conferring, observing, and using formative assessment to steer individuals and groups.

▶ Modeling: Think-Alouds at the Start of a Gradual Release Lesson

One vital structure for demonstrating thinking across all subject areas is called a *think-aloud*. The teacher first selects a short piece of text (a paragraph from the textbook, a related article, a primary source document, a photograph or diagram) and projects it in front of the class. Here's a think-aloud our colleague Greg Baldauf did with a sixth-grade science class in New Mexico.

OK, guys, I am going to read this article aloud for you, and when I notice myself doing some thinking, I'm going to stop and open up my head and try to show you what's going on in my mind. You just listen and notice what kind of thinking I am doing, and we will talk about it afterwards.

Here we go:

Scientists Fear Exotic Snakes. WASHINGTON, Feb. 24, 2008 (UPI) — Scientists fear that Burmese pythons, already known to be breeding in South Florida, could spread through much of the southern United States.

Holy moly, Pythons! Aren't those really big snakes? I'm not a snake person. I don't want these things around. Let me see what's going on.

According to the new U.S. Geological Survey report, the pythons would find about one-third of the United States— including much of California—to be comfortable for its expansion.

Whoa, that includes us. I'm looking ahead at that map down the page. There's New Mexico. We don't usually think of ourselves as being southerners, do we? But there it is, we do live in the southern part of the country. And we already have enough rattlesnakes, right? I'm going to read on.

Although other factors, such as type of food available and suitable shelter, also play a role, "Burmese pythons and other giant constrictor snakes have shown themselves to be highly adaptable to new environments," the report says.

Wait. I have a question here: where are these snakes coming from? I don't think they are indigenous to North America. They're called Burmese, like from Burma right? Let me see if I find that out.

The snakes weigh up to 250 pounds and slither at a rate of 20 miles per month, according to USGS zoologist Gordon Rodda. "We have not yet identified something that would stop their spreading all the way to San Francisco," Rodda said. If pet pythons were introduced into the wild in California by irresponsible pet owners, as happened in Florida, they could become established here even faster, without need of a cross-country journey.

There's my answer! People get these things as pets and then turn them loose when they get tired of them, I guess. This reminds me of our unit about invasive species, where we studied animals that get transported to new habitats and then mess up the ecosystem there. Remember feral pigs, mongoose, Asian carp, all those critters? I wonder if this is the same kind of phenomenon. Let me read on.

Pet pythons sometimes kill their owners, probably because they have mistaken the human for food and are unable to stop their instinctive reaction to coil and squeeze. In Florida, they eat bobcats, deer, alligators, raccoons, cats, rats, rabbits, muskrats, possum, mice, ducks, egrets, herons and song birds. They grab with their mouth to anchor the prey, then coil around the animal and crush it to death before eating it whole.

Wait. Did I get that whole list of animals? I have to go back and read this over.

. . . they eat bobcats, deer, alligators, raccoons, cats, rats, rabbits, muskrats, possum, mice, ducks, egrets, herons and song birds.

Deer for breakfast? That's just creepy. But it shows me how big and powerful these snakes really are.

Rodda said the real danger posed by the pythons is to wild animals. "Several endangered species," he noted, "have already been found in the snakes' stomachs. Pythons could have even more significant environmental and economic consequences if they were to spread from Florida to other states." Control of exotic species is often prohibitively expensive once they have become established.

Well, my big question now is, can't we find some way to control these critters? Even if it is expensive, it might be worth it. Tell you what, turn and talk with a partner for a few minutes and see if you can brainstorm some ways to stop these snakes from migrating across the U.S., maybe right up Cerrillos Road!

Notice how natural and nontechnical this think-aloud is. For starters, the teacher is simply being an engaged, active, and curious reader. But under the casual surface, the teacher is modeling a whole range of reading strategies: monitoring his comprehension, making connections, asking questions, drawing inferences, determining importance, synthesizing meaning, and even taking action about the topic.

Though they are useful all across the curriculum, think-alouds with text are not the only variety of modeling that teachers can do. Also vital is the *write-aloud*, where the teacher goes on the whiteboard, smartboard, or other public space and composes a new text, right in front of the kids. As you do this, you open up your head and show kids what's going on in your writer brain, what decisions you are making as you compose. Same for *search-alouds*, where you project the Internet or sit down with a small group of kids at a computer, much like Katie did on page 35. You model for them how you think about doing research, using the topic kids already selected. You enter search terms, select promising results, scan websites, check their credibility, look for key information, bookmark winners, follow links, play videos—all the while narrating your process, vocalizing your thinking. *(Hmmm, look at who runs this website. They're not neutral, they're a partisan advocacy group, so we cannot trust their statistics unless we triangulate them with other sources first . . .)*

Think-alouds, write-alouds, and search-alouds are not something teachers do once and then move on. We do these over and over and over, with different sorts of texts, different topics, and different research tasks. Kids need lots of exposure to the ways that skillful adult thinkers operate. All these varieties of think-alouds should be brief, and as soon as you have made a clear demonstration of your own thinking, you should shift to a shared reading, writing, or search where kids can chime in, suggest ideas, or ask questions.

For those who feel hesitant about "going live" with our own thinking, here's a comforting detail—we don't have to be perfect thinkers to be good models. In fact, it would be quite unhelpful for kids to see us effortlessly negotiating challenging text or flawlessly churning out polished writings in a single draft. Kids often think "good readers" understand whatever they read the first time through, by magic. In reality, not even the most proficient reader in the world understands tough text from one full-speed reading. In fact, they have to *work* for understanding. Real reading is a complicated, messy, recursive process, filled with starts and stops, rereadings, making and revising predictions, and so forth. Same with writing: composing a polished text comes in steps and stages, filled with false starts, changes, revisions, and edits. So as we think or write aloud for kids, we are not only showing them how proficient thinkers actually run their brains—we are also busting their unhelpful misconceptions.

*W*e don't have to be perfect thinkers to be good models.

When you begin doing think-alouds, you'll usually want to rehearse them first, planning on spots where you will stop and share your thinking. But once you get that down, want to try something really educational? Think aloud a piece of text you've never read before. Then kids get to see you using your real thinking right on the spot. When Smokey taught sixth grade a couple of years ago, he always invited the kids to bring in an article for him to think aloud, cold, every day. "They loved trying to stump me, bringing in this ridiculously complicated text they'd find on the web. But the trick was, the harder or more exotic the piece was, the better a think-aloud it made, because kids got to see me truly, sincerely struggle, bringing to bear every strategy in my brain to try and have it make sense. And it was OK for me to say, 'I don't think I have enough background knowledge to understand this one; I'd need to do some easier reading on this topic before I could get more meaning out of this article.'"

2 CLASSROOM WORKSHOP

Probably the single most important teaching structure to be developed in literacy education is the reading-writing workshop. As Donald Graves, Nancie Atwell, Lucy Calkins, Ralph Fletcher, and others have explained, students in a workshop classroom choose their own topics for writing and books for reading, using large scheduled chunks of classroom time for doing their own reading and writing. They collaborate freely with classmates, keep their own records, and self-evaluate. Teachers take new roles, too, modeling their own reading and writing processes, conferring with students one-to-one, and offering well-timed, compact mini-lessons as students work. In the mature workshop classroom, teachers don't wait around for "teachable moments" to occur—they make them happen every day.

IN KATIE'S LESSON ▶

In Katie's opening lesson, from the moment the kids start pursuing their lingering questions, the class shifts to a "researcher's workshop," where time is allocated between teacher demonstrations, shared thinking, guided practice, independent practice, and whole-class debriefing. In classic workshop style, students pick their own topics and then take responsibility for developing work, while Katie holds conferences with individuals and teams.

As you are probably realizing, the workshop is a perfect embodiment of gradual release teaching in any subject. It enacts the same principles and sequence of stages. Workshop derives from the insight that children learn to read by reading, to write by writing, to learn math by investigating math concepts, and that too often schools have not provided enough shared, guided, or independent practice. The workshop model recognizes that kids need less telling and more showing how, more modeling from teachers, and more time doing literacy or science or history, and less time hearing what these endeavors look like. Even the term *workshop* harks back to the ancient crafts-place, where not only real products were made, but a master craftsman coached apprentices.

In school, a workshop is a long, regularly scheduled, recurrent chunk of time (i.e., thirty minutes to an hour or more) during which the main activity is to *do* a subject: reading, writing, math, history, or science. While the session typically commences with a whole-class mini-lesson during which the teacher models a skill or strategy useful to everyone, it promptly shifts to guided and independent practice. Workshops meet regularly, at least once a week. In many classrooms, students have workshop time every day. A defining element of a true workshop is *choice:* students choose books for reading, projects for investigating, topics for writing. They follow a set of carefully inculcated norms for exercising that choice during the workshop period. They learn that all workshop time must be used on some aspect of working, so when they complete a product, a piece, or a phase, they aren't "done" for the day. Instead, kids must begin something new, based on an idea from their own running list of tasks and topics, or seek a conference with the teacher. While there are regular, structured opportuni-

Time Allocations in a One-Hour Workshop

Two to Five Minutes: **Status of the Class.** Each student announces or jots down in a few words what she will work on in this session.

Ten Minutes: **Minilesson.** The teacher offers a short and practical lesson on a tool, skill, procedure, or piece of information potentially useful to everyone.

Twenty to Thirty Minutes: **Work Time/Conferring.** Students work according to their plan. Depending on the rules and norms, this may include reading or writing, talking or working with other students, going to the library, conducting telephone interviews, or using manipulatives or microscopes. The teacher's roles during this time are several. For the first few minutes, the teacher may experiment, read, or write herself, to further model her own doing of the subject. Then the teacher will probably manage a bit, skimming through the room to solve simple problems and make sure everyone is working productively.

Then the teacher shifts to her main workshop activity: conducting small-group and one-to-one conferences with kids about their work, either following a preset schedule or based on student sign-ups for that day. Sometimes this may take the form of guided practice, where the teacher works on a particular skill or issue with a child or group. But mainly, the teacher's roles in these conferences are to be a sounding board, facilitator, and coach.

Ten Minutes: **Sharing.** In many workshop sessions, teachers save the last few minutes for students to discuss what they have done that day. Writers may read a piece of work aloud, readers offer a capsule book review, math students show how they applied a concept to a real-world situation, scientists demonstrate a chemical reaction, social studies teams report the results of their opinion survey.

ties for sharing and collaborating in a workshop, students also spend much time working alone, taking personal responsibility for their work.

Today, pathfinding teachers are extending the workshop model outward from reading and writing, where many have already found success, into other parts of the curriculum—establishing math, science, and history workshops. Teachers are adapting workshop because they see that deep immersion is the key to mastery, whatever the subject: they want kids to *do* history, *do* science, *do* math. The generic schedule given for a single one-hour workshop session could happen in any subject. It shows just one way that teachers commonly manage workshop time and activities.

Obviously, the workshop classroom is not an entirely new phenomenon. Its decentralized, hands-on pattern, with kids "doing" the subject rather than just hearing about it, is familiar to teachers of art, science, home economics, physical education, and other "doable" subjects. Of these fields, however, only art has traditionally allowed for any measure of student choice in the work. The commitment to student autonomy and responsibility is rooted more in older experiments with independent study, the open classroom, and learning laboratories. This powerful vehicle for student-centered learning—the workshop classroom—works because it addresses the shortcomings of prior experiments: it gives students and teachers clear-cut roles to perform, it provides for careful balancing of social and solitary activities, and it respects the necessity of detailed training for students to work purposefully in this decentralized format.

▶ *Conferring: One-on-One Conversations with Kids*

What we're trying so hard to create is time and space to sit down with kids, one at a time, and work for a few minutes on just what each student needs.

Conferences are the heart of the workshop. In a very real sense, they are the main reason we go to all the trouble to set up the norms, structures, and processes of workshop in the first place. What we're trying so hard to create is time and space to sit down with kids, one at a time, and work for a few minutes on just what each student needs. Unfortunately, in spite of decades of evidence confirming the impact of teacher-student conferences—from Jerome Bruner's scaffolding research in the 1960s to the current explosion of profitable tutoring organizations, most American students still spend their school day deployed in groups of thirty, listening to the teacher or doing seatwork. A study done in 2007 by Robert Pianta and his colleagues found that average fourth graders were spending 91 percent of their time either listening to a teacher talk or doing commercially prepared seatwork—much of it test prep. Perhaps ironically, however, most teachers will readily agree that a three-minute private conversation with a child, timed at just the right moment and targeted precisely to that kid's own work, is often more effective than endless whole-class instruction.

Why haven't conferences caught on more widely outside of reading and language arts? There are several very understandable sticking points. Tradition, as usual, provides a first layer of resistance. Teachers' formal training, as well as their own experience as students, strongly conditions them to think of teaching as a one-on-thirty rather than a one-on-one activity. Experienced teachers already possess banks of lesson plans, some of them developed and polished over years, for teacher-centered classroom activities that seem to work. These treasured whole-class lessons are ready to use, and they don't carry the risks and uncertainties that are inevitably part of anything new.

Second, in contemplating more one-to-one conferences, teachers worry about "what to do with the other twenty-nine kids" while they hold conferences with individual pupils. This is a reasonable concern: until teachers can get a classroom of students working productively without constant monitoring, they won't feel safe introducing one-to-one activities like conferences. This, of course, is one of the main reasons why it is so important to establish the workshop structure described—not only does it provide practice time in key curriculum areas, but it also creates the basic frame within which conferences can occur. And, working farther backward, building a productive workshop depends on the initial climate-setting and social-skill-building activities we'll be talking about shortly (see collaborative activities later in this chapter).

Finally, teachers worry that they won't know what to say to a child in a conference. Many think that to have an effective conference, they must first study the learner's work and then ask "the right questions"—or have the right advice ready to give. For teachers just starting to consider instituting such one-to-one conversations, this sounds like a lot of work. But good conferences do not necessarily require extensive teacher preparation. In writing instruction, for example, we have found that kids who have regular three-minute conferences with their teachers gain significantly in writing achievement, even when the teacher does not read the papers or give advice in those conferences.

So what kinds of things can the teacher say? Back in 1983, Donald Graves laid out three simple questions that teachers can use in any subject: (1) What are you working on? (2) How is it going? (3) What do you plan to do next? or How can I help you right now? For each of these key questions, teachers will gradually develop some subprompts or helping questions, but these three basic queries serve just fine for starters. In such a conference, it is not the teacher's job to tell or teach or offer instruction; the task is to help the student talk and to listen. In fact, such "process conferences" actually can help teachers avoid one conferencing problem that they may not worry about, but should: dominating the student. Too many teachers, when they first begin conferencing, simply offer a kind of knee-to-knee lecture, talking at the student for three or four minutes. The simple, three-question conference transfers the conversational responsibility from teacher to student, providing the teacher with a good implicit reminder to keep quiet.

How do such short conferences actually promote the learning of content? These meetings work because they teach a habit of mind. They help students learn how to reflect on their own work, review their own progress, identify their own problems, set their own goals, and make plans and promises to themselves about steps they are going to take. As we regularly hold conferences with students, leading them through the pattern of where-am-I-and-where-do-I-want-to-go, we are truly modeling a way of thinking for themselves; we are holding out-loud conversations with kids that they can gradually internalize and have with themselves.

Implementing a workshop classroom, with its core of individual conferences, can be a challenge for teachers. The structure itself will be new to many students, administrators, and parents; it competes for time with the official curriculum; and it often contradicts teachers' professional training and their own childhood experience in school. Nor do students always take smoothly and effortlessly to the workshop model. Yet, once the workshop gets rolling, it turns the traditional transmission-model classroom upside down: students become active, responsible, self-motivating, and self-evaluating learners, while the teacher drops the talking-head role in favor of more powerful functions as model, coach, and collaborator.

3 STRATEGIC THINKING

Regie Routman says that every human being enters this life thinking, seeking meaning, and comprehending. Even before we are born, we come to know and trust our mother's heartbeat, and are listening to the other sounds we hear from outside. (Why else would parents play Beethoven at the mother's tummy during pregnancy?) The moment we do join the world, we are constantly trying to make sense of everything—what we see, what we hear, what we feel—and a few years later, what we read. We are thinking creatures, there's no doubt about it.

It's always been a platitude among educators that we should "teach students how to think," help them "learn how to learn," etc., etc. And we constantly are told that "the world is changing so fast that information is quintupling every nanosecond," etc., etc. Then someone beats us over the head with that moribund proverb: "Give a man a fish and he eats for today; teach a man to fish and he eats forever." OK, we get it. Teaching thinking should be a big deal. But if you look beyond these slogans, and examine what we actually do, there has been very little *teaching of thinking* going on in American classrooms.

IN KATIE'S LESSON ▶

Katie very explicitly teaches thinking by showing kids how she notices and investigates her questions after reading a book. Then, she releases them to try this in their groups, with her assistance. Later she shows Ike how to think through an online search by modeling her own click-path. Throughout the lesson, there's an emphasis on metacognition, taking responsibility for running your own brain. There's steady encouragement to monitor your research, make smart decisions (as when Brianna changes topics), and critically evaluate sources.

But before we blame teachers for this shortcoming, there's something to remember: until recently, we haven't even known how our own thinking works, so how could we teach it to kids? Insights about how people actually think, how they get their brains to read text or to solve math problems, are fairly new developments.

Let's take reading as our example here, since kids need to do this special kind of cognitive activity in every school subject. Whatever the domain—literature, math, science, history—the content, the subject matter, the information is stored in different sorts of written texts. If kids cannot effectively access that information through reading, they are blocked from becoming knowledgeable and skillful in those subjects. But the actual cognition around reading wasn't much understood until Pearson and Gallagher's landmark 1983 study identified the specific thinking strategies proficient readers rely upon to understand a piece of text. Today, these strategies are gradually coming to inform instruction, as Best Practice teachers explicitly model for kids how to:

- monitor your comprehension
- make sensory images
- make connections with background knowledge
- ask questions
- draw inferences

- determine importance
- synthesize meaning

Thanks to Pearson and subsequent researchers and translators, teachers can now develop explicit lessons based on how smart readers think. They can support kids to comprehend literary, scientific, historical, mathematical, and all the other kinds of texts encountered in school (Harvey and Goudvis 2008; Miller 2002; Keene and Zimmerman 2007; Tovani 2005).

As we explained earlier, one of the principal ways to teach strategic thinking is for teachers to provide think-alouds, during which they vocalize their own internal thinking processes as they read a text. This powerful kind of lesson dramatically undercuts students' common misconception that comprehension is smooth and effortless if you are a "good reader," and demonstrates that making meaning is careful, recursive, stepwise work, even for proficient adult readers. Further, think-alouds allow us to show learners the particular mental operations that skilled thinkers use in different subject fields: how historians weigh sources, for example, or how proficient scientists develop hypotheses.

▶ Into, Through, and Beyond

Though we often rely on think-alouds early in a lesson or unit, we need to support kids' cognitive work at all stages of a study or inquiry. And our instructional choices range well beyond think-alouds. With reading as our example, let's look at how we might provide thinking-centric scaffolds *before* kids enter a text, *while* they are reading it, and *after* they have read.

INTO: Activities that prepare students before they read. This includes (1) helping students get focused on and curious about the reading, (2) developing purposes for reading, (3) involving students in issues and concepts in the reading, (4) making connections with students' prior knowledge to help make sense of the reading, and (5) modeling or demonstrating for students a cognitive strategy, a way to negotiate the upcoming text.

THROUGH: Activities that help students construct, process, and question ideas as they read. Good readers *visualize* what is happening in a story or historical situation or science experiment. As they read they notice the *questions* or wonderings that pop into their heads. They make *connections* between various parts of the piece and their own lives as well as the larger world around them. They draw *inferences,* putting together clues in the text and their own background knowledge to go beyond the explicitly stated information. They are always working to determine which are the most *important ideas* and which are minor elements or digressions. And consistently, they *monitor* their comprehension,

The mind of a proficient reader is agile and active, demanding clarity of the text.

noticing when they understand and when they've lost the thread. The mind of a proficient reader is agile and active, demanding clarity of the text.

BEYOND: Activities that guide students to reflect on, integrate, and share the ideas after they're finished. This is when readers *synthesize* ideas within their reading and between what they've read and what they already knew about a topic, to make larger *inferences* and *connections.* They follow up on the *questions* and *purposes* they had and consider whether they've learned answers, found surprises, or developed a new perspective on the topic. And they share their thoughts to help others with this process.

▲ ▲ ▲

As you can foresee, dividing the tasks of reading into these stages and providing students with support at each step takes more time than traditional teaching. It would be easier to simply command kids to "read this for Friday" and then pop a quiz on the appointed day. But, as all of us ex-students know, with that kind of reading assignment the kids generally won't understand or remember material two minutes after the test—and sometimes not even that long. The new approach to content-area reading invests time in having students deeply understand some important texts in the field rather than skimming over everything. The family of into, through, and beyond strategies includes several dozen related structures. Here, we offer just three examples, each one tied to a different stage of reading, and we encourage readers to explore further in the resources listed at the end of the chapter.

▶ *Before Reading: KWL*

This widely used strategy, developed by our National-Louis University colleague Donna Ogle (1986), is a sophisticated brainstorming process that works for students of all ages and in all content areas. Everything is built around an *upcoming topic,* a subject (whales, photosynthesis, Navajo culture, global warming, folktales) that students will soon read about. In successive stages, the teacher leads students, usually as a whole class, to first list what they think they already **Know** about the topic, then what they **Want** to find out about it, and later, after reading, what they've **Learned.**

The initial **K** step asks students to access their prior knowledge. As students brainstorm what they already know or "think they know" about the topic, the teacher lists the items on chart paper or an overhead. Why is evoking this "prior knowledge" so crucial? Because when their knowledge base is surfaced, students have an easier time making connections between new information and what they already know, which in turn helps make sense of the new material. It doesn't even matter if kids brainstorm misconceptions during a **K** session; this can actually be helpful, because incorrect ideas will be challenged by the upcoming reading, a much more effective kind of feedback than having the teacher simply say, "You're wrong."

While the **K** step usually goes smoothly, students sometimes need help getting started on the **W** questions—perhaps because they are hesitant to reveal their lack of knowledge, or because they're too infrequently asked to pose their own questions in school. To overcome any reticence, teachers can use items in the **K** column to tease out the questions: *I notice that you said Iraq was a desert. So what do you wonder about how people live in such a place?* This **W** process, generating questions about the topic, explicitly sets purposes and goals for the reading to come. Kids—and adults—read better and comprehend more when they enter the text thinking, with specific questions in mind. After completing the **K** and **W** columns, students can group and label the items in categories they decide on, to streamline their goals for reading.

Later, after the reading is done, students return to **L**—what they've learned—and record how they achieved the reading goals they set for themselves. When the students are completing the **L** list, teachers make sure to compare it to the **K** and **W** columns. Students should not only become more aware of what they've learned but also realize—as is often the case in learning—that some questions didn't get answered, while unexpected new ideas turned up. Used in this full form, KWL is really a complete into-through-and-beyond strategy, one of its elegant attributes. Developer Donna Ogle has written about elaborated versions of KWL that take this valuable idea even further (Carr and Ogle 1987).

The KWL strategy can be used to commence any unit of study in any subject: science, social studies, technology, math, health, you name it. For example, in his high school art classes, our colleague Arnie March doesn't just plunge into teaching Manet, Monet, Sisley, Pissarro, and the rest—he asks kids first to jot what they "know or think they know" about Impressionism and Impressionist painters. Then they make a whole-class list of K's, which does several nice things: it honors what kids do know (names like Picasso go up, stories of trips to the museum are told); kids' misconceptions are revealed for correction later (Andy Warhol was not an Impressionist); and best of all, a kind of implicit class-wide contract or agenda is created about going forward together in this topic. When we are required to teach topics on which kids have little or no background knowledge to activate, then we go must go back one more step and build that knowledge, immersing students in images, books, videos, conversations, and ideas about the topic. When they are up to speed, then we rejoin the KWL model, saying: "*Now* what do you wonder, what questions do you have, what would you like to find out?"

▶ During Reading: Text Coding

Veteran readers often have ways of marking or coding text they want to remember. Maybe they use a yellow highlighter, underline or box words, or put marks in the margins to flag questions, exclamations, or wonderments as they read. Indeed, marking up the text may be the most simple, practical, and widespread thinking tool that real-life readers use. In school, however, students often are discouraged from making any marks in the books they're using. In fact, the more challenging the material (like science or history textbooks), the less likely that kids will be allowed to use this effective tool for enhancing comprehension. Too bad. But we compensate by issuing small Post-it notes for kids to record their thinking as they read, leaving their questions, comments, connections, and reactions right on the page where they experienced them. The same technique can be used with their math, history, or science texts.

When books or other reading materials *can* be marked up (or when we make photocopies for this purpose), it's important for students to have a useful set of response codes. This is especially helpful with dense, content-loaded texts where every word matters, like poetry, math, or fact-filled nonfiction books. When addressing such text, students need to penetrate the surface, and dig out the meaning. Annotating text encourages kids to monitor their thinking, to stop, think, and react. Comprehension is enhanced when students notice their responses as they read, and quickly mark those spots (Vaughan and Estes 1986).

Figure 2.3
*Sample text codes
from Daniels and
Steineke, 2011.*

Text Codes	
✓	when you read something that makes you say, "Yeah, I knew that," or "I predicted that," or "I saw that coming."
X	when you run across something that contradicts what you know or expect.
?	when you have a question, uncertaintly, puzzle, need clarification, or are unsure.
!	when you discover something new, surprising, exciting, or fun that makes you say: cool, whoa, yuck, no way, awesome.
★	when you read something that seems important, vital, key, memorable or powerful.
👁	(an eye) when the reading really makes you see or visualize something.
⬭⬭	(interlocking chain links) when you have a connection between the text and your life, the world, or others things you've read.
ZZZ	this is boring, I'm falling asleep.

Teachers don't just hand out these codes; they *show* kids how to use them. Projecting a short story or news article, the teacher thinks aloud and puts down the appropriate marks where she herself is stopping to think. The teacher tries to vocalize her thinking process: "Well, I already knew that" (check). "What? I don't understand this" (question mark). "Now that's really important" (exclamation point). Next, students can begin using the coding system on short class readings. Words can be part of text coding, too. Students may jot words or brief phrases in the margins to flag big ideas, note strong reactions, or highlight puzzling questions. If the book belongs to the school or a library, the codes can be placed on small 1½-inch Post-it notes, with the edge sticking out for easy locating.

Once students become skilled at coding text, these special notes can be used to feed classwork in a variety of ways. Many teachers send students into small groups for reading discussions, using the coded sections of the text as conversation starters (e.g., "I was really puzzled here on the bottom of page 23 where Romeo says, 'What light from yonder window breaks?' How can light break?"). The teacher can also lead whole-class discussions using prompts like these: Who had a question mark in the first section? Exactly where was it? What puzzled you?

In Terrell Montgomery's middle school biology class, the district curriculum requires her to teach about invasive alien species. So Terrell creates text sets of short articles covering a host of invasive species—Burmese pythons, wild boars, Asian carp, killer bees, fire ants (she knows the kids love the creepiest ones). Then she lets each student choose the article about their favorite critter. Before they start reading, Terrell teaches a special text coding system. "Successful invasive species go through three stages," she explains. "They have to arrive, survive, and thrive. So, while you are reading your article, if you come upon some information that tells you how your critter arrived in the new ecosystem, put an *A* in the margin and jot a few words about what you learned. If the article explains how the species survived, mark that part of the text with an *S* and jot some words to help you remember. And if you read about the creature really thriving, dominating a niche and outcompeting other species, mark that information with a *T* and some words to help you remember the details. Ready? Happy reading, everyone." Later, the whole class gathers to share their learning, using the text codes to remember and quickly locate vital information.

▶ *After Reading: Written Conversation*

We often use class discussion as a key after-reading activity. But when you think about it, what is a class discussion? It is usually one person talking and twenty-nine others sitting, pretending to listen, and hoping that their turn never comes. Not quite what the standards documents call "engaged learning."

In fact, whole-class discussions may be routine, but they are a pretty passive form of instruction, since most kids at any given moment are not actively engaging with the material. With written conversation, we can have a "discussion" where everyone is actively talking at once—though silently, in writing.

Here's how it works in practice. Every student starts with a blank piece of paper, and at the teacher's signal, gets one to two minutes to share their thinking about the material they read (or any other shared classroom experience, like a Civil War video or a lab experiment). Then the teacher calls out "pass," and everyone hands their paper to the next person in the group. They read their classmate's thoughts and then write a comment directly underneath. The teacher calls "pass" again, maybe three or four times, until the circulating "chain letters" are filled with ideas, and the discussion can shift from written to out-loud. This process ensures that every single student in the room is either reading about or writing about one specific chunk of curriculum, for every minute that this write-around lasts. Nobody sits waiting for a turn that never comes, nobody can wiggle out of participating because they are shy or uncooperative. Everybody plays.

Here's what one pair of kids' letters looked like when Wendy Burns' fourth graders had a written conversation about a play they had seen in the school auditorium the day before.

March 14   Room 104

Dear Tammy,

How did you like the play yesterday? Do you still remember their real names? What were their names in the play? The sence was terrific.

Sincerely, Alberto Gregory Savini

Dear Alberto,

I liked the play but, I wish they showed when Lincoln was shot. I don't know their real names, but the people played Abraham Lincoln and Marty Todd Lincoln. By the way, scene is spelled s-c-e-n-e.

Signed,

Tammy Lynette Franklin

Dear Tammy

That sounds kind of immplight that they would show you how Abraham Lincoln was shot. Well, I did know their names, OK.

Sincerely,

Alberto Gregory Savini

Hey, Alberto,

Did you notice how overprotective Mary Todd Lincoln was? Know wonder she kind of went crazy after Abraham Lincoln died. But Mary Todd did have fashion sense, right? Don't you wish they showed when Lincoln got shot? I do.

singed,

Tammy Lynette Franklin

Dear Tammy,

No I didn't. Yes, she made a dress, it looked cool but not that designable. Yes I really do.

Sincerely,

Alberto Gregory Savini

This last entry may seem slightly cryptic until you realize that Alberto is answering the three questions posed in Tammy's previous missive, one at a time. And, as we see, she has finally beaten him into agreeing that the Lincoln death scene (or "sence," as Alberto would spell it) should have been included in the school play.

4 COLLABORATIVE ACTIVITIES

Best Practice means big changes in the way classrooms operate. Across all content areas, state-of-the-art instruction requires much less teacher presentation and controlling, and far more active student learning, taking place in flexibly shifting, decentralized groupings. In Best Practice classrooms, students work together effectively in small groups—in pairs, threes, ad hoc groups, and long-term teams—without constant teacher supervision. Teachers all across the country have been discovering and adapting the powerful versions of collaborative learning described by Darling-Hammond et al. (2008), William Glasser (1990), David and Roger Johnson (1998), Shlomo Sharan (1999), and others. They have been reassured and excited by research showing that, using the customary standardized measures, students of all grade levels make significant achievement gains across the curriculum when they are organized into collaborative groupings and projects. In 2011, a meta-analysis by Joseph Durlak showed that in schools where social skills are explicitly taught,

◄ **IN KATIE'S LESSON**

The whole literature circle lesson sequence is a collaborative group activity. Throughout, kids are working in the same small groups, originally formed around their book choices. To ensure success through every phase, they make formal ground rules before beginning. Then the groups work together over four specific phases: discussing their historical novels, digging out lingering questions, conducting research, and sharing their learning with the rest of the class.

academic achievement rises about 13%, in both course grades and standardized tests. Collaboration works.

And we must be sure to apply these effective collaborative structures to a thoughtful, rigorous curriculum. Some popular cooperative learning applications are merely study teams that harness the power of social interaction to help kids memorize the same old curriculum content. In fact, kids *can* teach each other dates and facts and formulas more effectively when they study as a group, but why bother? Far more powerful and appropriate uses of collaboration occur when students set up and pursue group investigations, read and discuss novels in literature circles, or generate their own crafted pieces of writing with the input of peer response and editing groups. We want to see students discussing and debating big ideas, not memorizing minutiae. As the Common Core Standards put it, by high school, students should be able to:

- Initiate and participate effectively in a range of collaborative discussions (one-to-one, in groups, and teacher-led) with diverse partners on grade-level topics, texts, and issues, building on others' ideas and expressing their own clearly and persuasively.

- Propel conversations by posing and responding to questions that probe reasoning and evidence; ensure a hearing for a full range of positions on a topic or issue; clarify, verify, or challenge ideas and conclusions; and promote divergent and creative perspectives.

- Respond thoughtfully to diverse perspectives; synthesize comments, claims, and evidence made on all sides of an issue; resolve contradictions when possible; and determine what additional information is needed. (CSSS Initiative 2010)

▶ *Social Relationships Come First*

While reading about these seven structures of Best Practice teaching, you probably notice that many of them depend on a cooperative classroom climate and supportive relationships among everyone in the classroom. Back in Katie's lesson, we noticed what skillful collaborators those kids were: they could plan and execute group projects, divide up responsibilities, keep track of schedules and commitments, and have lively, on-topic conversations that included vigorous but respectful debate. In short, they acted friendly and supportive toward each other. Now, as wonderful as the kids at Burley are, they were not born knowing how to collaborate so skillfully—or even, wonderful as their parents are, trained to join in inquiry circles at home.

No, the reason Katie's kids can work, plan, think, and converse so well is because she, and other Best Practice teachers, teach the necessary social skills— some of what we now call "twenty-first century skills"—*explicitly*. Early in the year, Katie and all the teachers at Burley take specific and intentional steps to build acquaintance, friendliness, and support among the students. They don't leave it to chance that the kids will get along and work well with each other. They make sure.

▲ ▲ ▲

Class constitutions. Just down the hall from Katie's room are Debbie King and Michele Timble's fourth-grade classes. If you look on the walls of either room, you'll see two unique classroom compacts, mini-constitutions made by the teachers and their kids back during the first week of the year. Imagine those muggy early days of school, as Deb (and Michele across the hall) gathered kids on the rug in front of them:

Deb: You guys, I have a copy of the United States Constitution here. Let me read you the first part, the preamble:

"We the People of the United States, in Order to form a more perfect Union, establish Justice, insure domestic Tranquility, provide for the common defense, promote the general Welfare, and secure the Blessings of Liberty to ourselves and our Posterity, do ordain and establish this Constitution for the United States of America."

Remember we talked about the Constitution a little last year? Can you tell what they were doing? Why did they write this thing?

Jason: To say how they wanted to live, what kind of rules would help for living together.

Deb: Right, the people who started this country decided to write down the big ideas, the principles that they wanted to live by, together. And I was thinking, maybe the same applies to us. We are a new group, right? Maybe not a nation, but we are a new community. And we might want to think about the ways we want to live together and treat each other in room 303 this year. Does that make some sense? Turn to your partner for a minute and talk about this: what would make fourth grade a really good place to be this year? How should we treat each other and work together? What should be our principles as a new community?

Over the next few minutes, there's a lively hum in the room. Kids generate ideas as Debbie circulates, briefly sitting with different pairs of students. After a while, the group regathers and kids offer suggested clauses for the class compact. They negotiate, reword, winnow, rewrite, and finally come up with the compact shown in Figure 2.4.

Figure 2.4
*Room 303's
classroom compact*

Room 303's Classroom Compact

We, the students and teachers in Room 303, in order to form a more peaceful classroom, do establish this compact.

We agree to speak and listen to each other with respect.

We agree to work hard and encourage others.

Finally, We agree to care about each other so it feels just like home.

We sign below as a symbol of our commitment to keep our class happy, safe, and comfortable.

This is followed by twenty-six signatures, many with Founding Fathers' style flourishes, and surrounded by detailed self-portraits of each signatory.

▲　▲　▲

How different this lesson is from other start-the-year events teachers have sometimes used! Too often we launch Day 1 by presenting a list of rules, infractions, and their commensurate punishments. ("The third time, I call your parents . . .") When you think about it, this is tantamount to telling kids: "Before I even met you, I was thinking of all the things that you might do wrong and how I can punish you for it." It sacrifices any opportunity to jointly develop rules and expectations that the kids might actually buy into. It announces an adversarial attitude. And, most self-defeatingly, it serves not as a deterrent, but as a *menu* for any would-be provocateurs in class, who are likely energized by this "just try something, buster" attitude. Instead, Deb and Michele pull out the Constitution and use it as "mentor text" for a people coming together to give voice to their shared aspirations.

Well, what about high school? Probably it's not so easy to get kids talking about friendliness and support there? Come visit Nancy Steineke's English classroom in the first week of school, where five classes a day march through—a total of 150 kids, some who already know and like each other, and others who either don't know or don't like various classmates. If Nancy lets this situation persist unaltered, getting kids to collaborate in the classroom will be inconsistent and ineffective all year long. If she mistakenly sees this as a luck-of-the-draw phenomenon, she'll sigh and say, "Maybe next year I'll get a class that can collaborate, but for this year I guess I'll just have to lecture."

But Nancy knows that cooperative classes are made, not born. And all her lessons require every kid to work willingly and respectfully with anyone else in the class for the next 180 days. As Nancy tells them, "You don't have to hang out after school, but in here, you have to *act* friendly toward everyone."

▲   ▲   ▲

Home court advantage. To begin building that classroom camaraderie, Nancy has kids read the baseball standings in the *Chicago Tribune*. The research question she poses is: Why do teams win more games at home than away? She puts kids in small groups to puzzle over the Cubs and White Sox won-loss records to figure out what "home field advantage" really means. Kids slowly begin listing factors that create home court or home field advantage.

- You know the field well.
- Your fans are all there.
- You feel comfortable.
- People yell encouraging things.
- You can get excited from the cheering.
- They don't boo when you make a mistake.
- You can depend on your teammates.
- You try harder so you don't let your fans down.

When Nancy pulls the kids back together, she invites each group to share one factor they considered, and a definition of home court advantage begins to emerge. Teams win more games at home than away because they feel safe and supported, because their teammates are dependable and positive, because they are motivated to try even harder for the home fans, and because they don't fear being razzed for their mistakes. "And that's what I want this class to be for you all year long," Nancy concludes. "We have to work like a team, to make sure everyone feels safe and supported to take risks and try things and grow as readers and writers. I want you guys to come in here every day and feel that you have home court advantage as a learner."

Now, Nancy hands out big paper and markers, and each group creates a poster that depicts their own vision of home court advantage. Many have stick-figure scenes depicting bleachers filled with fans hollering out encouraging slogans. These posters go right up on the wall of the classroom and remain there for the rest of the year. This might sound like a kindergarten activity creeping into secondary school (sophomores coloring? the first week of school?). But Nancy explains the ongoing benefits. "All through the year, whenever somebody fires off a put-down of someone else in the class, kids will simply point at the wall of posters, and that's all it takes. Sometimes all kids need to do is tip their heads toward the wall, just that subtle gesture, to remind each other, we don't do that stuff in here, we support each other."

▲ ▲ ▲

Follow up lessons. Nancy's and Debbie's lessons are just getting started, building community, when the group first gathers. As the school year unfolds, Best Practice teachers continue to explicitly teach collaboration, using lessons around seven specific social skills (Harvey and Daniels 2009):

Collaboration Strategies
Be responsible to the group
Listen actively
Speak up
Prove your point
Share the air
Disagree agreeably
Reflect and correct

From this inventory of key collaboration skills, teachers build specific mini-lessons that help kids grow as coworkers. If kids have trouble "sharing the air" in a small-group discussion, with some acting like "hogs" and others as "logs," they don't bemoan the kids' shortage of collaborative DNA. Instead, they teach a lesson to fix it.

Next meeting, everyone gets five poker chips. Every time you talk, you have to spend one chip. The airhogs, being airhogs, will spend all their chips immediately—so they are prevented from talking any more (though they can ask questions of others). Now, the reticent or shy or formerly sleeping logs have room to speak up—indeed, they *must* speak up, because until their chips are expended, nobody can go back to the bank and get five new chips and start another round of better balanced conversation. Does this sound manipulative? Mechanical? You bet. It is also highly effective (Daniels and Steineke 2004).

Here's a kinder, gentler lesson to teach the social skill of sharing airtime. The teacher gathers the kids together and says: "When I was sitting in on your groups yesterday I noticed a lot of you were having the same problem—trying to balance the airtime in the conversation. Some people were talking a lot, while other people were hardly talking at all. So here's what I think we should work on: What could you say to someone who isn't participating very much in your group? I mean, specifically what words could you say that might invite or encourage someone to join in? Talk in your groups for a minute and jot down the ideas you come up with."

Typically, students will come up with phrases like:

Hey, _____, what do you think?

_____, we haven't heard from you in a while.

Do you have any ideas about that, _____?

What's your opinion, _____?

The class affirms the most helpful-sounding invitations, and group members copy their favorites onto folded index cards to make "table tents" that are placed right in their line of sight when the next group meeting convenes (see Figure 2.5). The cards cue students to invite quiet members in—all they have to do is read the card and fill in the name: "Brenda, we haven't heard from you in a while, what do you think?" (Steineke 2009).

▶ *Putting Social Skills to Work in the Classroom*

Once the classroom has developed a climate of friendliness and support, the teacher can utilize a whole range of sociable structures that engage and involve kids in higher-order thinking and discussion.

Turn and talk. (Also called pair share or partnerships.) This is the simplest building block of an engaged, interactive classroom. Pairs of kids turn to each other for one to two minutes and talk about a topic given by the teacher. That's it. Turn-and-talks usually happen within a large-group presentation, where the whole class is gathered for a teacher lesson, read-aloud, or other purpose. As the

Figure 2.5
Table tents with invitations

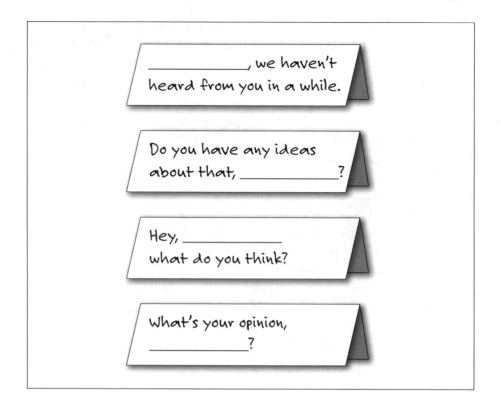

teacher shares, she periodically stops and asks kids to discuss the ideas with a partner, giving them a very specific prompt: *What do you think is going to happen next in this story? What would be some important sections to have in our science journals? What do you think was Lincoln's main reason for freeing the slaves?* After bringing the kids back, she will typically call on a few pairs for their ideas, examples, or questions. Then the presentation proceeds until the next turn-and-talk opportunity, usually not more than five or ten minutes later.

This simple structure gets kids involved in the content, makes learning a collaborative enterprise and not just a teacher show, acts as a check for understanding, and helps the teacher notice strengths and needs among the group. It's also a radical departure from more teacher-centered instruction, where kids are expected to sit through very long periods of teacher talk without moving or talking—which, from a cognitive point of view, prevents them from taking enough action to actually remember the content. For a moment, picture a traditional high school lecture class; now, interject a few turn-and-talks (say one every seven or eight minutes). This simple addition of student involvement and action can significantly transform the dynamic.

Of course, even for a collaborative activity like turn-and-talk, norms must be established first. Kids need to know who their partner is and be sitting right beside them before the lesson begins; they have to use their quieter "twelve-inch voice" so pairs can hear each other; they need to take turns talking; and they have to come right back when the teacher regathers the group. So we teach these skills in mini-lessons, right at the start of the year, knowing that kids will benefit for months to come.

Partner/buddy reading. Paired reading activities can come in many variations. Two students may take turns reading aloud to each other from a story or text-book, passing a single book back and forth if they don't have two copies. Or they can read silently, stopping to talk after each page. Pairs can read the same section outside of class and join to discuss the reading, or they can jigsaw the text, read-ing different sections and sharing their respective pieces of the puzzle.

Literature circles/book clubs. Groups of four or five students choose and read the same article, book, or novel. While doing their reading inside or outside of class, they make notes about topics or questions they want to bring up later with their friends. Then, student-led groups meet (once for an article, three or four times for a book) using everyone's notes as sources of discussion topics and debates. Afterward, the circle may report briefly to the whole class; then they trade members with other groups that are finished, select more reading, and move into a new cycle (Daniels 2002; Daniels and Steineke 2004). Alternatively, when finishing a book or other reading, students like Katie's may have lingering questions, topics that they have become curious about through the reading. In that case, they can re-form as inquiry circles (described on the next page) to pursue answers to those questions.

Writing circles. As we mentioned earlier, Jim Vopat developed this variant of literature circles with kids in Milwaukee. The model parallels book clubs quite directly: kids form themselves into small groups and choose topics they want to write about; then each member prepares a draft. The choice of genres is wide open; kids can write a poem, story, play, memoir, news article, whatever suits them. Periodically, the group gets together to share their drafts, reading them aloud and receiving constructive, low-risk feedback from their group-mates. Key to this interaction is the teacher's careful training of kids in myriad ways to give helpful responses. After sending multiple first drafts through this peer response process, each group member picks one piece that they feel has poten-tial to develop into a larger, polished, public piece of writing—and they go to work on it. In this phase, members take on new roles designed around helping every writer reach their audience: publisher, editor, copyeditor, agent, illustra-tor, marketing director, and so forth. Working as partners, everyone helps to bring a piece to "publication"—and then the cycle of exploratory drafts and feedback begins again.

Inquiry circles. Developed in 2009 by coauthor Harvey Daniels and our colleague Stephanie Harvey, inquiry circles, the authors joke, "are like literature circles on steroids." Instead of simply picking a book to read and discuss together, kids select a *topic* to investigate. And that opens up the whole world of resources—magazines, newspapers, journals, primary sources, websites, databases—not to mention other research techniques: observation, experimentation, surveys and questionnaires, and interviewing. Harvey and Daniels outline four types of these inquiry circles:

- Mini-inquiries, also called "quick-finds," in which teachers and students notice interesting questions as they pop up and stop to find answers, honoring their curiosity rather than rolling on.

- Curricular inquiries, where teachers take mandated curricular content, whether it's community helpers, photosynthesis, or factoring polynomials, and organize kids into small investigative teams that research different aspects of the topic, and later, teach others what they have learned. This is the meat and potatoes of inquiry: taking on subjects that students must learn about anyway, and turning them into active, challenging, and memorable experiences that require kids to take responsibility and build knowledge that lasts.

- Literature circle inquiries, as described in Katie's story at the very start of this chapter, are investigations that begin at the end of a book. Most lifelong readers recognize that when they finish a book of any merit or substance, they usually have more questions than they started with. Maybe you didn't originally care much about the Great Depression, but after reading *Bud, Not Buddy*, there are a million things you wonder about—the issues raised in the book, the time period, or the author. We begin by asking kids to notice their lingering questions from the book, and form them into inquiry groups around the questions that most attract each student.

- Open inquiries, where small groups of kids investigate hot topics and burning issues they have chosen for themselves. In open inquiries, we form kids into research teams based on their topics, and then coach and support them as they seek information, evaluate material, vet sources, lay out their findings, and develop a performance that shows others what they have learned. Sometimes this version feels hard to fit into a school year, when every day feels filled by mandates and the need to "cover the curriculum." But kids aren't really working at the highest level of rigor until they take responsibility for *every* stage of inquiry, which begins with identifying (not being assigned) an important, worthwhile, and researchable topic.

When teachers commit to the inquiry circle model over a whole year, they begin to develop major inquiry units; for more about this, see Integrative Units, coming up just ahead.

Whole-class meetings. One of our favorite school improvement approaches is called the Responsive Classroom (see their website, www.responsiveclassroom .org). In part of their model, community is built through very well-designed whole-class routines, rituals, meetings, and processing. It is not a cute and minor thing that students begin the day tossing a nerf ball around the room while saying "good morning" to whoever catches it, by name. This is about allocating time and creating activities that build and sustain the fellow-feeling needed to have hard-working, kid-driven classrooms.

So, we don't gather the whole classroom community only for teacher lectures. We also come together for participatory, democratic meetings during which the group can brainstorm ideas, set goals, make plans, learn new structures for working, solve problems, and evaluate their own work. While this kind of session may sound simple, most teachers are experienced in giving whole-class presentations and instructions, not in chairing meetings that invite genuine interchange and decision making by the students.

William Glasser outlined a recurrent cycle of classroom meetings that builds both content learning and democratic involvement (1990). The class:

1. meets regularly to talk about its own learning activities and social processes;
2. identifies learning goals or group problems;
3. prioritizes its goals or problems;
4. proposes and discusses alternative courses of action;
5. makes a formal, group commitment to action; and
6. regularly meets to share and review the outcomes of group decisions.

While this pattern of whole-class meetings obviously can nurture the socioemotional development of the classroom community, its academic uses are just as vital: at these meetings, students can decide what to study, divide into working groups, plan how and when to report their learnings with others, and more.

Whole-class meetings are also important for sharing completed work that students are proud of or for which they want feedback to help them revise further. Many elementary teachers end their daily writing workshop time with ten minutes for a few students to occupy the "author's chair," read their work aloud, and call on peers who ask questions, offer specific praise, or explain where they felt confused. A whole science class can profitably talk through the qualities that characterize an effective lab explanation, report, or small-group presentation—so that everyone participates in setting criteria for meaningful evaluation. And when any small-group project is finished, the teacher can help her class internalize the underlying concepts by outlining together not only the major ideas explored, but also the activities the class used and how groups overcame various obstacles and solved problems in the course of their learning.

5 INTEGRATIVE UNITS

In Best Practice schools and classrooms, administrators and teachers refuse to accept the randomness in learning that comes with the traditional march of separate subjects through the school day. They believe that content does matter and that for school to work, it must *make sense* to students—ideally, make sense all day long. Therefore, whether on their own or with input from students, teachers identify a few big subjects of interest and importance, and then build extended units around those topics. In elementary grades, we know teachers who've built multiweek chunks of curriculum around topics as diverse as whales, rain forests, exploring, castles, the ocean, climate, Australia, fairy tales, and homes.

In a whales unit, for example, the children might read (and hear read aloud) lots of different whale stories, build a library of favorite whale books, do a whale readers' theater, study the biology of whales, work in research teams to investigate different kinds of whales (e.g., blue, killer, and beluga), go to the aquarium (if there's one nearby) and observe real whales, write and illustrate whale stories and reports, do whale mathematics (calculating the days of gestation or the quantity of plankton a baleen whale eats daily), and, of course, do lots of whale art. When teachers design such thematically coherent activities, they usually find that they can quite easily fit in many of the standard mandated curriculum elements; these topics simply come up in a different way, at a different time, and in a different order. But the main benefit of such teaching is that it provides children with the choice, continuity, order, challenge, and genuine responsibility they need to both enjoy school and stay engaged with the work.

Deepening content. Extended lessons are often called "themes" or "interdisciplinary units," denoting their cross-content nature. And while they are a step ahead of the uncoordinated, disjointed experiences kids may have with school subject matter, they don't necessarily represent the very highest level of curriculum development without some thoughtful planning. In fact, these themes can sometimes be downright superficial—a leading example being the seemingly mandatory "Apple Unit" in October. Now, there's nothing wrong with reading apple books, doing apple art, and taking a bus to the apple orchard (we're all about authentic experiences). But is a unit like this mostly for fun, or is there some content with staying power—about agriculture, seeds and pollination, nutrition and diet, or about the apple's symbolism in American lore and literature? And are kids' own questions about apples being answered, or even asked? Or is a predetermined series of attractive experiences simply unfolding for the umpteenth year in a row? Instead of adapting preplanned units from a lesson-planning website or from an educator's magazine, teachers can search out readings, books, videos, magazines, and websites with lots of great materials about

> *In Best Practice schools and classrooms, administrators and teachers refuse to accept the randomness in learning that comes with the traditional march of separate subjects through the school day.*

the topics that will be coming up during the school year (always a huge task in creating thematic units), but then bring kids into the planning process when the school year convenes.

What about high school? Curriculum integration often seems easier in elementary schools, where teachers may have the same thirty kids all day long. If a self-contained elementary teacher decides to integrate curriculum, her own goodwill and resolve can get it done. But in high school, things are a little tougher. Creating a truly integrated curriculum would require the cooperation of six or seven teachers who have no mandate to cooperate nor history of doing so, who have no common planning time, and who all still have on their desks a weighty scope-and-sequence document for their own segment of the school day—a curriculum that they probably have spent many increasingly comfortable years delivering.

Still, there are many ways high school teachers can move toward integrated, thematic instruction. If schools are ready to make courageous institutional reform, they can follow the pattern of Addison Trail High School in Illinois, where a large group of freshmen meet in a thematic three-course program that integrates the study of English, science, and social studies. At Best Practice High School in Chicago, teachers developed their own timeshare plan: Tuesdays and Thursdays for block-scheduled integrated curriculum units; Mondays and Fridays for regular seven-period, separate-subject days; and Wednesdays for students' community internships.

Even where there's no schoolwide sanction for innovation, teachers still can reform their own forty-five-minute slice of the school day, reorganizing material into more meaningful, coherent, even integrative chunks. If the textbook presents a jumbled or arbitrary sequence of materials, the teachers can rearrange it, finding and identifying organizing themes that the curriculum writers didn't notice or mention. Teachers can help kids by identifying and stressing the few "big ideas" that strand through the welter of seemingly disparate material often presented to students.

Sometimes, two secondary teachers can get together to provide integration across more than one period of the day. For years, this has been done in American Studies programs, in which history and literature are taught in a combined two-period, team-taught class. Taking this idea a step further, several schools we've worked with have begun projects where a group of seventy-five kids and three teachers get a half-day together to pursue a big topic. At Stagg High School near Chicago, one pilot group studied U.S. history, literature, and German—an approach that, among other things, highlighted the often-overlooked Germanic roots of American colonial culture. Although curriculum integration in high schools is especially challenging, there's increasing hope as schools around the country break down the barriers of student and teacher scheduling, departmental boundaries, ability grouping, and subservience to standardized test scores.

This integrative curriculum model involves students in content inquiry right from the start—identifying topics, developing questions to be pursued, planning the inquiry, dividing up tasks, gathering information, and sharing in the whole process. We have learned the most about this approach from pioneering work of James Beane (1997, 2005). His version of integrated, negotiated curriculum does more than cross subject areas: it makes students real, responsible partners in their own education.

IN KATIE'S LESSON ▶

Katie's integrated units on novels meet the requirements of the Chicago Public Schools curriculum for social studies, and also address Common Core State Standards for reading classic and contemporary works. But Katie has met these standards the Best Practice way, melding all the skills and content into a big inquiry unit that engages kids' curiosity and hands them responsibility for working, thinking, and building knowledge that will last.

In its purest form, integrative curriculum is designed around specific concerns students have about themselves and their world. Inquiries begin with a series of brainstorming and listing activities designed to gather students' questions and issues. From these lists of topics, units of the curriculum are developed collaboratively by teachers and students. If needed, teachers can later "back-map" from students' genuine questions to many of the mandated ingredients in district or state curriculum guides. If middle schoolers say they want to study racism (as they often do), teachers can plug in plenty of history, math (compiling statistics from racial-attitude surveys), and science (the literature of scientific racism, from phrenology to mental measurement, contrasted with today's fascinating tracing of DNA histories), along with plenty of reading, writing, researching, and representing skills.

Yes, but . . . how do I fit in these big integrative units when there is so much other content we are required to cover?

We teachers are always selecting from a whole universe of curriculum. Academic subjects are so rich and extensive that in the course of one unit or semester or year, there's simply too much material for anyone to learn in any deep or significant way. Indeed, one of the most counterproductive elements of traditional American schooling has been its relentless emphasis on "covering the material" in a prescribed curriculum guide. Typically, such a mandated curriculum is an overstuffed compendium of facts, dates, concepts, books, persons, and ideas—a volume of material so enormous that no one can remember *anything*, if *everything* must be mentioned. And this pressure pushes teachers toward lecture-style classes, with emphasis on student note-taking, followed by multiple-choice tests stressing temporary memorization and factual recall.

In Best Practice classrooms, teachers realize that every student needn't study every possible topic—or even the same topics. Indeed, it is good educational practice (and solid preparation for adult life) to be part of a community where topics are parceled out to work groups, task forces, teams, or committees. When teachers jigsaw the curriculum, they seek natural ways to divide a given topic, assigning small groups of students to investigate the different parts, each team bringing back its piece of the puzzle to the whole group later on. In U.S. history, for example, not every student needs to learn about every Civil War battle. Instead, a Best Practice teacher might let groups of kids each pick a single battle to study—Antietam for one group, Gettysburg for another, Bull Run for a third, and so on. Then the kids' job is to really dig in with reading and research and talking, taking time to carefully explore and grasp the events involved, pursuing a deep understanding of their particular battle.

Later, when the class reconvenes, each group has a responsibility to share the highlights that emerged from its study. To pull the whole experience together, the teacher helps students find the similarities, differences, connections, and key concepts in the subtopics all have studied. In following this procedure, everyone learns one subject in detail, while still gaining a familiarity with related topics by way of reports from other classmates. For students, as future citizens and voters, what's most important to remember about the Civil War? We'd argue it's not the names of the generals or the dates of the battles, but the distinctive weapons, strategies, tactics, political implications, and injuries sustained in *all* the battles that happened in this horrific new level of warfare.

One last point about integrative units: kids love them. Think back on your own most positive and memorable experiences in school, at different grade levels. Think of subject-matter topics that you really got into, engaged with, and learned—that maybe you still remember, or even studied further on your own. Among the grown-ups we have talked to, those memories very often trace back to rich, holistic, extended, and deep investigations.

REPRESENTING TO LEARN

We talked in Chapter 1 about how important students' expression, as well as their reception, is to their learning. For most of us, just hearing something mentioned is not enough to "learn" it. To really grasp and own a concept, we must *act upon it*, using every possible sensory modality to do so: write it, tell it to others, draw it, debate it, sing it, dance it around the room. Whatever it takes to light up those key brain regions for maximum impact. And we need to do this often, regularly, and long enough for ideas to "stick." But how, specifically, do teachers make this happen in the classroom? What's the pedagogy of expression?

Obviously, the first step in inviting students to represent their thinking is by allowing them—indeed, requiring them—to

◀ **IN KATIE'S LESSON**

Kids build thinking in several modalities throughout these lessons. When first reading their books, they jot their responses and questions on Post-its, using words, phrases, quick sketches, or doodles to capture their thinking as they read— and to provide good discussion starters when the group convenes. Kids represent their learning in lots of peer talk throughout a lesson. And at the end, they choose from public performances like a symposium to represent what they have learned.

talk about what they are studying. When we said earlier that silence should be downplayed in the classroom, what we meant was, if kids aren't talking about the subject matter quite a lot, they probably aren't learning it. Look back at all the talking kids did in Katie's lessons—in pairs, teams, the whole class, conferences with the teacher, presenting research findings. And remember also our section on collaborative activities earlier, where we named a number of structures that make kid-kid talk in the classroom accountable, meaningful, and memorable.

Another preeminent tool we have for representing our thinking is *writing*, which we will spend some time on here. But when we talk about writing as representing, as a kind of expression and a tool for learning, we are not talking about note-taking. Anyone who has been to college can testify that you can become a note-taking robot, mindlessly writing down words from a professor's lecture without understanding them—or even, in any real sense, listening. No, for writing to qualify as taking intellectual action, the ideas under study must be transformed into the student's own words, her own language, her own thinking.

▶ *Writing to Learn*

Many teachers are already familiar with the notion of *writing to learn,* developed in the 1970s and 1980s and widely disseminated though National Writing Project in-service programs. The idea is simple: writing can be a tool of thinking as well as a finished product. There are many quick and simple writing activities that help students to encounter, probe, explore, and remember the content of the curriculum. While the traditional view of school writing envisions only polished compositions, when students act on information by using informal, spontaneous writing, they actually understand and recall more of what is taught. Remember in Katie's lesson how kids sat down in a group and jointly created a whiteboard list of lingering questions they had about the Depression? They didn't revise, spell-check, or seek to publish those lists; instead they *used them* to advance their thinking and organize their further research.

Since the early days of writing to learn, we've discovered that writing down *words* is not the only valuable modality. Drawing, sketching, jotting, mapping, and other artistic and graphic representations are equally valuable—and when combined with words, in strategies like clustering, semantic mapping, or cartooning, they can powerfully leverage students' thinking about the curriculum. Indeed, research is quickly accumulating that documents the contribution artistic expression offers to the development of basic-skills learning in subjects like math, science, and literature. So, to acknowledge this important broadening of writing to learn, we refer to this cognitive work as *representing to learn* (Daniels and Bizar 2004).

Learning logs. While there are many individual writing-to-learn activities that can be used à la carte from time to time, Best Practice teachers tend to be a bit more systematic about having kids represent and develop their thinking. The classic manifestation of this is a journal (or learning log, notebook, or sketchbook), in which students regularly do short, spontaneous, exploratory, personal pieces of writing (or drawing; see Figure 2.6) about the content they are studying. Instead of filling in blanks in worksheets and jotting short answers to textbook study questions, students respond to fewer, broader, more open-ended prompts: What would have changed if Lincoln had been shot six months earlier? What are the advantages of an indicator over a meter? What are three questions from last night's reading that we ought to discuss in class today? In logs, teachers ask students to react, record, speculate, compare, analyze, or synthesize the ideas in the curriculum. Students aren't writing to be graded on grammar or artistic ability, but rather to pursue ideas and try out thoughts. These notebooks are a way of running their brains, monitoring their thinking, and making reflection habitual and concrete. This is writing and drawing for thinking, not as a polished product.

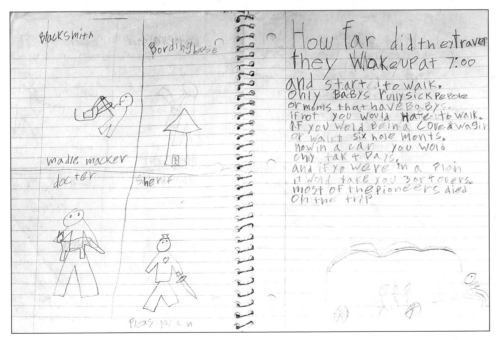

Figure 2.6
Learning Log

As a cognitive tool, learning logs can work for learners in any content field, and at any grade level. Even kindergartners can draw one of the community helpers they are studying and helpful adults can add captions, labels, or talk balloons as kids direct. Whatever the subject matter, learners can always jot down their responses, record their own prior knowledge, probe their thinking patterns, map predictions, diagram connections, or sketch plans for what to do next. When they are shared, notebooks also open a private channel of communication between the teacher and each student. In learning logs, teachers report, students will often share things that they would never announce to the class, thereby providing teachers a new and valuable kind of feedback.

Teachers don't just collect students' short writings and take them home—they *use them during class*, reading random entries aloud to start off the class, feeding them into small-group discussions, giving each student someone else's text and having them jot a quick response, or parceling sets of writing out to teams for review or action. Many teachers, like our friend Wayne Mraz, assign "admit slips" and "exit slips," short bits of writing used to start and end a class. Others run classroom discussions about a topic—a poem or Manifest Destiny or a chemical process—using the kind of written conversation we described earlier (pages 55–57). For teachers who use these representing-to-learn strategies regularly, the compiled entries become an increasingly thick record of what each student has done and learned.

Although these logs are often called journals, they are *not* diaries. Some teachers are wary of trying journals because of the confessional connotations of that word, but academic journaling is expressly for recording and advancing subject-matter learning in school. Other teachers worry about implementation problems, perhaps because they have seen too many ill-advised English teachers trudging home from school on Friday afternoon, lugging a sky-high stack of student spirals that they "have to" respond to over the weekend. But learning logs needn't increase the workload of either students or teachers. They are supposed to *replace* textbook study questions, ditto sheets, or other low-level, memorization-oriented activities. Students should spend the same amount of time working and teachers the same amount of time responding, with everyone engaged in higher-order, more valuable thinking. In fact, many teachers find that when the students' representing-to-learn pieces are used as the starting point for class activities and discussions, they don't even need to collect and read the work separately; hearing the ideas discussed aloud provides plenty of feedback about what kids are thinking.

Sketch-to-stretch. This is one of the many valuable writing-to-learn strategies introduced in Short, Harste, and Burke's classic *Creating Classrooms for Authors and Inquirers* (1996). In this simple strategy, instead of taking notes on a reading, a lecture, or a common experience, students draw quick sketches to stretch their thinking and understanding of concepts. The Annenberg Teacher website offers a simple example (Annenberg 2011).

After reading a description of the nesting habits of hummingbirds, students draw a sketch that shows how they visualized the details: the place a nest would be found, the size of a hummingbird's nest, materials used to build the nest, the number of eggs in a nest, the color of eggs, and how parent(s) of baby hummingbirds take care of their young. Students can draw a series of sketches to reveal the development of baby hummers from egg to first flight.

Next, students share their drawings with a partner, in a small group, or with the whole class, explaining how they made connections and drew inferences from the information provided to make their drawings. Finally, the teacher helps students clarify their thinking and discard misconceptions, using different drawings as talking points.

Figure 2.7
Hummingbird nest

▶ *Drama*

One of the things we three have noticed over our many years of teaching is that anytime you switch the class activity to something dramatic, suddenly there's a whole new cohort of kids who are leading and excelling. When this happens, it first makes you happy as a teacher, as you think to yourself things like, *Wow, I never realized how smart Cherie and Brad and Gina are.* And then about one second later you're worrying, *Yikes, have I been giving those kids enough moments to shine?* The whole idea of students having different learning styles, developed by Howard Gardner and others at Harvard's Project Zero, certainly has a lot of surface appeal. It helps us understand why certain kids respond to some classroom activities far better than others. At the very least it is a powerful reminder of the need for cognitive variety in the classroom, for offering students plenty of entry points and plenty of ways of to engage with the curriculum.

One of the most accessible dramatic structures for classroom learning is *tableaux.* Ever seen the Iwo Jima Memorial statue, or a picture of it? Those soldiers raising a flag in a WWII battle? That's a tableau—a group of people frozen in a scene that tells a powerful story, a depiction that crystallizes an idea. In this case, duty, honor, country. In school, we use tableaux as a way for students to represent ideas and concepts of all kinds: historical events, philosophical ideas, or scientific processes (depicting the stages of cell mitosis is always fun). We add a narrator who reads aloud a passage, quotation, or title that lets the audience know what is being represented by the dramatically arranged group of two to eight students. One of the great things about tableaux is that no one but the narrator has to say anything or remember any lines, so the stage fright potential is almost nil.

Nancy Steineke (2009) shares this set of Homeric tableau prompts that her sophomores choose from, when they are showing their understanding of the end of the Trojan War.

QUOTES AND CAST MEMBERS FOR TROJAN WAR TABLEAUX

1. On a beach hidden from sight of the walls, Ulysses ordered carpenters to build an enormous wooden horse. **Ulysses, carpenters, narrator**

2. Then Ulysses, Diomedes, Menelaus, and sixteen other of their best warriors hid themselves in the belly of the horse. **Ulysses, Diomedes, Menelaus, narrator**

3. They marveled when they found the giant wooden horse and tried to guess its purpose. "Clearly, an offer to Poseidon," said Chryseis. **Chryseis, Priam, Trojans, narrator**

4. Chryseis continued, "If we take the horse into the city and set it in our temple we shall be the ones to earn the favor of the Earth-shaker Poseidon, who has been so hostile to us." "Brilliant," said Priam. "Fatal!" shrieked Cassandra. "That horse will devour Troy!" **Chryseis, Priam, Cassandra, Trojans, narrator**

5. Ulysses crept out. Seeing no one, he tapped on the horse's belly. Diomedes and the others slipped silently out of the trapdoor. **Ulysses, Diomedes, Greeks, narrator**

6. Ulysses led the others to the wall where they surprised and killed the drowsy sentries. **Trojans, Ulysses, Diomedes, Greeks, narrator**

7. Of all the Trojan princes, Aeneas was the only one to escape the massacre. Heedless of his own safety he lifted his old father to his shoulders, and carried him through the burning city. And the Greeks were so struck by his courage that they let him go. **Greeks, Ulysses, Diomedes, Aeneas, Aeneas' father, narrator**

Before performing, students must check back through the book to determine how their chosen scene fits in the overall story and what clues are available to help visualize the moment. Then they block out and rehearse their tableau, and the narrator practices the lines carefully. When it is time for tableaux performances, audience members close their eyes briefly as each team sets up, and only when the tableaux are frozen and ready may onlookers open their eyes and view the performance. In Figure 2.8 we see Mike, Erik, Trevor, Frank, Brad, Kyle, and Luke creating their enactment of Trojan War tableau **number 2.** (Steineke 2009)

Figure 2.8
*Tableau
(Photograph
courtesy of
Nancy Steineke)*

 FORMATIVE-REFLECTIVE ASSESSMENT

In Kristin Ziemke's first grade in Chicago, there's a dedicated computer in the room, labeled with a sign that says "Reflection Booth." When Kristin introduced this resource to her six-year-olds, she gathered them around the computer for a mini-lesson.

Kristin: You guys, we have so many ways of showing what we know in Room 106, don't we? We can write things, we can draw things, we can make giant posters, we can teach each other out loud. And you know I'm always asking you to look back and *reflect* on your work, on your research, on your collaboration with each other. Today, we are adding a new tool to help you reflect on your learning, and the great thing is, you don't have to find me to share your reflections. You can just step into the Reflection Booth here (it's not really a booth, but we are pretending a little bit, right?), press the Control key, and video your reflections on your work. Then just press Stop when you're done, and I'll come look at it later. Isn't that cool? Watch and I'll show you how it works.

Immediately after the demonstration, predictably, there's an eager lineup at the Reflection Booth; everyone wants to share their thinking in this new fun way.

And, of course, the minute a kid has recorded something, they go find Kristin, tug on her pant leg, ask her to please watch their reflection right now! But as the booth becomes a more routine part of the classroom resources, traffic drops to manageable levels, and kids steadily stop by to leave their thinking for Ms. Ziemke, who watches these short clips after school or during conferences with them.

Kids can report on their individual efforts or, if they have been working with a team, they can crowd around the camera and reflect together. Here, two first graders reflect on the poetry unit they have been studying.

Vivian: Hi. I'm Vivian and this is Connor and today we are going to talk to you about poetry.

Connor: Well, first, onomatopoeia is when something goes like, "boom, zoom, pow, drip"—it's like a word that makes a sound.

Vivian: Poems are stuff that you work on. It's kind of like a song, like the Black-eyed Peas, "Tonight's gonna be a good night," but it's something you do all throughout your life. Like if you want to grow up you can be a poetry writer, and do poetry and help the world.

Connor: Or you can use line breaks. Those help the reader. And it doesn't have to rhyme.

Vivian: There's also repetition where you use the same word a lot and alliteration. And it's really fun to write and . . .

Connor: And you learn new stuff.

Vivian: Sometimes it's calm and sometimes it has action. But it's just not too long, because if it's too long then it becomes kind of like a story. And you have to do something really pacific [specific], like you can't just do something like, "I saw a thing. It was cool."

Connor: It's just really interesting to see how there's many different ways to make poems.

Vivian: So I think it's been working really well for the class learning to write poetry.

Connor: Yeah, and it feels great to write poetry.

These reflection videos become a part of each child's assessment portfolio, are used to help track growth all year long, and are viewed in parent conferences, which the kids host right along with Kristin.

In Best Practice classrooms, teachers don't just make up tests and put grades on report cards. They are less interested in measuring students' recall of individual facts or use of certain subskills than in how they perform authentic, complete, higher-order activities: reading whole books, drafting and editing stories or articles, conducting and reporting a scientific inquiry, applying math to real problem solving. Because progressive teachers want deeper and more practical information about children's learning, they monitor students' growth in richer and more sophisticated ways. More and more, teachers are adopting and adapting the tools of ethnographic, qualitative research: observation, interviews, questionnaires, collecting and interpreting artifacts, and performances. They use information from these sources not mainly to "justify" marks on a report card, but to guide instruction, to make crucial daily decisions about helping students grow. And above all, they see the main goal of assessment as helping students set goals, monitor their own work, and evaluate their efforts. Nothing more conclusively marks the well-educated person than the capacity to run one's own brain, have clear self-insight, and follow through on projects.

Observational records. Many teachers keep anecdotal, observational records, saving a few minutes each day to jot notes about students in their classes—some call this "kid-watching." Instead of using numbers, letters, or symbols, teachers create written descriptions of what students are doing and saying. Some teachers put these observations on a schedule, tracking five particular kids on Monday, another five on Tuesday, and so forth; others might watch just one kid per day. Some simply jot notes on any kids who show noteworthy growth, thinking, problems, or concerns; others prefer to record observations of the class as a community. The common feature of these observational notes is that teachers save time for regularly recording them; they develop a format that works for them; and they consistently use these notes, both to guide their instruction and to communicate with parents and others about children's progress.

Teachers also teach students to become self-observers in increasingly powerful ways. In face-to-face interviews, written questionnaires, or learning logs, teachers ask kids to record and reflect on their own work (e.g., books read, experiments conducted). In Best Practice classrooms, it is common for students to have periodic "evaluation conferences" with their teachers, where both parties use their notes to review the learner's achievements and problems over a span of time, and then set goals for the upcoming weeks or months. In a curriculum that values higher-order thinking as well as individual responsibility, such self-evaluation teaches multiple important lessons.

Student portfolios. One of the most promising mechanisms for authentic evaluation is the student portfolio, a folder in which students save selected samples of their best work in a given subject. The practice of keeping such cumulative records has many benefits. First, of course, it provides actual evidence of what the child can do in writing, math, art, or science, instead of a mark in a grade-book—which is, after all, only a symbolic record of a long-discarded piece of real work. These portfolio artifacts also invite all sorts of valuable conversations between the child and the teacher, children and peers, or kids and parents: How did you get interested in this? How did you feel while you were working on this? How did you solve the problems you encountered? What would you tell another student about this subject? What are you going to do next? The process of selecting and polishing items for inclusion in the portfolio invites students to become increasingly reflective about their own work and more skillful at self-evaluation. And the portfolio makes it possible to concretely observe the trajectory of students' progress.

This approach also lends itself very nicely to a wonderful strategy that provides parents with an in-depth understanding of their child's learning—student-led parent conferences. When a parent listens as his or her child explains the work she has done and what she's learned from it, displayed with artifacts from the experience, that parent can see very clearly just how the child is doing. It's virtually a look inside the child's head, not just a mark on a piece of paper. And if the teacher is concerned that not all parents may readily grasp the import of this activity, she can prepare a guidesheet that tells the parents what to look for. We've also found that the children's preparation for their presentations becomes an excellent time for reflection on learning—the child's own self-assessment and thinking about how she's progressed and what she can aim for next.

Learning exhibitions. In an inquiry-based, integrative curriculum, kids do a lot of research, gather information, and build concepts on their own. Obviously, teachers want to assess the extent and quality of that learning. One way of doing so is to require a written report, certainly a time-tested way of gauging kids' learning (or at least their craftiness with freetermpapers.com). But written reports make teachers the only audience, overstress kids' reporting in a single modality, and squander a conspicuous resource in the room—the twenty-five other kids in the class! In this twenty-first-century world, where we are trying to get students "career and college ready," we have to think hard about what life really requires of high school graduates. While many college students and some workers have to create written reports, and certainly should be adept at doing so, almost every adult in America has to get up on their hind legs and report, explain, or present, out loud in front of a group of people—a department meeting, a video conference, a team gathering, a trade convention. Indeed, the CCSS speaking and listening standards quite pointedly state this: students must practice showing what they know—about science, math, literature, history—out loud, in front of an audience.

In *Assessment Live*, Nancy Steineke crystallizes this idea and puts it to work. As Nancy says:

> There's an old saying that school is a place where young people go to watch old people work. Live assessments offer us a way to turn this backwards arrangement around. Live assessments reinforce vital subject matter while expanding kids' preparation and performance skills. They honor the learning goals you've set for your students while also reflecting the standards your state has mandated. They are rigorous yet offer students the opportunity for flexibility, creativity, and innovation. (2009, 19)

She goes on to give instructions and scoring rubrics for ten such performance assessments.

▶ *The Timing and Efficiency of Assessments*

When teachers try to add these new, more productive forms of assessment to their classrooms, they will run into a time crunch unless they either subtract some old assessment activities or overlap the new assessments with something else. A good starting point is to review all the forms of evaluation under way in the classroom, terminating those that don't usefully steer instruction, advance kids' learning, teach students to self-evaluate, or produce artifacts worth saving. For many teachers, this may mean grading far fewer busywork handouts, workbook pages, study questions, and worksheets. Instead of tabulating the errors in stacks of identical fill-in-the-blank worksheets, teachers can spend their precious evaluation time analyzing and responding to each kid's whole original reports or stories, perhaps writing a personal note of response that gives guidance as well as models solid adult writing.

Another key to implementing better assessments is to overlap assessment with instruction, instead of always relying on evaluations that occur separately, after the work is done (and when it is too late for students to improve their product or learn from the assessment!). Many progressive forms of assessment are integral to learning itself. Reading and writing conferences are a case in point; when sitting down to talk with a child about her writing, the teacher can simultaneously and seamlessly gather information about the child's development as a writer. As the teacher jots down a few notes following each conference, a powerful record of growth is created. Similarly, when students and teachers together design scoring rubrics for class presentations, science experiments, or persuasive essays, they are explicitly being taught the ingredients of a successful performance, right along with creating a tool to evaluate their efforts.

All these adjustments mean that teachers are making a time trade: they're not spending any less time on assessment, but they're also not spending more. They're differentiating their efforts, looking at children's growth in a wider variety

When teachers try to add these new, more productive forms of assessment to their classrooms, they will run into a time crunch unless they either subtract some old assessment activities or overlap the new assessments with something else.

of ways. They are committed to the principle that the most valuable assessment activities are *formative,* aimed at understanding a child's development and making instructional decisions about that child. *Summative* evaluation, the process of converting kids' achievements into some kind of ranked, ordinal system that compares children to each other, has mainly external purposes, and needs to happen far less often.

Overall, when we think about meaningful and useful assessment of our students, we should keep in mind the following principles.

Best Practice Assessment

▶ focuses on the knowledge and abilities that are key to Best Practice learning, and on complex whole outcomes and performances of writing, reading, researching, and problem solving, rather than only on isolated subskills

▶ most of the time is formative, not summative—and then applies the data to guide individual students' further learning and to adjust our own teaching

▶ employs data that is descriptive or narrative, not just scored and numerical

▶ involves students in developing meaningful responses (for example, asks students to describe what makes a good research report), and calls on them to keep track of and judge their own work

▶ triangulates, looking at each child from several angles, by drawing on observation, conversation, artifacts, and performances, and by looking at learning over time

▶ operates as a part of instruction (as in teacher-student conferences), rather than separate from it

▶ occupies a moderate amount of time, not ruling a teacher's professional life or consuming lots of instruction time

▶ where possible, abolishes or deemphasizes competitive grading systems

▶ involves thoughtful collaboration and discussion with other teachers as they visit each other's classrooms and look at student work together

▶ employs parent-education programs to help community members understand the value of new approaches, and then invites parents to participate in the process

Can Teachers Still "Teach"?

▶ *The Seven Structures and Traditional Presentation*

There are at least three reasons why teacher-centered, whole-class instruction can and should remain part of the school day. First and most important, teachers have great things to teach—they have knowledge, wisdom, experience, ideas, and content that can be shared through whole-class presentations they design. All of us who teach have developed great units—favorite sequences of activities that engage students, year after year. We have worked to design and refine and enrich these units; they are our treasures, and we're not about to give them up. We also realize that as we present these favorite lessons, we are modeling for students our own passion for knowledge. Even if they don't understand or remember everything, we hope they'll catch our excitement about ideas. Oh, and by the way, remember the Gradual Release of Responsibility model of instruction? It *begins* with the teacher modeling and explaining.

On a more pragmatic level, some teacher-directed lessons are still necessary because most teachers work within a mandated curriculum. They are responsible for students' learning (or at least briefly remembering) many required elements of an official syllabus of content. We argued earlier that many ingredients of the typical school curriculum can be learned "along the way," amid innovative, student-centered techniques. For example, kids who have regular writing workshops will acquire many English spelling and editing skills even though they are not taught them through teacher presentations or workbook drills. However, the average school curriculum still contains much other material that isn't learned collaterally through applied experience in the subject. In language arts, for example, all the writing workshops in the world will not teach students the names of the parts of speech. If kids and teachers are to be held accountable for learning about gerunds, subordinate clauses, and the like, and there's not enough time for an active inquiry project on the nature and structure of language, the teacher will probably have to take the initiative to conduct such lessons.

Finally, as learners and as people, teachers deserve to feel safe and comfortable in school too. They need the security of doing something familiar for some of the day: we cannot expect teachers who have been trained and socialized to think of teaching as presenting to suddenly cast aside that whole model for the entire six-hour day. The fact is that teachers *will* continue to present whole-class lessons; the point is for them to get better at it and at the same time, start doing it less.

Annenberg Learner. 2011. Instructional Strategies for the Journey North: A Global Study of Wildlife Migration and Seasonal Change. www.learner.org/jnorth/tm/InstrucStrat29.html.

Atwell, Nancie. 1998. *In the Middle: New Understandings About Writing, Reading, and Learning* (2nd edition). Portsmouth, NH: Boynton/Cook Heinemann.

Beane, James. 1997. *Curriculum Integration: Designing the Core of Democratic Education.* New York: Teachers College Press.

———. 2005. *A Reason to Teach: Creating Classrooms of Dignity and Hope.* Portsmouth, NH: Heinemann.

Carr E., and Donna Ogle. 1987. KWL Plus: A Strategy for Comprehension and Summarization. *Journal of Reading* 30: 626–631.

Common Core State Standards Initiative. 2010. *Common Core State Standards, Speaking and Listening.* National Governors Association and the Council of Chief State School Officers.

Daniels, Harvey. 2002. *Literature Circles: Voice and Choice in Book Clubs and Reading Groups.* Portland, ME: Stenhouse.

Daniels, Harvey, and Marilyn Bizar. 2004. *Teaching the Best Practice Way: Methods That Matter, K–12.* Portland, ME: Stenhouse.

Daniels, Harvey, and Nancy Steineke. 2004. *Mini-Lessons for Literature Circles.* Portsmouth, NH: Heinemann.

———. 2011. *Texts and Lessons for Content-Area Reading.* Portsmouth, NH: Heinemann.

Darling-Hammond, Linda, et al. 2008. *Powerful Learning: What We Know About Teaching for Understanding.* San Francisco: Jossey-Bass.

Durlak, Joseph. 2011. The Impact of Enhancing Students' Social and Emotional Learning: A Meta-Analysis of School-Based Universal Interventions. *Child Development* 82(1): 405–432.

Fountas, Irene, and Gay-Su Pinnell. 1996. *Guided Reading: Good First Teaching for All Children.* Portsmouth, NH: Heinemann.

Glasser, William. 1990. *The Quality School: Managing Students Without Coercion.* New York: Harper.

Graves, Donald. 1983. *Writing: Teachers and Children at Work.* Portsmouth, NH, Heinemann.

Harvey, Stephanie, and Ann Goudvis, 2008. *Strategies That Work: Teaching Comprehension to Enhance Understanding.* Portland, ME: Stenhouse.

Harvey, Stephanie, and Harvey Daniels. 2009. *Comprehension and Collaboration: Inquiry Circles in Action.* Portsmouth, NH: Heinemann.

Hayes, Erin. 2008. Google's 20 Percent Factor. ABC News Online. http://abcnews.go.com/Technology/story?id=4839327&page=1.

Hiebert, Elfrieda, et al. 2007. Opportunity to Read: How Much? What Kinds of Texts? For What Reasons? International Reading Association Annual Convention, May 13, 2007, Toronto, Ontario, Canada.

Hyde, Arthur. 2006. *Comprehending Math: Adapting Reading Strategies to Teach Mathematics, K–6.* Portsmouth, NH: Heinemann.

Johnson, David, and Roger Johnson. 1998. *Learning Together and Alone.* New York: Allyn and Bacon.

Keene, Ellin Oliver, and Susan Zimmermann. 2007. *Mosaic of Thought: The Power of Comprehension Strategy Instruction*. Portsmouth, NH: Heinemann.

Managing Google's Idea Factory. 2005. *Bloomberg Business Week*. October 3. www.businessweek.com/magazine/content/05_40/b3953093.htm.

Miller, Debbie. 2002. *Reading with Meaning*. Portland, ME: Stenhouse.

Ogle, Donna. 1986. The KWL: A Teaching Model That Develops Active Reading of Expository Text. *Reading Teacher* 39: 564–570.

Pearson, P. David, and Meg Gallagher. 1983. The Instruction of Reading Comprehension. *Contemporary Educational Psychology* 8: 317–344.

Pianta, Robert, et al. March 2007. Opportunities to Learn in America's Classrooms. *Science Magazine*.

Routman, Regie. 2008. *Teaching Essentials*. Portsmouth, NH: Heinemann.

Sharan, Shlomo. 1999. *Handbook of Cooperative Learning Method*s. New York: Praeger.

Short, Kathy, Jerome Harste, and Carolyn Burke. 1996. *Creating Classrooms for Authors and Inquirers* (2nd edition). Portsmouth, NH: Heinemann.

Steineke, Nancy. 2009. *Assessment Live: Ten Real-Time Ways for Students to Show What They Know and Meet the Standards*. Portsmouth, NH: Heinemann.

Tovani, Cris. 2005. *I Read It But I Don't Get It: Comprehension Strategies for Adolescent Readers*. Portland, ME: Stenhouse.

UPI. February 24, 2008. Scientists Fear Exotic Snakes.

Vaughan, Joseph, and Thomas Estes. 1986. *Reading and Reasoning Beyond the Primary Grades*. New York: Allyn and Bacon.

Vopat, Jim. 2009. *Writing Circles: Kids Revolutionize Writing Workshop*. Portsmouth, NH: Heinemann.

Suggested Further Readings

Gradual Release of Responsibility

Copeland, Matt. 2005. *Socratic Circles: Fostering Critical and Creative Thinking in Middle and High School*. Portland, ME: Stenhouse.

Fisher, Douglas, and Nancy Frey. 2008. *Better Learning Through Structured Teaching: A Framework for the Gradual Release of Responsibility*. Alexandria, VA: Association for Supervision and Curriculum Development.

Miller, Donnalyn. 2009. *The Book Whisperer: Awakening the Inner Reader in Every Child*. San Francisco: Jossey-Bass.

Wiggins, Grant, and Jay McTighe. 2005. *Understanding by Design*. Upper Saddle River, NJ: Prentice-Hall.

Classroom Workshop

Anderson, Jeff. 2006. *Mechanically Inclined: Building Grammar, Usage, and Style into Writer's Workshop*. Portland, ME: Stenhouse.

Blaumann, Leslie. 2011. *The Inside Guide to the Reading-Writing Classroom*. Portsmouth, NH: Boynton/Cook Heinemann.

Boushey, Gail, and Joan Moser. 2006. *The Daily Five: Fostering Literacy Independence in the Elementary Grades*. Portland, ME. Stenhouse.

Fletcher, Ralph, and JoAnn Portalupi. 2001. *Writing Workshop: The Essential Guide.* Portsmouth, NH: Heinemann.

Ray, Katie Wood, and Lisa B. Cleaveland. 2004. *About the Authors: Writing Workshop with Our Youngest Writers.* Portsmouth, NH: Heinemann.

Saul, Wendy, Jeanne Reardon, and Charles Pearce. 2002. *Science Workshop: Reading, Writing, and Thinking Like a Scientist.* Portsmouth, NH: Heinemann.

Strategic Thinking

Daniels, Harvey, and Steven Zemelman. 2004. *Subjects Matter: Every Teacher's Guide to Content-Area Reading.* Portsmouth, NH: Heinemann.

Hand, Brian, Lori Norton-Meier, and Jay Stalker. 2009. *Negotiating Science: The Critical Role of Argument in Student Inquiry.* Portsmouth, NH: Heinemann.

Hoyt, Linda, and Tony Stead. 2011. *Explorations in Nonfiction Writing.* Portsmouth, NH: Heinemann.

Keene, Ellin Oliver. 2008. *To Understand: New Horizons in Reading Comprehension.* Portsmouth, NH: Heinemann.

MacGregor, Tanny. 2007. *Comprehension Connections: Bridges to Strategic Reading.* Portsmouth, NH: Heinemann.

Sobel, David. 2008. *Childhood and Nature: Design Principles for Educators.* Portland, ME: Stenhouse.

Collaborative Activities

Harvey, Stephanie, and Harvey Daniels, 2009. *Comprehension and Collaboration: Inquiry Circles in Action.* Portsmouth, NH: Heinemann

Joyce, Bruce, Marsha Weil, and Emily Calhoun. 2003. *Models of Teaching* (7th edition). Englewood Cliffs, NJ: Prentice-Hall.

Kluth, Paula, and Alice Udvari-Solner. 2007. *Joyful Learning: Active and Collaborative Learning in Inclusive Classrooms.* Thousand Oaks, CA: Corwin.

Lundy, Kathy, and Larry Swartz. 2011. *Creating Caring Classrooms: How to Encourage Students to Communicate, Create, and Be Compassionate of Others.* Portland, ME: Stenhouse.

Steineke, Nancy. 2002. *Reading and Writing Together: Collaborative Literacy in Action.* Portsmouth, NH: Heinemann.

Integrative Units

Barell, John. 2006. *Problem-Based Learning: An Inquiry Approach.* Thousand Oaks, CA: Corwin.

Buhrow, Brad, and Anne Upczak Garcia. 2006. *Ladybugs, Tornadoes, and Swirling Galaxies: English Language Learners Discover Their World Through Inquiry.* Portland, ME: Stenhouse.

Hallerman, Sara, John Larmer, and John Mergendollar. 2011. *Project Based Learning in the Elementary Grades: Step-by-Step Guidance, Tools and Tips for Standards-Focused K–5 Projects.* Novato, CA: Buck Institute for Education.

Harvey, Stephanie. 1998. *Nonfiction Matters.* York, ME: Stenhouse.

Harvey, Stephanie, and Harvey Daniels, 2009. *Comprehension and Collaboration: Inquiry Circles in Action.* Portsmouth, NH: Heinemann.

Markham, Thom, John Larmer, and Jason Ravitz. 2003. *Project Based Learning Handbook: A Guide to Standards-Focused Project Based Learning for Middle and High School Teachers.* Novato, CA: Buck Institute for Education.

Representing to Learn

Burnaford, Gail, Arnold Aprill, and Cynthia Weiss. 2000. *Renaissance in the Classroom: Arts Integration and Meaningful Learning.* Mahwah, NJ: Routledge.

Countryman, Joan. 1992. *Writing to Learn Mathematics.* Portsmouth, NH: Heinemann.

Ehrenworth, Mary. 2003. *Looking to Write: Students Writing Through the Visual Arts.* Portsmouth, NH: Heinemann.

Ernst, Karen. 1997. A *Teacher's Sketch Journal: Observations on Learning and Teaching.* Portsmouth, NH: Heinemann.

Fineberg, Carol. 2004. *Creating Islands of Excellence: Arts Education as a Partner in School Reform.* Portsmouth, NH: Heinemann.

Horn, Martha, and Mary Ellen Giacobbe. 2007. *Talking, Drawing, Writing: Lessons for Our Youngest Writers.* York, ME: Stenhouse.

Rief, Linda. 2007. *Inside the Writer's-Reader's Notebook: A Workshop Essential.* Portsmouth, NH: Heinemann.

Formative-Reflective Assessment

Bernebei, Gretchen, Jayne Hover, and Cynthia Candler. 2009. *Crunchtime: Lessons to Help Students Blow the Roof Off Writing Tests—and Become Better Writers in the Process.* Portsmouth, NH: Heinemann.

Conrad, Lori, Missy Matthews, Cheryl Zimmerman, and Patrick A. Allen. 2008. *Put Thinking to the Test.* Portland, ME: Stenhouse.

Graves, Donald. 2002. *Testing Is Not Teaching: What Should Count in Education.* Portsmouth, NH: Heinemann.

Johnston, Peter H. 2004. *Choice Words: How Our Language Affects Children's Learning.* Portland, ME: Stenhouse.

Miller, Debbie. 2011. *Teaching with Intention: Defining Beliefs, Aligning Practice, Taking Action.* Portland, ME: Stenhouse.

Tovani, Cris. 2011. *So What Do They Really Know?* Portland, ME: Stenhouse.

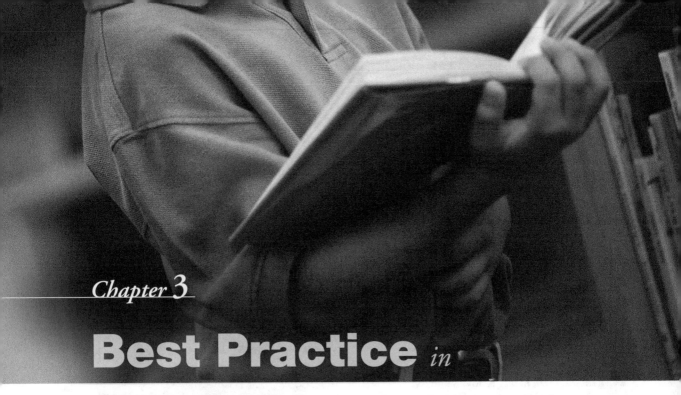

Chapter 3

Best Practice *in*
Reading

Sara Ahmed teaches eighth grade at Burley School in Chicago. She welcomes us into her classroom on a warm spring day to show how her students dig deeply into a historical memoir and its themes. Today, instead of only reading printed text, Sara's students will study, "read," and discuss some powerful visual images, using the same comprehension strategies they have been applying to their books.

Sara explains. First-period PE is over and my eighth graders come sifting through the door with a bit more energy (and body heat) than when I greeted them earlier this morning. They are welcomed back to class by this note on the projection screen:

> *Good morning! Grab a clipboard, a pencil, Post-its, your* Warriors Don't Cry *book, your reading brains, a buddy, and meet me on the rug!* ☺

My kids know to expect something like this every time they enter the room. This kind of invitation gets them thinking right away. Instead of shouting across-the-room questions like, *What are we doing, now? What do we need, again?* and *What did she say?* they buzz: *I wonder what we are going to do?* or *Do you think this has to do with those pictures hanging in the hallway?*

Figure 3.1
*Sara Ahmed and her
eighth graders*

Actually, that last question was one I expected to hear. Before school that day, I had hung a gallery of photographs outside our classroom. Each one contained an image related to our current focus on the civil rights movement and our reading of *Warriors Don't Cry*, a historical memoir by Melba Pattillo Beals, one of the nine black teens who integrated Little Rock Central High School in Arkansas in 1956. Some of the photos I found were images of the very events being portrayed in Beals' book—the nine African American students entering the school, soldiers guarding them, crowds of angry white people screaming and waving signs at the children. Other pictures were from the same era, but depicted different images of school integration, including black and white children happily studying together, saluting the American flag, and even holding hands. I set up these photos in the hallway before kids arrived purposely to pique a little interest and curiosity. It's tough to wake a teenager up in the morning, but this one is in my bag of tricks.

Now, I give a ready helper a stack of blank paper and ask her to give one sheet to each student. Then I shift kids' attention to an image on our big classroom screen (shown in Figure 3.2), with a simple instruction.

Me: Why don't you have a look at this picture and talk about it.

Kids view the photograph and chat for a minute while I take attendance. And by the time the last few stragglers join us, most of my students realize that

Figure 3.2
*Little Rock school
integration "Black
Students Escorted by
Soldiers"* © *Bettman/
CORBIS.*

the people in the image are the main characters of our book. Some are digging into their copies of *Warriors* to connect to a related photo or find a clue that confirms their prediction.

Dylan: That's Melba!

Ivelis: Terrence Roberts is the tall one, right?

Vanessa: OMG, Elizabeth Eckford isn't in this because she didn't make it that first day, remember?

Before their burst of curiosity fades, I darken the screen and tell them we will get back to that image in just a minute. I quickly set the scene for today's work, reminding students that now we are a few chapters deep into reading our novel. We've met the characters and identified with some, placed ourselves in the setting, grasped some introductory themes, and noticed some early "up-standers" and "bystanders." (This is some terminology we use in my classes to contrast people who take courageous stands in tough situations, versus those who stand by and allow injustice to happen. This organizing concept comes from my years of experience with Facing History and Ourselves, an international organization that supports teachers who are concerned with social justice, not just social studies.)

Me: Now it's time to really start asking how and why these individuals and historical events interact as we read our way through this text. All year, we have been talking about how effective readers make visual images as they read, right? I know that when you guys read, you always have that film strip or that movie of mental images running in your mind. I've shown you many times how I stop and carefully think about my own mental images when I read, and how sometimes I even sketch them in my notebook or margin?

There's some good-natured eye-rolling, as it if to say, "Yeah, only three million times."

Me: Today, I'm going to flip-flop things on you and give you the image before the text. In fact, it is going to be like one of those wordless picture books you read when you were in first grade, where you had to infer what was happening just from the pictures.

Isaias: Oh, I loved those. Those were awesome.

Me: Good, I have Isaias' approval! So, in just a sec, you are going to be "reading" some images and hopefully gaining a better understanding of what was really going on when the Little Rock Nine integrated Central High. Now I am going to put that same image up again, but this time we're going to slow down and see it, analyze it, in sections. Take that blank paper that Ana gave you and fold it into three equal sections like this. Follow my lead on the projector or have a buddy help you. Label each part just as I do up here. *(When I am doing this viewing exercise with other images, I'll use quadrants, circles, or whatever other subdivisions encourage thoughtful attention to all the details in a picture.)*

Left	Middle	Right

By now, everyone has their sections labeled as I give the next set of directions.

Me: Each section on your paper goes with the section of the image you are going to see. In that box, I want you to write down what you see. To start with, you can just be literal. The idea is to look slowly and patiently into the image and notice all the details that are there, in the foreground and the background. What does the image make you see, hear, feel, and wonder? And if you are not sure what something is, pose it as a question. So listen to me "read" a little of the first section. You guys can steal from me if you are seeing the same things.

I vocalize my thinking and jot down key words to label my noticings.

Me: I see a tire. I see men with soldier hats.

Forrest: You mean helmets, Ms. Ahmed.

Me: Right, helmets! Thanks, Forrest! I wonder, is that a weapon that soldier is carrying? The picture is old, black and white.

Now I turn it over to the kids, letting them quietly view and write about the first section of the image for another minute.

Me: It looks like you all have some observations down and I know you're eager to talk, so turn to your buddy and share. Feel free to borrow their ideas; it shows you are really listening to them.

I listen in on several conversations as I roam the room, starting with Denzel and Gabe.

Denzel: I noticed all the soldiers are white.

Gabe: Yeah, me too, and there are a lot of them. I also noticed that it is sunny outside, so it is morning or afternoon.

Denzel: They must be the soldiers that turned them away, or maybe they were protecting them?

Gabe: It's hard to tell who would be upstander soldiers or bystander ones.

After a few minutes of talk time, I invite pairs to report out their thinking to the whole class.

Me: I have been hearing some great observations. Anybody want to share?

While a few kids offer their thoughts to the group, I scribe them on my projected version, so everyone's thoughts are recorded. Then, over the next four or five minutes, we go through the same process for the middle and right sections of the image (shown in Figure 3.3).

When we finish the last section, I show the full image once more. This time, I have kids flip their sheet over and write down their final thoughts. *What are your reactions to the image? What questions would you ask the people in this photo? How do you connect this image back to the* Warriors *book?* And finally, I ask them to give this photo a title or caption. They set to writing pretty eagerly because they are so consumed with this image and have lots of thoughts and opinions. I let them write for about three minutes before switching to discussion. This time, to add some fresh interaction, I have buddies join with a nearby pair to discuss in a group of four.

I roam the room again, listen and take notes about what I hear (I will use my observations in my assessment of kids later on, as well as to plan for tomorrow's

LEFT	MIDDLE	RIGHT
jeep, tire	kids in white, walking	this seems to be the
– 3 soldiers,	to school	end of the procession
officers?	sergeant leading them	(or recession)
no parking sign	two more soldiers, young	girl has white skirt
phone pole	who's standing behind?	must be 50's or 60's
trees	building in back?	so — big full skirt
people crossing	guns pointed in same	belt on one guy
street	direction	what are they
	is the girl holding books?	guarding?

Figure 3.3
Responses to sections of the Little Rock integration photograph

lesson). I hear a lot of talk about that overarching theme in our class—upstanders and bystanders. There is quite a lot of conversation about whether you can tell what kind of "stander" someone is, just by their body language in a picture.

Me: I know you were all eager to share with each other. I would love to hear all the titles you guys gave this image, but first let me tell you a few I heard while visiting around the room. *(I do this to honor the students with great thoughts who aren't always comfortable sharing in the whole group.)*

Me: "The Price of Education." Anyone want to claim that title? *(Brenda raises her hand.)* Can you say a word or two about what you were thinking?

Brenda: *(Quietly)* I just thought, this integration is costing everyone so much to go through it, the kids, their families . . .

Me: That's very thoughtful, really true. Thanks for that.

I share two more titles, and then I pose an added challenge.

Me: Most of you have noticed there are a lot more photos hanging outside in the hallway today, and some of you have asked about them. All of us are going to go out and "read" those images. Except I am going to challenge you to something, you ready? You are going to have to read with a different type of hat on. This side of the room—everyone from Celeste over—is going to view these images with the attitude of an integrationist. Meaning?

Evan: We want the schools to mix black and white students.

Me: Did you all hear Evan? *(Nods and yeses. Now I point to the opposite side of the room with my arms.)*

Alexis: Oh no!

Sympathetically smiling at Alexis' reaction, I nod.

Me: You are going to take on the role of a segregationist. Meaning?

Juan: We are the most terrible people in the room?

Everyone lets out an awkward tiny laugh.

Me: Not you personally! But everyone, what does Juan mean by that?

Sieanna: That we are supposed to pretend to be like the segregationists, who are racist and don't want the black students in the white schools.

Me: Sadly, yes. Just like some of the characters you are meeting in *Warriors*, right? Thanks, Sieanna and Juan.

I stop a few kids who are trying to inch their way over to the integrationist side.

Me: With the Post-its on your clipboards, you are going to do all the things we just did together with the first picture. You are going to walk through the gallery out in the hall and study several of those pictures. You will look deeply into the details, analyze, connect, draw inferences, visualize further, and think about the photographer's motives for taking this photo. You're using your same repertoire of comprehension strategies, except the text is a picture, not a page of print. Does that make sense?

I get a few nods, and I can see that the kids are chomping at the bit to get into the hall.

Me: When you feel you fully understand an image, I want you to give it a title. But you are going to do it with either your integrationist or segregationist hat on, so you are really going to take on the attitudes, beliefs, and feelings of these people, got it? So, your job is to write down the title you would give the specific image you are looking at, put your initials on it, and stick it on the chart paper behind the picture. Try and get to at least four or five.

After reminding the kids about hallway norms and expectations, I set them loose. They pour out into the hall, clipboards in hand. I watch them as they rove around from poster to poster, quietly studying and gradually posting titles. After I see that everyone is working autonomously, I rove from chart to chart, grabbing compelling Post-its from each one, from both integrationist and segregationist viewpoints.

Once activity starts winding down, I usher the kids back to our meeting area on the rug. Now, on my document projector, I put up one of the images with two of the kids' suggested titles, one integrationist and one segregationist. There is a murmur of wonder and looks are shot across the room. The first image shows six students of mixed races, pledging their allegiance to the flag.

Dylan: That's mine.

Me: Thanks, Dylan. Read us your caption.

Dylan: "One Nation Under God."

Figure 3.4
Alexis titles a photograph

Me: Explain your thinking on that?

Dylan: Well, I was an integrationist and it sounds like a positive message because they are all together doing the pledge like we do.

Me: Thanks. What about the other side?

Jeremy: I had that same one, but I was a segregationist and I put, "Never the *United* States," because no segregationist thinks or wants blacks and whites to be united.

Me: Thanks, Jeremy and Dylan. Everyone, I know you all want to share yours, and that's important because I saw some great thinking out there. So I will post them all for a few days so you look them over and make some notes in your journal about ones that stand out or connect to your own reading. But now, let's dig back into our discussion of the book. Why do you think this was important to do today as we try to get a better idea of what really happened down in Little Rock in 1955? The book already gives us eyewitness testimony from our author, who was one of the Nine and lived through it, right?

Chloe: Well, we are all reading about it and trying to visualize it, but we will never really know what it felt like. Looking at real pictures gives us a better idea because it's not like fiction or with bias . . . it's a picture.

Vanessa: Yeah, back then they didn't have Photoshop, so they like couldn't make it up.

Me: Ha! Good point. Anybody else?

Mikayla: Well, for me personally, I had a hard time in some parts trying to really visualize what it was like in that mob scene or what being escorted by troops really looked like. Then I saw that picture of Elizabeth Eckford and how that woman was screaming at her in that mob and I realized that they really did hate them. It's kinda scary.

Me: Thanks for being honest, Mikayla. I can get stuck like that too, so I'll sketch it out or try and find an image if I don't get it. Thumbs up if you were in the same boat as Mikayla at some point as a reader. *(Lots of thumbs go up.)* So how did reading all of these images help? How will it change the way we go back into *Warriors Don't Cry* and really make sense of what's going on?

Evan: I think it makes us go a little deeper. Like, you will never know how they really felt because it didn't happen to us, but seeing the actual pictures and reading about it at the same time is pretty cool. Well, not cool that it happened, but you know, like cool that it helps us get it.

Me: I'm with ya, Evan. He is right on! Think of all the things you guys did in just that one image. You connected, you questioned, you inferred, you made judgments about what was important, you analyzed, you thought about point of view, and you immediately recalled and retold parts of our novel. Those are all the things that great readers do all the time! You're geniuses. So let's get back into the book with these new understandings and see how this shapes our reading. Let's keep using the author's words, your own mental images, and any historical evidence or artifacts to help us understand this difficult journey of school integration.

A Look at the Reading Standards

Reading invariably comes first on everyone's list of basic academic skills, and we certainly endorse that ranking. After all, much of the information that school (and life) offers us is stored in print, and students' ability to unlock and use all this knowledge depends on fluent, skillful, critical, and independent reading. And while reading instruction always has its passionate controversies, today the professional consensus about state-of-the-art reading instruction is stronger and clearer than ever. The act of reading is no longer the "black box" mystery it was thirty years ago. We now understand quite well how reading works, and we agree—well, pretty much—about how to teach it to the vast majority of children.

Several landmark documents have defined Best Practice in reading. An early base for national standards was established by the influential *Becoming a Nation of Readers,* published by the National Institute of Education (Anderson et al. 1985), and *New Policy Guidelines for Reading,* issued by the National Council of Teachers of English (NCTE) (Harste 1989). In 1996, the NCTE and the International Reading Association (IRA) issued the definitive *Standards for the English Language Arts.*

▶ The NCTE/IRA Standards for the English Language Arts

1. Students read a wide range of print and non-print texts to build an understanding of texts, of themselves, and of the cultures of the United States and the world; to acquire new information; to respond to the needs and demands of society and the workplace; and for personal fulfillment. Among these texts are fiction and nonfiction, classic and contemporary works.

2. Students read a wide range of literature from many periods in many genres to build an understanding of the many dimensions (e.g., philosophical, ethical, aesthetic) of human experience.

3. Students apply a wide range of strategies to comprehend, interpret, evaluate, and appreciate texts. They draw on their prior experience, their interactions with other readers and writers, their knowledge of word meaning and of other texts, their word identification strategies, and their understanding of textual features (e.g., sound-letter correspondence, sentence structure, context, graphics).

4. Students adjust their use of spoken, written, and visual language (e.g., conventions, style, vocabulary) to communicate effectively with a variety of audiences and for different purposes.

5. Students employ a wide range of strategies as they write and use different writing process elements appropriately to communicate with different audiences for a variety of purposes.

6. Students apply knowledge of language structure, language conventions (e.g., spelling and punctuation), media techniques, figurative language, and genre to create, critique, and discuss print and non-print texts.

7. Students conduct research on issues and interests by generating ideas and questions, and by posing problems. They gather, evaluate, and synthesize data from a variety of sources (e.g., print and non-print texts, artifacts, people) to communicate their discoveries in ways that suit their purpose and audience.

8. Students use a variety of technological and information resources (e.g., libraries, databases, computer networks, video) to gather and synthesize information and to create and communicate knowledge.

9. Students develop an understanding of and respect for diversity in language use, patterns, and dialects across cultures, ethnic groups, geographic regions, and social roles.

10. Students whose first language is not English make use of their first language to develop competency in the English language arts and to develop understanding of content across the curriculum.

11. Students participate as knowledgeable, reflective, creative, and critical members of a variety of literacy communities.

12. Students use spoken, written, and visual language to accomplish their own purposes (e.g., for learning, enjoyment, persuasion, and the exchange of information).

Obviously, these admirable but general goals don't say much about what instruction might lead students to achieving them. (And they go well beyond reading into writing, technology, and other domains.) But the NCTE and IRA quickly filled the gap with three books showing the standards in action in elementary, middle, and high school classrooms (Wilhelm 1996; Sierra-Perry 1996; Smagorinsky 1996). Next, the NCTE created a companion website called Readwritethink.org, filled with lessons correlated to the standards. And in 2009, the NCTE and IRA, concerned about the steep rise of standardized testing and its effects on classroom practice, issued *Standards for the Assessment of Reading and Writing*, which spelled out best practices for monitoring, evaluating, and reporting students' growth in literacy. So, all together, these resources created a clear picture of reading instruction that was student-centered, challenging, and interactive—and the NCTE/IRA standards were incorporated into many state and district standards documents around the country.

The National Board for Professional Teaching Standards (NBPTS) has been another important voice in defining Best Practice in reading. Established in 1987 and funded by prominent national philanthropies, including the Bill and Melinda Gates Foundation, the board has by now certified over 91,000 American teachers as being the "best of the best." The NBPTS identifies the nation's most accomplished teachers by setting explicit instructional standards, and then evaluating each candidate's practice in light of those high standards. The NBPTS goes even further than the NCTE/IRA in detailing the exact climate, materials, processes, conversations, interactions, and assessments that characterize state-of-the-art classrooms. Among other traits, the NBPTS says that highly qualified reading teachers:

- are avid readers themselves and share their own reading life with students
- model their own cognitive processes for reading
- explicitly teach comprehension strategies
- tap students' curiosity and motivation
- create a climate of collaboration and mutual trust
- invite students to make connections between texts and their own experience, events in the world around, and previous texts they have read

- understand that meaning does not reside solely within a text, but is created in a transaction between a reader and the author's words

- promote close reading of texts

- preview important material for students before reading and help them make predictions

- invite rich kid–kid talk about books, in peer groups of all sizes

- encourage students to become skillful self-assessors, as well as evaluating students' growth themselves

Many echoes of the NCTE/IRA standards resound here, and the pedagogy is clearly in the foreground.

Both the NCTE/IRA and NBPTS standards were built on an emerging view of reading as a kind of thinking, a special type of cognitive work. Since then, this reading-as-thinking paradigm has been further investigated and strongly validated. Thanks to researchers like Keene and Zimmermann (2007) and Duke and Pearson (2002), we better understand the repertoire of cognitive strategies that proficient readers use to enter, unlock, comprehend, remember, and use text. Though many different inventories of reading-as-thinking skills have been proposed, most researchers agree that all skillful readers:

- monitor their comprehension (actively keep track of their thinking, adjust strategies to the text at hand, reread, slow down, etc.)

- visualize (make mental pictures or sensory images)

- connect (link to their own experience, to events in the world, to other readings)

- question (actively wonder, surface uncertainties, interrogate the text and author)

- infer (predict, hypothesize, interpret, draw conclusions)

- evaluate (determine importance, make judgments, weigh values)

- analyze (notice text structures, author's craft, purpose, theme, point of view)

- synthesize (retell, summarize, remember information)

In our opening story, we could see Sara Ahmed's students drawing actively on these very strategies, as they tried to comprehend both their book and an array of historic images.

Now that we know definitively how proficient readers think, teachers can design and offer lessons that teach these crucial mental operations explicitly. We no longer have to just hope that students will become strong comprehenders; we can show them exactly how it is done and guide them in practicing it. The above list, which represents a consensus among reading researchers and classroom practitioners, is adapted from Harvey and Steve's book *Subjects Matter: Every Teacher's Guide to Content-Area Reading* (2004). For more recent thinking about

Both the NCTE/IRA and NBPTS standards were built on an emerging view of reading as a kind of thinking, a special type of cognitive work.

reading strategy instruction, see *Comprehension Going Forward* (Daniels 2010), which has articles by eighteen noted reading researchers.

In recent years, the field has amassed further research that confirms the thrust of the NCTE, IRA, and NBPTS recommendations. The latest edition of the authoritative *Handbook of Reading Research* validates and extends many of the principles and practices outlined in these standards (Kamil, Pearson, Moje, and Afflerbach 2011). Over the same time, literacy educators have been steadily developing classroom structures and activities that put the standards to work. Today, teachers can draw upon research-based models of reading instruction at all grade levels, thanks to developers like Harvey and Goudvis (2007), Keene and Zimmerman (2007), Atwell (1998; 2013 [in press]), Beers (2003), Calkins (2000), Miller (2002), Gallagher (2004), and Wilhelm, Baker, and Dube (2001).

THE COMMON CORE STATE STANDARDS FOR READING

Released in 2010, the Common Core State Standards for English Language Arts sounded some familiar notes (Common Core State Standards Initiative 2010a).

▶ Common Core State Standards for the English Language Arts

KEY IDEAS AND DETAILS

1. Read closely to determine what the text says explicitly and to make logical inferences from it; cite specific textual evidence when writing or speaking to support conclusions drawn from the text.

2. Determine central ideas or themes of a text and analyze their development; summarize the key supporting details and ideas.

3. Analyze how and why individuals, events, and ideas develop and interact over the course of a text.

CRAFT AND STRUCTURE

4. Interpret words and phrases as they are used in a text, including determining technical, connotative, and figurative meanings, and analyze how specific word choices shape meaning or tone.

5. Analyze the structure of texts, including how specific sentences, paragraphs, and larger portions of the text (e.g., a section, chapter, scene, or stanza) relate to each other and the whole.

6. Assess how point of view or purpose shapes the content and style of a text.

INTEGRATION OF KNOWLEDGE AND IDEAS

7. Integrate and evaluate content presented in diverse media and formats, including visually and quantitatively, as well as in words.

8. Delineate and evaluate the argument and specific claims in a text, including the validity of the reasoning as well as the relevance and sufficiency of the evidence.

9. Analyze how two or more texts address similar themes or topics in order to build knowledge or to compare the approaches the authors take.

RANGE OF READING AND LEVEL OF TEXT COMPLEXITY

10. Read and comprehend complex literary and informational texts independently and proficiently.

One immediately notices a high level of congruence between these outcome statements and previous reading recommendations. The full Common Core language arts standards documents run for over two hundred pages, including lengthy appendices and addenda, many of which either affirm the present standards or make laudable advances on past practice.

The CCSS call for students to be active, wide-ranging, and discriminating readers, a prescription that everyone, inside and outside of the school world, certainly agrees with. The standards also explicitly link effective reading with citizenship in a democracy, another widely held goal among reading professionals. And the CCSS make the vital point—embedded in the very title of the standards—that literacy development must not be confined to the reading block or the English language arts classroom. Instead, there should be much more reading, beyond the textbook, and more reading *instruction*, in content areas like social studies, history, science, and technical fields. In this, the CCSS join a wide cry in the reading world: every teacher must be a teacher of reading.

It is particularly valuable that the CCSS call for a rebalancing of the text types studied in school, recommending much more nonfiction reading. Despite many efforts by past researchers and organizations, there has continued to be an overemphasis on fictional text in American schools. Now, we do recognize that chronological narrative is arguably the Mother Genre from which all other texts derive. And it seems completely sensible to start with stories for beginning readers in the primary grades. But we have overdone it for decades. Sure, kids love stories, but they also love *information*, about dinosaurs, whales, glaciers, civil rights, technology, and climate change. Some teachers even believe that our traditional emphasis on stories, myths, and poetry have disproportionately disadvantaged boys, who sometimes prefer facts to fables. Given all these concerns, there's a pretty wide consensus in the profession that students need to encounter considerably more nonfiction text as they move up through the grades toward college and career readiness.

There are many other details we won't address here, since the standards are easily accessible online. For the most part, they extend and refine many established strands of good reading practice. But in a couple of important ways, the CCSS are out of step with mainstream reading research and practice. Sometimes this stems not from the standards themselves, but the way they're read or represented by various readers. Briefly, here are our concerns and, we hope, an even-handed view of these controversial elements.

▶ What Kids Read

One of the most frequently appearing words in the Common Core English language reading standards is *complexity*. The authors assert that school reading programs have gradually dumbed down the materials kids read, and that students should simply be reading harder books (CCSS Initiative 2010, 31–32, 57–58). Within the standards themselves and in its Appendix A are listed specific titles that illustrate this preference for more challenging texts. Along with a great many educators and researchers, we were quite concerned by our initial scan of the grade-level "Exemplar" lists. There is a very high premium placed on older, classic, American-Anglo literature, with language and settings that can be remote from today's students and their interests. Many of the titles are recommended for much younger readers than skilled teachers might consider appropriate for promoting children's reading development. And there's a relative dearth of contemporary authors or topics of immediate appeal to students.

But as the CCSS authors state, this is not a national required book list, but merely some examples of how students might step up to the next level. The standards do not say that students must *always* be reading books that are hard. Nor do they require that kids *always* read "at grade level," no matter what the child's actual reading level might be. On the contrary, the document says: "Students need opportunities to stretch their reading abilities but also to experience the satisfaction and pleasure of easy, fluent reading, both of which the Standards allow for" (CCSS Initiative 2010, Appendix A, 9). And the standards writers also realize that in America some kids do come to school as language learners, or as struggling readers, and that they must practice with books they are able to read: "Teachers who have had success using particular texts that are easier than those required for a given grade band should feel free to continue to use them so long as the general movement during a given school year is toward texts of higher levels of complexity" (CCSS Initiative 2010, Appendix A, 9).

In the official "publisher's criteria" for the CCSS, lead authors David Coleman and Susan Pimentel (2011, 4) explain that highly challenging works need not be read in their entirety; that short excerpts can instead be used in class, so that students can be exposed to important thinkers and authors without the need to push through whole, very difficult works. And further, the standards authors encourage teachers to read such selections aloud to assist students in comprehending them.

When thinking about what young people should read, we must always seek balance. As many veteran teachers will attest, young readers need to encounter both *windows* and *mirrors*. All readers need window-books they can look through, discovering whole other worlds, times, places, peoples, struggles, and events. Works by Shakespeare, Emily Dickinson, and other CCSS-recommended authors help kids expand their vision in this way. But children also need mirrors, authors like Christopher Paul Curtis, Kate DiCamillo, and Sherman Alexie, who create characters and situations that reflect students' real lives. In these books, kids immediately see themselves, and they feel: this is about me, my people, my community; these are the issues my friends and I are dealing with; these are the things I wonder and care about.

The CCSS exemplar texts open many windows, but offer few mirrors. Following the guidance of so many of the other standards documents and the strong research on reading, it's essential that teachers use the flexibility the CCSS explicitly offer to improve on this balance. Today, we're blessed with a vibrant, creative, challenging universe of fiction and nonfiction books written expressly for young people. Children's and adolescent literature is at a peak of quality and quantity. At the beginning of this chapter, Sara Ahmed showed us how *Warriors Don't Cry*, a historical memoir written expressly for young adults, galvanized her eighth graders' curiosity and spurred their deep and analytical thinking about the civil rights movement. As many teachers know, current topics like this one are often the very works that lure kids into reading, help them build fluency and stamina, and build the habit of thinking about and discussing books. Kids need the best of all worlds.

As many veteran teachers will attest, young readers need to encounter both windows and mirrors.

▶ Leveling Texts

There is a great emphasis in the CCSS on computing difficulty ratings for books. And, of course, it is valuable to have a general, comparable sense of how hard a book might be for the average reader. But among school kids, just as among adults, that "average reader" can be pretty hard to locate. Indeed, assigning levels to books can be the mother of all slippery slopes. As our venerable colleague Steve Krashen says, "I am seventy, but I read at a seventy-four level." Take the Harry Potter books, for one example. Their official lexile score is around 880, which places Harry at "the same grade level" as *Crime and Punishment, Jane Eyre*, and *To Kill a Mockingbird*. But Harry is much easier, as tens of millions of quite young readers will attest. A high-complexity score for a book I am really eager to read may not deter me at all. And a low-complexity-scoring book about a topic I have zero interest in doesn't necessarily make it an "easy read" for me.

What really affects the "level" of a text is a whole host of factors. Here is a list of ingredients we use when working with kids and teachers (Daniels and Steineke 2011).

WHAT MAKES TEXTS MORE ACCESSIBLE

- The text is shorter rather than longer.

- The reader has chosen the text, versus it being assigned.

- The reader has relevant background knowledge.

- The text embodies familiar settings and cultural values.

- The topic has personal interest or importance.

- The text evokes curiosity, surprise, or puzzlement.

- The text has high coherence, meaning that it explains itself (e.g., "The pleisiosaur, a Mesozoic period dinosaur . . .").

- The text makes ample use of pictures, charts, and other visual and text features that support and add meaning.

- The teacher evokes and builds the reader's background knowledge.

- The teacher teaches specific strategies, such as visualizing, inferring, questioning, and rereading.

- Readers can mark, write, or draw on text as they read.

- Readers can talk about the text during and after reading.

- Readers can hear text read aloud by the teacher, by a classmate, or in a small group.

- Readers have experience writing in the same genre.

Notice that this list includes many factors not inherent to the text itself, including what the student knows, what the teacher does, and under what conditions the reading occurs. These ingredients are not machine scorable; they require teacher action and judgment. So, in addition to consulting the book-leveling scores developed for the CCSS, teachers should expand their understanding of text difficulty to include all the above factors as they match students to books. In all, it is important for teachers to recognize that the Common Core Standards, though very serious about complexity, need to be balanced with a thoughtful understanding of classrooms and kids.

▶ Comprehension Strategy Instruction

Earlier, we cited the vibrant thirty-year-old body of evidence about the mental operations skilled readers use to make meaning from text: monitoring thinking, visualizing, inferring, connecting, questioning, analyzing, synthesizing, and the rest. These studies, often referred to as the "proficient reader research," show that effective readers possess a finite, internal repertoire of cognitive "moves" they can use to make sense of difficult text—and that these strategies are teachable at a very young age. This research has given rise to a nationwide trend toward more explicit and direct teaching of comprehension. Unfortunately, reading strategy instruction gets short shrift in the Common Core Standards.

According to the CCSS authors, meaning exists inside of texts themselves, and neither the reader's background knowledge, nor the cognitive strategies she is able to deploy before or during reading, can help attain this fixed meaning. Accordingly, the only reading strategy recommended is repeated "close readings." Now, without a doubt, rereading is one of the moves that smart readers can make if they run aground while reading. But it is only one of many "fix-up" strategies that skilled readers have in their toolboxes. Further, the CCSS want students to enter texts "cold," without thinking or predicting about them in advance. As they put it, "Teachers should never preempt or replace the text by translating its contents for students or telling students what they are going to learn in advance of the text." As the authors go on to explain: "when productive struggle with the text is exhausted, questions rather than explanations can help focus students' attention on key phrases and statements in the text, or in the organization of ideas in the paragraph" (Coleman and Pimentel 2011, 8). In other words, more rereading.

Many teachers we work with have been puzzled by this neglect of explicit comprehension instruction in the standards, which seems so contrary to current research, and which is belied by the success they have achieved with children by doing just such teaching. Just think about all the work Sara Ahmed was doing to build her students' background knowledge of the civil rights era, so they could understand *Warriors Don't Cry* more deeply. We worry that these CCSS positions could mislead teachers into abandoning the preteaching of academic vocabulary, the previewing of text, helping students to set purposes for their reading, or even teaching comprehension at all. It has been amply shown, and supported by strong existing recommendations such as those from the National Board for Professional Teaching Standards, that students understand and remember better when they enter the text thinking. Effective teachers make sure that students read actively and consciously, and build lasting knowledge by using the same, complete arsenal of reading strategies that lifelong readers employ. So while many aspects of these new standards can help educators plan for successful teaching of reading, effective teachers and schools will make sure they also employ the research-proven practices we describe in this chapter.

Qualities of Best Practice in Teaching Reading

Below we explain the basic qualities and characteristics of Best Practice in reading instruction, approaches validated by the most reliable research—and the model toward which thousands of teachers are moving. As you'll soon see, some of these recommendations especially apply to beginning readers, some to older ones, and many, to all.

Focus on meaning. Reading is not phonics, vocabulary, syllabification, or other "skills," as useful as these activities may be. Reading means getting meaning from print. The essence of reading is a transaction between the words of an author and the mind of a reader, during which meaning is constructed. This means that the main goal of reading instruction must be comprehension.

Read aloud. Hearing books read aloud is a key to learning to read. Regie Routman writes: "Reading aloud allows children to hear the rich language of stories and texts they cannot yet read on their own or might never have chosen to read. Our students learn vocabulary, grammar, new information, and how stories and written language work, especially when we talk about the background of a piece of writing and encourage active participation and discussion" (2003, 20). This recommendation is not just for the little ones; teachers of all grade levels (including middle and high school) should set aside time each day for reading aloud, selecting good literature or nonfiction of high interest to young people.

Do everything in your power to get kids to read—anything and everything. Reading is the best practice for learning to read. The quantity of children's reading experience is related directly to their achievement levels (Allington 2011). Free, voluntary reading, both in school and out, is strongly associated with gains in reading achievement (Krashen 2004). Effective teachers provide time for independent silent reading every day, using structures like literature circles and reading workshop, as well as by encouraging at-home reading of a wide variety of materials.

Provide beginning readers with many opportunities to interact with print. These include listening to stories, participating in shared book experiences, making language-experience stories and books, composing stories through play, enacting dialogue, and reading and writing predictable books. From the first day of school, books and paper and pencils should be in the hands of children. If children do not have extensive book experiences before coming to school, teachers must begin by providing the reading experiences they have missed. But children should never be treated as though they have not had meaningful encounters with print; in fact, even those from the most struggling families have experienced much more interaction with written symbols than most teachers realize (Paratore 2001). Instead, teachers should build from and extend what children already know about language, whether that knowledge begins with fairy tales in parents' laps or from the ample (and educationally underestimated) print appearing on computer or TV screens.

Surround readers with opportunities for success. Children learn to read best in a low-risk environment. Reading experiences should allow children to take risks, make inferences, check their conclusions against the text at hand, and be wrong. Reading teachers should help children understand that predicting what will happen next in stories, jumping to conclusions, and confirming or disconfirming their hypotheses are effective and powerful reading strategies rather than errors. For the most part, teachers should avoid questions that require right answers and instead ask questions that encourage a diversity of well-supported responses. Constant penalties for being wrong, as well as an overemphasis on correctness, grades, and being right, undermine the climate of safety that young readers need to take risks and grow.

Teach phonics. Young children should have well-structured instruction in phonics. For children just beginning to read—typically in kindergarten and first grade—it is vital to learn the sound-symbol relationships of written language. Indeed, if children do not crack the alphabetic code, reading (i.e., getting meaning from print) is effectively blocked to them. Therefore, skillful teachers provide young children with a variety of high-involvement activities that help them understand, manipulate, and use sound-symbol correspondences. But even as teachers offer this important experience, they also keep in mind that *phonics is not a subject in itself*, but rather a tool, and that the goal of teaching phonics is comprehension. Smart teachers carefully balance the time given to phonics in the early grades with other key beginning reading activities, and group their students carefully (though temporarily) so that those who have already mastered phonics can go on and read, rather than sitting through whole-class phonics lessons they do not need. In any case, such brief, well-designed lessons in phonics normally should be concluded by the end of second grade for all but those who have identified special learning problems.

Constant penalties for being wrong, as well as an overemphasis on correctness, grades, and being right, undermine the climate of safety that young readers need to take risks and grow.

The so-called reading wars have lasted over fifty years, pitting skills-centered instruction against more holistic approaches. The contrasting paradigms are often expressed as phonics versus literature, or drill versus play, or teacher control versus student autonomy. The opposing sides constantly launch research studies, invective, and accusations at each other, making primary-grade teachers feel even more nervous about whether they are doing the right thing for the beginning readers in their care.

It is important to remember that even the very conservative National Reading Panel (2000) prescribes just ten minutes a day of phonics activities. We also must remember that the majority of children, 60 to 80 percent by most estimates, can learn all the phonics skills they'll ever need from ample real reading and (especially) from practicing spelling in their own writing. Indeed, many children crack the alphabetic code at home before ever coming to school. All this puts the role of phonics in perspective: in a responsible and balanced K–12 reading program, phonics amounts to less than 5 percent of the instructional efforts teachers make.

Provide access to a wide and rich array of print. Basal readers are not enough. Chances to read many interesting and informative books are the base of a successful reading program. Selections should go well beyond the basal reader to include a variety of materials, both narrative and expository, provide experiences with children's literature, and encourage students' self-selection of books. The Best Practice classroom is stocked with a broad assortment of print of all kinds, including poetry, newspapers, and trade books as well as content-area books and magazines. Fiction and nonfiction materials should be selected on the basis of quality and student interest and should represent a wide range of difficulty, not only so kids can experience successful independent reading regardless of their level, but also so they can challenge themselves by moving up in difficulty. Content-area teachers should use multiple textbooks and trade books, and set up environments in which students work on self-selected topics within the required units of study. High-quality digital resources are vital for students at all grade levels, along with web access that's both safe for learners and free from the censorship of undiscriminating website-blocking programs.

Give kids choices. Choice is an integral part of literate behavior. Children should be encouraged to choose reading materials, activities, and ways of demonstrating their understanding of the texts they have read. Remember how in Sara Ahmed's classroom, kids were allowed to choose five or six out of twenty different photographs to study? Reading skills and strategies should be presented as options rather than as rules to be universally applied under all reading conditions. Teachers should schedule regular time periods for reading and writing, rather than giving brief, narrow reading and writing assignments. Teacher-directed instruction in which all children in a classroom or reading group are constantly required to make the same response limits rather than empowers young readers.

Balance challenging texts with easy ones. Kids need easy books. We've already questioned the assumption that students should spend most of their school days reading books they can understand only with a teacher's active support. Studies show that young readers need much more of what adult readers sometimes call "beach books"—easy, predictable, enjoyable, quick reads, books you can zoom through at full speed, with a high rate of comprehension (Allington 2010). Success, not frustration, is what builds reading power and fluency. If you doubt this, interview some highly sophisticated adult readers (maybe even yourself) and you'll usually find that, as children, these folks spent thousands of hours "practicing reading" with Goosebumps (350 million copies sold), Boxcar Children, the Babysitter's Club, or even, God forbid, comic books or *Mad* magazines.

Teach reading as thinking. Reading is a cognitive process: an active, constructive, creative, higher-order thinking activity that involves distinctive thinking strategies before, during, and after reading. Students need to learn how skillful, experienced readers actually manage these processes.

Model reading. In her lesson, Sara Ahmed talked several times about her own thinking and modeled directly how to dig out important details in an image. Teachers should read widely along with their students, sharing their reading lives and talking about how they select books, authors, or genres. It is vital that children get to observe a joyfully literate adult who loves and uses reading in a variety of ways every day. And teachers should do more than talk about books and authors they love; they must *show* their students how they think while they read. Using a powerful teaching strategy called "think-alouds," teachers can read aloud unfamiliar selections in front of their students, stopping frequently to "open up their heads" and vocalize their internal thought processes (See Chapter 2 for a more detailed look at a think-aloud.)

Name and teach reading strategies directly. Research tells us that proficient readers actively visualize, question, connect, predict, and evaluate, among other skills. Teachers shouldn't keep these cognitive strategies a secret, even from the youngest children. In a developmentally appropriate way, they should describe each strategy explicitly, model the strategy in action, do it collaboratively with kids, allow guided practice time, and then let kids use it on their own. This

Reading is a cognitive process: an active, constructive, creative, higher-order thinking activity that involves distinctive thinking strategies before, during, and after reading.

combination of explicit teaching and gradual transfer of responsibility from teacher to student is especially critical for struggling readers (Routman 2006).

Support readers before, during, and after reading. Assigning reading is not *teaching* reading. Simply saying "read this for Friday" can leave kids to struggle with the text alone. Instead, wise teachers "front-load" instruction (Wilhelm, Baker, and Dube 2001). Before kids read a particular text, teachers help students activate prior knowledge, set purposes for reading, and make predictions. During reading, teachers help students monitor their comprehension and construct meaning. We can see how artfully Sara Ahmed did this in her story at the start of this chapter. After reading, teachers help students savor, share, and apply meaning, and build connections to further reading and writing.

Help children use reading as a tool for learning. Teachers can demonstrate the usefulness of reading and writing by offering opportunities for children to engage in meaningful reading and writing during content-area instruction. Brainstorming questions before a subject is explored, pursuing library or Internet research projects, integrating reading and writing in content-area learning logs, and designing classroom activities that engage students in reading and writing in the ways they are used outside of school—all these strategies help kids see reading as a powerful tool for answering real questions.

Give kids daily opportunities to talk about their reading. What do enthusiastic adult readers do when they finish a great (or disappointing) book? Usually, they look for someone to talk to, to share their views, recount their reactions, and start a conversation. Kids need the same experience. Daily sharing time, book club meetings, written conversations, dialogue journal partners, book buddies, author's chair presentations, peer-tutoring groups, and collaborative research projects are opportunities for kids to practice this kind of literate talk. Observing kids in these conversations also provides teachers with much information for gauging students' progress.

Replace workbooks and skills sheets with authentic activities. There is little evidence that workbooks and skills sheets enhance reading achievement, and they often consume precious chunks of classroom time (not to mention book budgets). Effective teachers critically evaluate so-called skill activities before giving them to students and replace them, where appropriate, with authentic, original activities. An oral summary of a text in preparation for discussing it with a book group or a response to a text in a reading journal is far more meaningful than a worksheet on main ideas or a workbook exercise on fact and opinion. Once students have internalized the behavioral norms of reading and writing workshops, these structures provide far more valuable and individualized "seatwork" than any prepackaged worksheet.

Provide writing experiences at all grade levels. As well as being valuable in its own right, writing powerfully promotes ability in reading. Indeed, for our youngest emerging readers, writing with developmental spelling is often their "lead strategy" for deciphering the sound-symbol relationships of written language. At all grade levels, effective teachers provide a balance of different kinds of writing activities, including both individual, self-sponsored writings like those in journals or writing workshops and teacher-guided writing activities that help students try new genres, topics, and forms for writing.

Match reading assessment to classroom practice. Many of the current standardized reading achievement and basal series tests focus on atomized subskills of reading, and do not stress the essence of reading, which is comprehension. The best possible assessment occurs when teachers observe and interact with students as they read authentic texts for genuine purposes, and then keep anecdotal records of students' developing skills, problems, changes, and goals in reading. Regie Routman (2003, 105) describes one-to-one assessment conferences in which the teacher leads a child through these steps:

- Bring me a book you can read pretty well. Why did you choose this book?
- What is the reading level of this book for you?
- Tell me what the book is about so far.
- Read part of this book for me.
- Tell me what you remember about what you just read.
- Let's discuss your strengths and what you need to work on.

How different this caring conversation is from a multiple-choice test that children fill out in silence and even fear.

▲　▲　▲

We think that the foregoing list of principles and practices is amazingly simple. These recommendations don't require any complex, futuristic innovations. To begin with, they invite a recommitment to some fundamental instructional strategies: reading good literature aloud; having kids read lots of whole, real books; providing much writing practice; encouraging the patient and varied discussion of the ideas in books. And these recommendations invite teachers to step into some powerful new roles, modeling their own reading, diversifying kids' reading materials, offering students more choice and responsibility, and rebalancing time allocations so that the most powerful experiences get the time they need.

Reading in Science, Social Studies, and Other Subjects

Not all school reading takes place in reading or English classes. Nor should it. Our opening example, about the civil rights movement, took place in a social studies classroom. Indeed, one of our most urgent national initiatives is "reading across the curriculum," which means providing students with much more practice with the kind of nonfiction text they'll encounter in college and at work. As students move up through the grades, they meet increasingly difficult concepts in mathematics, science, and history, and the kinds of text they encounter pose new challenges. The reading skills learned in the primary grades are no longer enough; kids need to constantly redevelop their repertoire of ways of thinking about text. So we are also working to give teachers of those "content-area" subjects the support they need to not just assign more readings, but to explicitly teach kids how to understand disciplinary materials.

For generations, America's young readers have been hamstrung by our system's overdependence on textbooks, and the concomitant neglect of important shorter texts, fiction and nonfiction trade books, primary sources, and web content. But things are changing. To both engage and educate young readers, content-area teachers are moving toward a more balanced mix of real-world material in a variety of genres. They use textbooks selectively, helping students to dig deeper into a smaller number of topics. They supplement textbooks with an array of other sources—especially ones with alternative interpretations, contrary views, or competing hypotheses. They create time for free voluntary reading, not just in English but across the curriculum. In science, technology, engineering, social studies, and even math classes, teachers are building classroom libraries where kids immerse themselves in biographies, historical novels, journals, magazines, and current trade books related to the field. As they create these collections, teachers recognize that *all kids need books they can read,* which means gathering reading materials at a wide range of reading levels, from comics to online databases.

The reading-as-thinking approach takes on added significance as kids move up through the grades, encountering new genres, tougher, more technical text, and more challenging writing styles. Students continue to need teacher demonstrations, think-alouds, and strategy lessons that help them tackle ever more difficult materials. Lately, a number of authors have offered workable models and materials that help students understand and remember subject-matter material, while stressing enjoyment, engagement, and positive reading attitudes

(Robb 2010; Tovani 2004; Daniels and Zemelman 2004). And big kids still need to study *words*; at this age level, with phonics long since mastered, word study can focus on academic vocabulary. But this doesn't have to mean word-list drudgery: authors like Holbrook and Salinger (2010), Whitaker (2008), and Blachowicz and Fisher (2009) offer lively, playful approaches that help words really stick with kids. Encouraged by a strong research base and backed by the CCSS, teachers are focusing kids' attention on "Tier 2" vocabulary (Beck 2002), those especially powerful words like *boundary, evidence, abstract, domain*, and *matrix* that reach across many disciplines.

A Feast of Books in First Grade

PAT BARRETT DRAGAN

Martin Elementary School, South San Francisco, California

The more passionate I am about children's literature and sharing it with my students, the more success I have in creating readers—children who love books, take them home each night, and talk about them as if they are old friends. This approach works for my English learners as well as the rest of my first-grade class. Of course, in my "reading workshop," I balance all types of instruction in literature, comprehension, writing, and phonics, but the heart of it is when I read aloud to the children. Several times a day, as kids listen to me bring books alive, they are getting access to stories that resonate with heart and soul, grow vocabulary, embed language rhythm and structure, and expand their content knowledge.

▶ *Reading Literature Aloud*

Sometimes I get an almost electric tingling up my spine as I am reading a book aloud. When I get this same sort of silent "electric hum" coming from the children as well, then I *know* the book is reaching all of us!

This happened when I read the kids David Shannon's picture book, *A Bad Case of Stripes.* Shannon's book is the story of Camilla, who wakes up covered with stripes. The stripes turn into other patterns throughout the story. Ultimately we find out what causes these odd happenings, and how Camilla solves her problem. Crucial to the plot is the fact that she is craving lima beans, but doesn't think she should eat them because her friends don't like them. Here are some brief samplings of the children's thoughts about what is causing Camilla's spots, stripes, and other difficulties:

"I know! It's bacteria!"

"Ohhh! Camilla didn't wash her hands."

"She should wash her hands all the time."

"If somebody says something, she changes into it."

"Or she changes into the color of it."

"If somebody said, 'Make Camilla turn normal,' she'd turn normal. But nobody said it."

"The lima beans are magic."

"Maybe she ate too many lima beans when she was little."

There is much discussion over whether doctors should give Camilla worms, jellybeans, magic beans, medicine, or lima beans to turn her back into herself. There is a lot of use of the word *normal*. Some of this discussion—a few minutes at interludes—is with partners, doing what we call "turn and talk," after which we go back to the whole-group session and share more ideas.

> "Maybe there's regular, normal lima beans and magic lima beans. Is that what you're thinking about, buddy?" (One child said this to another, to help his friend sort out his thoughts.)
>
> "Patrick said this story is like *Imogene's Antlers*! I think so too."
>
> "It's like *I Wish That I Had Duck Feet.*"
>
> "Camilla wanted lima beans SOOOOOOO bad!"
>
> "She's not eating what her body wanted."
>
> "If she ate lima beans and changed back into normal she should eat lima beans every day. I solved the case!"
>
> "You know how you say, 'I got a frog in my throat?'" (This child grabs his throat, so I'll "get it.") "She mighta said, 'I got a chameleon!' Get it? You know, Camilla, chameleon?"
>
> "And now she has a bow with a rainbow color."
>
> "And now she eats lima beans always."

I was pleased to hear the detail and imagination reflected in the children's discussions, as they made meaning together and built on each other's ideas. They were *thinking* as they talked and listened to the story. My six-year-olds were acting just like proficient adult readers: mulling over visual connections, making inferences and predictions, determining what is important in the unfolding story, and evaluating the events and the story solution.

Now, let's go back to the beginning of the morning and I'll tell you how we use the rest of our reading time. Children have got to have it *all*—many different types of reading instruction—phonics, shared and guided reading and writing, literature books, thematic units, big books and basals, fiction and nonfiction, large- and small-group instruction. Who knows what specific lessons will help all the pieces fall into place for a child?

▶ *Overnight Reading*

After coats and lunches have been quickly put away and I have taken attendance, I look at tables to see who has returned "overnight books." These are the choice treasures selected by the children to take home to read and have read to them. Students put books and homework at their seating places, so I can easily see if a book or paper is missing. Then children take turns, table by table, returning their books to their special bookcases, and choosing another book to take home "for overnight." There is a lot of competition to get popular books, and students are quick about making selections. Each table team has an assigned day of the week to choose first, and children know the routine. There is great joy in getting to take a special book home. Esmeralda hugged her reading choice one morning, on the eleventh day of school, and said, "I've been waiting *forever* for this book!"

I have already read these books aloud, so children are familiar with them. This particularly helps our English learners. They have heard me read the story, have seen the pictures, and have spent time with a partner who speaks their language. They have looked at the book, retold the story, and *read* together. When possible, I have paired copies of some books, one in English, one in another language. Children may take one or both home. I try to make sure that there are some books for each of the home languages represented in our class. I keep just a few more books available for overnight than there are students. This makes it easier for children to focus on the reading material they *really* want to spend time with. Each child prints the title and reads it to me, getting help from classmates if needed. I write the title on my weekly grid. The whole process goes very fast. And while this is going on, children are already beginning to read.

▶ *Independent Reading*

We always have daily free choice time for children to choose a book, magazine, or any other reading material, and read it wherever they wish, alone, with a partner, or in a group. Children cherish and count on this social reading time. Because it is so important to them, they organize themselves, make their own choices, and make the time meaningful. I have gradually released the responsibility to my kids for using this time well, and results are far-reaching. As Darnell said to me one day as he went back to his table with a stack of books, "I just love to come to school in the morning so I can read and read and read!"

This special time for books helps turn children into avid, lifelong readers, but it doesn't have to be lengthy. Sometimes the period is as short as ten minutes, and other times we enjoy a whole rainy-day recess. Many children want to read in our "book nook"—a cozy classroom area with over a hundred books placed "covers out" on rain gutters on the wall. Stuffed animals lurk there, waiting for children to read to them. The nook has a race car rug to sit on and some special pillows (one in the form of a giant frog), as well as additional tubs and tubs of books. Only four or five children fit comfortably in this special space, so we take turns by table teams. Other children read on the carpet in the library area, while some hole up under tables, or in little clusters in other places in the classroom, alone, in pairs, or in little groups.

There's nothing like sharing a good book with friends. "Look," says Brenda, with great excitement: "A mouse lemur!" She is reading an issue of *Ranger Rick* magazine with Irvin and Edgard. All three children are thrilled to learn about the mouse lemur. I'm pretty thrilled too. I didn't know there was any such kind of lemur. I mention this to the children so they will see my enthusiasm, and will realize that I am a learner too. I'm also delighted that Brenda is able to figure out the information about this animal. Edgard, who is fluent in both English and Spanish, explains all about lemurs to Irvin, who is just beginning to learn English. The *Ranger Rick* magazine article has wonderful photographs, and these visuals help all three children access the text.

There's nothing like sharing a good book with friends.

Several children are sitting on the floor surrounded by open books and reading about reptiles together. Maria and Obdulia are choral reading *Sheep in a Jeep* by Nancy Shaw. Other children are comparing editions of *Come Along Daisy* by Jane Simmons in English and Arabic. And Jesús, Ariel, and Cesar are folding paper airplanes and hovering over a large book full of different designs for planes to make (and fly after school or occasionally during a brief afternoon break). Believe me, I thought long and hard about making this paper airplane book and copy paper available to children during free choice independent reading time!

During free choice reading time in my classroom, many of the students excitedly peruse large reference books they can't really read, but they learn a lot from the captions, photographs, and pictures. The children's intense interest in specific topics carries them past the difficulties of the text. They just take in whatever information they can and use the "group brain" to figure things out. At the beginning of the year, when we are just starting to develop special relationships with books and reading, I do a lot of pretending and acting "as if." I just act "as if" the children are real readers, passionate about books and learning. And pretty soon I find that this really is the case. Most of my students are English learners and may not have much access to books or reading material at home. They *desperately* need this time to connect with books (and to watch me model my own excitement as I read).

▶ *The Basal Program*

Now we put independent books away and join up at the class meeting area for the flag salute, some music, and of course, more reading. I am obligated to teach a basal reading series and I do so during this part of the day. The program includes organized lessons that encompass phonemic awareness, phonics, a story to read, comprehension activities, and other literacy skills that relate to the text we read. While I prefer more authentic activities with literature, I can adapt these basal lessons to my own students and their needs. For example, because phonics makes more sense to children in the context of the story, we "scavenger hunt" in our basal readers for the words that go with the phonics part of the lesson.

At the beginning of the year, the basal stories are frequently too difficult for my children, so I project them with the document camera and we read them like a homemade "big book." Doing these shared readings together gives children lots of successful practice. They are sharing the experience of figuring out the words as well as working to comprehend meaning. It helps them to transfer this experience to reading the actual paper copy. This kind of practice also provides a way for our English learners to participate with us, even getting the gist of the story by just looking at the pictures.

This week the basal has a story for children to listen to and visualize as the teacher reads the text. But there are no pictures. Because the majority of my students are second-language learners, it is imperative that I modify this lesson. No one will get anything out of a solely auditory activity without any illustrations, props, realia, or clues about the text. I decide to turn the story into a "drawing tale," and I draw pictures of characters and events as I read. These are not great drawings, but they give some meaning to the text, and my class is fascinated watching pictures appear on screen or whiteboard.

At the end of the story we form a circle, sit down, and choose characters to enact the tale, "creative dramatics" style. I "feed" characters the lines, but they can say them however they wish and are free to make up their own dialogue. Children act out the story, without props—we just imagine them. The class is enthusiastic about the drama, and our follow-up discussion indicates that children have understood the story. At the end of the lesson, Betsy, a child with an emerging command of English, comes up to me with her arms folded, hands across her heart. She is all eyes. "That was a lovely story," she says.

▶ Small-Group Instruction: Guided Reading

After recess, children go to small guided reading groups with me. Guided reading is where I teach a small number of children, usually four to six, to read books at their *instructional* reading levels. I determine these levels by taking a "running record" for each child. When children are reading at their instructional levels (92 to 97 percent accuracy), they have to struggle just a bit but can read the material with a short introduction and a little personal help from the teacher. In my guided reading groups, children are spending their time engaged in the learning activity that will help them the most in their efforts to become literate: actual *reading*—not doing workbook pages, checking on spelling or vocabulary, or similar follow-up activities.

The guided reading format is simple. I briefly share two or three titles at my group's level, and let the kids pick the book they want to read. I provide some quick background information and give children a moment to share any prior knowledge of this topic. We take a "picture walk" through the book together, talking about what is going on in different illustrations. This overview of the story is especially important for ELLs. I work for a tone that is relaxed and lighthearted. I make a point to work vocabulary words from the story into the conversation as we look through the book. Sometimes I ask children to "frame" a specific word with two fingers. I remind children of the questions they can ask themselves if they become stuck as they read:

- Does that sound right?
- Does that look right?
- Does that make sense?

I stress the importance of rereading so we will understand the text. All of this is done quickly, in order to maximize children's time to read.

I have children read aloud quietly, at their own pace, and as they read, I listen to each child. I ask children whether they need help. I ask everyone to keep reading, even if they have finished the story. Some children then read with a partner or with me. I'm there to help anyone who needs a boost. There is time later for students to reread books we have already read, independently or with a partner or group, as they wish. To wrap up the lesson, I take time for kids' "meta-cognitive" comments, like what they did to figure out tricky words or clarify confusing parts of the story.

The group lasts fifteen to twenty minutes, and the emphasis is on children getting as much solid reading time as possible. The last five minutes or so, we have some word study or word play with magnetic letters or marking pens on whiteboards. I dictate words and children write or form them, and then read them back to me. We make new words from these, changing beginning or ending sounds, erasing or adding final *e*'s, and so on. Nothing we do is too big a struggle: we all learn more when an experience is upbeat and positive.

▶ *Thematic Teaching*

Much of the reading kids are doing during all these different workshop times is connected to a common topic. Each Friday, the kids and I pick a theme to explore the following week. I try to steer my group toward units that are coming up in the curriculum as well as topics we are interested in. For example, one of the upcoming units in our basal program had a story about the rain forest. So the kids and I decided to make rain forests our weeklong focus of inquiry. We created a large "KWL" chart, listing things we knew (K), things we wanted to know (W), and, later, things we learned (L).

I supplement the basal by bringing in some special read-alouds, as well as other books and magazines on the theme. I invite the children to peruse and talk about these theme materials during independent reading time or while classmates are working with me on guided reading. Then we'll get together again in whole group to add to our KWL chart, discuss ideas and information, and listen to related read-alouds.

A favorite was Lynne Cherry's wonderful book, *The Great Kapok Tree.* In their partner discussions after my reading, the children wondered whether the protagonist should listen to the voices of animals and an Aboriginal child—who spoke to him in the guise of a dream—or follow the orders of his employer and cut down the tree. A great conversation sprang up between Avit and Henry. "The man should not cut down the tree," they said. "The people should let things grow. Then they should gather nuts and fruit and plants and take them to town and sell them at the market for money for their families."

With that comment alone, revealing children's deep passion and interest for investigating and learning, I counted the unit a success. We made sure to wrap up our investigations with some time for both shared writing and individual children's writing. And during our art period, we built a torn-paper rain forest around the classroom wall and learned some related poetry and songs.

▶ *Becoming Investigative Reporters*

Once kids get interested in doing research, there are no limits. Another way we gather information—as well as contribute to our school community—is through our weekly newspaper. This project is detailed in my own book, *Kids, Cameras, and the Curriculum* (2008). Again, we pick a theme (and it could be the same one we are already looking into) and focus on finding out as much about it as we can. I have small digital cameras the kids use to photograph their findings, and a small printer dock so that we can print out an individual photo or two. Each weekly "newspaper" is one ledger-sized page (14 by 17 inches) and generally has one or two stories and one or two photos.

The project is very hands-on. Because we usually pick a story that is going on in our classroom or at school, or involves school personnel or students, we can investigate by asking questions, doing interviews, and making notes. We write up our story on Wednesday and Thursday, shared-writing style (I scribe; the kids talk and "help" me spell and punctuate). We reread our chart story many times to make sure our text sounds right and makes sense.

Then, on Friday, we print out a couple of the photos taken by our classroom photographers, and attach them to the story version I have typed. We make copies of our newspaper in the faculty room and take it to the office, where we all announce, "Hot off the press!" The principal or other office staffer reads our news aloud to us. The new edition is placed in the window for all to see, and each classroom receives a copy of our news. My class keeps copies in binders for proud rereading practice.

One of the most exciting editions featured a letter and photograph from Antarctica from famed *National Geographic* photographer Paul Nicklen. One of the most fun side effects of this reportorial coup was catching sight of some upper-grade students looking at the newspaper in the office window, and reading and talking about the article. As we passed them on the way to lunch, I heard one of them say, with some frustration, "How do they *DO* that, get a letter and picture from Antarctica?!!!" (It's *OUR* little secret!)

Some other stories we have reported in *The Kids' Press* are Safety Patrol, Our Librarian, Famous Author Visits, Aryanna Wins Contest, *The Polar Express* Party, Jump Rope for Heart, News Team Visits Office, and School Board Visits. Our school board members did indeed visit, to see our newspaper and talk to the kids about how they wrote it. In one of my favorite "student take-over moments," my kids went for their pencils, small notebooks, and a camera and started interviewing the school board members! I was a proud teacher/publisher that day.

▶ First Graders Can Accomplish More Than We Can Dream

In one short year, first graders can go from dependent learners to children with strong, independent ideas—kids who can figure out a text, read it, comprehend it, and sometimes, care enough to take action. Through all their independent reading, small-group discussions, and investigative group work and writing experiences, they have gained a language to rely on. Still, I believe the heart of their success is the read-aloud. Children begin to speak the language of the stories they hear and read; play with the words, phrases, and ideas; and try them out in their own lives. As the great children's author Bill Martin, Jr., said, "Students will only learn to read when they have language inside of themselves." Hearing and reading glorious works of children's literature fills the children up with heaping helpings of language and story. And my kids seem to understand the importance of the work we are doing with literature and with each other. As one of my children, Sabine, told me, "Reading is for getting smart."

▶ Helping English Learners Practice Reading

While I am busy with guided reading groups, one little independent group may read together at the listening center. They have organized stacks of four or five leveled books in front of them, coordinated with a cassette tape they helped make. They create these tapes with me, all of us reading in unison, after we read the books in the guided reading group. These children speak little English yet, but they are able to read book after book, following along as they listen to these taped stories. The stories are comprehensible because of simple pictures and our prior activities and discussions.

Students are successful at all the reading activities because they have already had small-group lessons with these materials. The books selected for this independent practice are at their specific learning levels, and children are relaxed and in charge.

There are many background scaffolds or supports for these reading practice sessions. Children experience written text in many ways: by listening to real literature read aloud, through "big book" shared readings, and by reading trade books and basal texts together, often on an overhead projector "shared-reading style." They take part in guided reading lessons in small groups with leveled texts. They read and create poetry charts, act out books they love, and have many writing experiences—with mini-lessons, classroom interviews, and writing their own poems, memoirs, and stories. There is an emphasis on oral language and on connecting language with visuals to help language learners understand what is being said.

As they connect with text and life and each other, there is an atmosphere of play. I think that is what the children are doing: playing. They are using spontaneous expression and gaining fluency as they work to say the words, read with understanding, and make the books come to life. And they are having a great time doing it.

Works Cited

Allington, Richard. 2010. *Essential Readings on Struggling Learners.* Newark, DE: International Reading Association.

———. 2011. *What Really Matters for Struggling Readers: Designing Research-Based Programs* (3rd edition). New York: Allyn and Bacon.

Anderson, Richard C., Elfrieda H. Hiebert, Judith A. Scott, and Ian A. G. Wilkinson. 1985. *Becoming a Nation of Readers: The Report of the Commission on Reading.* Washington, DC: National Institute of Education.

Atwell, Nancie. 2013 (forthcoming). *In the Middle: Writing, Reading, and Learning with Adolescents* (3rd edition). Portsmouth, NH: Heinemann.

Beck, Isabel. 2002. *Bringing Words to Life.* New York: Guilford.

Beers, Kylene. 2003. *When Kids Can't Read, What Teachers Can Do.* Portsmouth, NH: Heinemann.

Blachowicz, Camille, and Peter Fisher. 2009. *Teaching Vocabulary in All Classrooms* (4th edition). New York: Allyn & Bacon.

Calkins, Lucy McCormick. 2000. *The Art of Teaching Reading.* New York: Allyn and Bacon.

Coleman, David, and Susan Pimentel. 2011. *Publishers Criteria for Common Core State Standards in English Language Arts and Literacy in History/Social Studies, Science and Technical Subjects*. National Governors Association and Council of Chief State School Officers.

Common Core State Standards Initiative. 2010. *Common Core State Standards for English Language Arts and Literacy in History/Social Studies, Science and Technical Subjects*. National Governors Association and Council of Chief State School Officers.

———. 2010. *Common Core State Standards for English Language Arts and Literacy in History/Social Studies, Science and Technical Subjects; Appendix A: Research Supporting Key Elements of the Standards*. National Governors Association and Council of Chief State School Officers.

Daniels, Harvey, ed. 2010. *Comprehension Going Forward: Where We Are, What's Next*. Portsmouth, NH: Heinemann.

Daniels, Harvey, and Nancy Steineke. 2011. *Texts and Lessons for Content-Area Reading*. Portsmouth, NH: Heinemann.

Daniels, Harvey, and Steven Zemelman. 2004. *Subjects Matter: Every Teacher's Guide to Content-Area Reading*. Portsmouth, NH: Heinemann.

Dragan, Pat Barrett. 2008. *Kids, Cameras, and the Curriculum: Focusing on Learning in the Primary Grades*. Portsmouth, NH: Heinemann.

Duke, Nell, and P. David Pearson. 2002. Effective Practices for Developing Reading Comprehension. In Alan E. Farstrup and S. Jay Samuels, eds. *What Research Has to Say About Reading Instruction*. Newark, DE: International Reading Association.

Gallagher, Kelly. 2004. *Deeper Reading*. York, ME: Stenhouse.

Harste, Jerome C. 1989. *New Policy Guidelines for Reading: Connecting Research and Practice*. Urbana, IL: National Council of Teachers of English.

Harvey, Stephanie, and Anne Goudvis. 2007. *Strategies That Work: Teaching Comprehension to Enhance Understanding*. Portland, ME: Stenhouse.

Holbrook, Sara, and Michael Salinger. 2010. *High Definition: Unforgettable Vocabulary-Building Strategies Across Genres and Subjects*. Portsmouth, NH: Heinemann.

Kamil, Michael, P. David Pearson, Elizabeth Moje, and Peter Afflerbach. 2011. *Handbook of Reading Research, Vol. 4*. New York: Routledge.

Keene, Ellin Oliver, and Susan Zimmermann. 2007. *Mosaic of Thought: Teaching Reading Comprehension in a Reader's Workshop*. Portsmouth, NH: Heinemann.

Krashen, Stephen. 2004. *The Power of Reading: Insights from the Research*. Portsmouth, NH: Heinemann.

Miller, Debbie. 2002. *Reading with Meaning: Teaching Comprehension in the Primary Grades*. Portland, ME: Stenhouse.

National Board for Professional Teaching Standards. 2003. *Standards for Generalist/Middle Childhood*. Arlington, VA: NBPTS.

National Council of Teachers of English and International Reading Association. 1996. *Standards for the English Language Arts*. Newark, DE, and Urbana, IL: International Reading Association and National Council of Teachers of English.

———. 2009. *Standards for the Assessment of Reading and Writing (Revised Edition)*. Newark, DE, and Urbana, IL: International Reading Association and National Council of Teachers of English.

National Reading Panel. 2000. *Report of the National Reading Panel: Teaching Children to Read.* Washington, DC: National Institute for Child Health and Human Development, Department of Health and Human Services.

Paratore, Jeanne R. 2001. *Opening Doors, Opening Opportunities: Family Literacy in an Urban Community.* New York: Allyn and Bacon.

Robb, Laura. 2010. *Teaching Reading in Middle School: A Strategic Approach to Teaching Reading That Improves Comprehension and Thinking* (2nd edition). New York: Scholastic.

Routman, Regie. 2003. *Reading Essentials: The Specifics You Need to Teach Reading Well.* Portsmouth, NH: Heinemann.

———. 2006. *Writing Essentials: The Specifics You Need to Teach Writing Well.* Portsmouth, NH: Heinemann.

Sierra-Perry, Martha. 1996. *Standards in Practice, 3–5.* Urbana, IL: National Council of Teachers of English.

Smagorinsky, Peter. 1996. *Standards in Practice, 9–12.* Urbana, IL: National Council of Teachers of English.

Tovani, Cris. 2004. *Do I Really Have to Teach Reading?* Portland, ME: Stenhouse.

Whitaker, Sandra. 2008. *Word Play: Building Vocabulary Across Texts and Disciplines.* Portsmouth, NH: Heinemann.

Wilhelm, Jeffrey D. 1996. *Standards in Practice, 6–8.* Urbana, IL: National Council of Teachers of English.

Wilhelm, Jeffrey D., Tanya N. Baker, and Julie Dube. 2001. *Strategic Reading.* Portsmouth, NH: Heinemann.

Suggested Further Readings

Allen, Janet. 2007. *Inside Words: Tools for Teaching Academic Vocabulary.* York, ME: Stenhouse.

Blachowicz, Camille, and Donna Ogle. 2001. *Reading Comprehension: Strategies for Independent Learners.* New York: Guilford Press.

Boushey, Gail, and Joan Moser. 2009. *The Café Book: Engaging All Students in Daily Literacy Assessment and Instruction.* York, ME: Stenhouse.

Daniels, Harvey, and Nancy Steineke. 2004. *Mini-lessons for Literature Circles.* Portsmouth, NH: Heinemann.

Dragan, Patricia. 2007. *Literacy from Day One.* Portsmouth, NH: Heinemann.

Fay, Kathleen, and Suzanne Whaley. 2004. *Becoming One Community: Reading and Writing with English Language Learners.* Portland, ME: Stenhouse.

Fountas, Irene, and Gay Su Pinnell. 1996. *Guided Reading: Good First Reading for All Children.* Portsmouth, NH: Heinemann.

Frey, Nancy, and Douglas Fisher. 2009. *Learning Words Inside and Out.* Portsmouth, NH: Heinemann.

Smith, Michael, and Jeffrey Wilhelm. 2002. *Reading Don't Fix No Chevys: Literacy Lives of Young Men.* Portsmouth, NH: Heinemann.

Steineke, Nancy. 2002. *Reading and Writing Together: Collaborative Literacy in Action.* Portsmouth, NH: Heinemann.

Tovani, Cris. 2000. *I Read It, But I Don't Get It: Comprehension Strategies for Adolescent Readers.* Portland, ME: Stenhouse.

Reading Resources on the Internet

The International Reading Association is the largest and most influential reading society and the co-creator of our national literacy standards. For association news, research bulletins, publications, and conference announcements.

www.ira.org

Although a K–12 organization, the membership of the National Council of Teachers of English is predominantly middle and high school teachers, and NCTE is the top source of information on reading, literature, and writing for secondary students.

www.ncte.org

The Daily Café: Sisters Gail Boushey and Joan Moser are among today's most popular literacy educators. Their books and workshops give teachers just the blend of practicality and inspiration they crave. This subscription website digitizes the sisters' magic with more text, lessons, videos, and resources for teachers seeking a balanced literacy approach in their classrooms.

www.thedailycafe.com

ReadWriteThink: The NCTE and IRA partnered with the MarcoPolo Education Foundation to create a highly teacher-friendly website that offers lesson plans and student materials in the spirit of the IRA/NCTE standards, and increasingly correlated with the Common Core Standards. Lesson quality is variable.

www.readwritethink.org

Edutopia is a program of the George Lucas Educational Foundation, which supports project-based learning, social-emotional learning, and access to new technology for students, with a special focus on "information literacy." Lots of useful materials here, with a strong pro-tech bent.

www.edutopia.org

Accomplished teachers who are ready to seek national certification can learn about the rigorous one-year process, find out the benefits of a successful review in their own state, and locate a support group at the website of the National Board for Professional Teaching Standards.

www.nbpts.org

Literature teachers of all grade levels, and especially teachers facing censorship issues, rely on the American Library Association.

www.ala.org

Founded in 2006 by the respected author and editor Brenda Power, the subscription website Choice Literacy offers innovative, high-quality resources for K–12 literacy leaders. The website has grown to include over 700 professionally produced and edited video and print features from top educators in the field, as well as promising new voices.

www.choiceliteracy.com

The Book Whisperer: Donnalyn Miller is an extraordinary middle school teacher who has a gift for matching kids to books that change their lives. She also gives highly cogent and engaging workshops for teachers around the country. We've already recommended her book, and now read her blog at

http://blogs.edweek.org/teachers/book_whisperer/

English Companion Ning: Our colleague and fellow author Jim Burke has done an amazing thing: over the past few years he has created a web space where more than 31,000 teachers now gather to support each other. There are book clubs, topical discussions, interest groups, classroom videos, idea exchanges and more. This resource leads the field.

http://englishcompanion.ning.com/

Recommendations on Teaching *Reading*

▲ INCREASE	▼ DECREASE
Teacher reading good literature aloud to students	Students compelled to read aloud to whole class or reading group, being corrected and marked down for errors
Time for independent reading	Exclusive emphasis on whole-class or reading-group activities
Children's choice of their own reading materials	Teacher selection of all reading materials for individuals and groups
Balance of easy and hard books	Exclusively difficult "instructional-level" books
Exposing children to a wide and rich range of literature	Relying on selections in basal reader
Teacher modeling and discussing his/her own reading processes	Teacher keeping his/her own reading tastes and habits private
Primary instructional emphasis on comprehension	Primary instructional emphasis on reading subskills such as phonics, word analysis, syllabication
Teaching reading as a process: • Use strategies that activate prior knowledge • Help students make and test predictions • Structure help during reading • Provide after-reading applications	Teaching reading as a single, one-step act
Social, collaborative activities with much discussion and interaction	Solitary seatwork
Grouping by interests or book choices	Grouping by reading level
Silent reading followed by discussion	Round-robin oral reading
Teaching skills in the context of whole and meaningful literature	Teaching isolated skills in phonics workbooks or drills
Writing before and after reading	Little or no chance to write
Encouraging invented spelling in children's early writings	Punishing preconventional spelling in students' early writings
Use of reading in content fields (e.g., historical novels in social studies)	Segregation of reading to reading time
Evaluation focused on holistic, higher-order thinking processes	Evaluation focused on individual, low-level subskills
Measuring success of reading program by students' reading habits, attitudes, and comprehension	Measuring success of reading program only by test scores

Just-Right Technology

No doubt about it, we are living in a digital wonder age. There is so much that teachers can do with twenty-first-century technology—not to mention what students are *already* doing with it outside of school! While we are quite fond of many new technologies ourselves, we believe that the true power of teaching resides mainly in the interaction between the mind of a teacher and the minds of learners. Sometimes a piece of modern technology can enhance that connection; other times, old tools work fine; and sometimes, no technology beyond the human voice is needed. Following are a few examples of the former—what we call just-right technology.

Projectors

The iconic blackboard is appropriately becoming extinct, and has been replaced with a whole range of projecting equipment with vastly expanded (and differing) capabilities. With today's phenomenal accessibility of information, images, and videos in all school subjects, teachers absolutely must have the tools to flexibly and effortlessly display that content on a big, bright screen. No matter what the hardware, teachers must be able to project:

▶ all daily classroom instructions and directions, as an accommodation for English language learners and students with special needs, and as a multisensory advantage for everyone

▶ any article, story, or Internet page while doing think-alouds, write-alouds, and search-alouds

▶ text, images, videos, and real objects like a historic artifact or a tree leaf, models for writing, and materials for study and student inquiry

CAUTION: *Smart and smarter boards can be amazing. At their best, they can help with all the above functions and much more. But they are still a centralized, teacher-controlled, front-of-the-room device that kids mostly watch. On the other hand, a class set of tablet computers allows kids to scatter throughout the room, pursuing their own learning, conducting research, and developing reports. We haven't been everywhere that new technologies are being tried, but the most powerful ones we have encountered—the classrooms where we find ourselves saying "Wow, this is the future"—are using kid-driven devices.*

Still, with all technology, content is the key. The school world is now flooded with electronic software of highly uneven quality. Some programs are spectacularly interactive; others are digital worksheets. For just $70, you can buy an excellent

document camera that can do most of the functions listed above. For the vast majority of teachers who will never get a $4,000 board or twenty-five tablets (or the training to use them effectively, or someone to fix them when they break), a doc cam can be a great first step.

Online Research and Publications

It is an undeniable paradigm shift that kids and teachers can now get detailed, up-to-date information about virtually any topic in the world at the click of a mouse, right in the classroom. And also on the web, today's students can become not just researchers but content creators, sharing their thinking with audiences ranging from classmates and parents to other kids around the world. In this day and time, if a classroom does not have enough web-enabled devices for small groups, or better yet, for each student, to get online each day, this should be viewed as an educational emergency and promptly corrected.

At the same time, as with any educational technology, the web can be harnessed to low-level, factual-recall drills—or to higher-level creative inquiry. Best Practice teachers ensure that kids engage and create meaningful, challenging content.

> **CAUTION:** *Most school districts install blocking software to prevent students from navigating to inappropriate websites. Fine. But many of the programs sold to schools for this purpose are absurdly censorious. One program blocks access to all marine biology research institutes. Why? Because one such center, the Woods Hole Oceanographic Institute, has a bad word in it. Hole, get it? Teachers need to be empowered to override such meat-axe software easily and quickly, without having to file a weeks-ahead waiver request.*

Cell Phones

Some schools are still banning cell phones from classrooms. Savvier ones incorporate them into instruction. When they researched the Coney Island amusement park during the turn of the twentieth century, Sara Ahmed's eighth graders had a problem: they lived in Chicago. So through some web searching and teacher networking, the kids found several contemporary residents of the Coney Island area who happily shared their recollections in cell phone interviews.

If a classroom does not have enough web-enabled devices for small groups, or better yet, for each student, to get online each day, this should be viewed as an educational emergency and promptly corrected.

Down the hall in Katie Muhtaris's fifth-grade classroom, kids were studying insects and needed some expert input. So they went right to Skype, the free online video conferencing tool, and the whole class watched as a small group interviewed a Louisiana entomologist about caterpillar populations.

Digital Assessment

Kristin Ziemke uses podcasts to assess her first graders' reading comprehension. With an iPad, students use a drawing app like Whiteboard to create an image that reflects their thinking. Then they open the image in a podcasting app like SonicPics, where they dictate their thinking, creating an auditory and visual representation. These short podcasts can show a range of comprehension strategies—making a mental image, listing questions about a text, or giving a summary of what they read. Kids then email these to the teacher so she can watch them at home or share with parents. Using a series of these digital samples, Kristin can assess student learning over time.

> **CAUTION:** *Computerized gradebooks are popular, and are even mandated in some districts. But most are designed with quizzes, tests, and point accumulations as the default forms of student assessment. They make it almost impossible for teachers to enter open-ended data from one-to-one conferences, classroom observations, or extended inquiry projects. Thus, if used uncritically, these seemingly benign programs can drive low-level instruction.*

Teaching with Images

There is virtually no school lesson that cannot be enhanced by projecting relevant images gathered from the web. In his high school driver's education class, Roger Walters launches "defensive driving" by projecting a series of photographs that hint at different causes of accidents (cell phone use, overcrowded cars, traffic, sleeping, drinking). As kids view the pictures, they talk out loud in pairs to identify each risk portrayed and later read articles about each risk.

Flipping the Classroom

Here is a radical use of technology being developed around the country, especially by secondary science and math teachers. Instead of lecturing for most of the class period, these teachers create ten-minute online lecturettes that hit key textbook points. Students view these presentations as homework, on YouTube or the school website. Then, when kids come to class, teachers devote 90 percent of the time interacting with learners through experiential learning, application, discussion, conferring, and clarifying ideas. Now *that* is high-tech! For more, see Paul Andersen's materials from Bozeman, Montana, schools (www.bozemanscience.com/science-videos/) or Google "flipping the classroom" and enjoy.

Digital Differentation

In Katie Muhtaris's fifth-grade classroom, digital recordings help differentiate instruction for individual kids. "We talk so much about giving kids access to nonfiction by highlighting visual features like images, tables, maps, et cetera," says Katie. "But nowadays it is so easy to take an iPod, cell phone, or classroom computer and create a quick recording of any text you are using. When I have students read a short article on the Great Wall of China, I know a few kids will struggle, even with all the visual supports. So quickly before school I read and record the text and then load it into iTunes. When we work on the article in class, I can casually say, 'Oh, Reggie, if you want to listen to that article, I've got it over here on this computer.' The student can sit side by side with the article and this little piece of technology and elevate his comprehension. A quick way to provide access for the kids that need it! Often, other kids who don't really need help decoding the text still want to listen to the audio recording anyway, just because it is FUN."

Chapter 4

Best Practice *in*

Writing

Jessica Lopez-Rosario's second graders at McAuliffe School, in a predominantly Mexican-American Chicago neighborhood, enter Room 107 to find on the chalkboard a gentle not-quite assignment about connecting their writing with their science unit:

> Hey! Maybe some students would like to do a sea animal poem. You could write a poem about the animal you are researching! How many of you think you can give it a try today during morning work?
>
> *—Your teacher, Mrs. L-R*

Not surprisingly, most of the kids eagerly get to work on this, while Jessica moves around the room, conferring with individual students. She recently taught a brief mini-lesson on line breaks in poems and now helps kids with this step as needed. She encourages the first student to read her poem aloud to see how it sounds, to locate possible line breaks. Then the girl draws lines between words in a second poem to choose her line breaks. "Yes, you've got it!" Jessica declares as she stands up to move on to another child.

The next kid is stuck, with nothing written, which calls for a different intervention: "OK, just tell me about it. Where were you? Playing tag in the park? . . . OK, write it down just like you told me. First get your ideas on paper. After that you can arrange them into a poem."

After about fifteen minutes of writing and conferring the kids move to the rug, where Jessica conducts a mini-lesson on a writing skill. She proceeds to explain:

> Good morning writers! [Good morrrrning Mrs. Lopez-Rosario!] Yesterday
> we talked about showing instead of just telling. Rather than just saying,
> "She was very sad," you can describe your character looking down at her
> feet with her mouth turned way down at the corners. But I noticed that
> some people are still trying to figure out how to use this in their writing. So
> to help you, we'll read a story that shows us how to do this.

Jessica and special education teacher Amy Hegener take turns reading from the book *The Way I Feel*, by Janan Cain. While this is a book about feelings (obviously), the teacher uses this "mentor text" to help students recognize the effectiveness of active descriptions of each feeling instead of just naming them. After each feeling is described, the kids "turn and talk" with a neighbor to discuss the answer before the feeling is stated.

The conclusion of the mini-lesson then aims to help make sure the kids begin to incorporate the strategy in their writing. Jessica instructs: "If you're not sure that you are showing-not-telling, you can read your poem to someone else. Remember, *you're all writing teachers in this class!*"

The kids head off to their seats for more writing, and Jessica moves out into the room once more to help individuals who need it.

There are plenty of writing-oriented materials around the room from brainstorming and mini-lessons during the year:

- a chart listing "mood" words
- a list of basic punctuation marks
- a chart describing revision strategies—reread, check for capitals and punctuation, underline the first word of each sentence, and change any words that are frequently repeated
- a sample poem on a chart, with labels for various features like line breaks and rhymes
- a word wall with words from the science unit
- a collection of students' writing, titled "Authors' Celebration," displaying essays about family—personal, but explanatory in nature

There's plenty of writing going on all year long in Room 107—and in fact in every classroom throughout the school, because the teachers have decided it's high priority. After several weeks orienting students to writing workshop procedures, the second-grade teachers lead eight writing units on various types of writing during the rest of the year, with at least two published pieces for each unit. Workshop runs forty minutes per day, five days a week, including oral sharing several times each week and an authors' celebration at the end of each unit.

Jessica started implementing writers workshop just two years ago. In the winter of that year, the school organized an Instructional Leadership Team, with coaching help from a Chicago school network group called the Partnership for Instructional Leadership and training by Jeff Nelsen of Targeted Leadership Consulting. The team decided, after input from all the teachers, to focus on building writers workshop into everyone's teaching, using a carefully planned step-by-step approach so as not to overwhelm people. Jessica explains that this year's start-up went much more smoothly than last because her second graders had already experienced workshop. She reflects on her own professional learning:

> What *was* I doing before I implemented writers workshop? . . . My writing instruction was something like that, but not nearly as interactive, and not as much sharing took place. Kids didn't do as many different types of writing, and they weren't writing as much as they could or as well as they could. It was more one-size-fits-all. However, I was fitting in more writing in the content areas, and now I'm looking to reconnect with that.

On the day we've described, that certainly was happening as science met poetry.

A Look at the Writing Standards

Over the past thirty-five years, research on writing has blossomed to create a clear picture of the kind of effective writing strategies found in Jessica Lopez-Rosario's classroom. And as you'll see below, Jessica makes use of almost every one of the principles outlined in this chapter. George Hillocks summarized the early work on these strategies in *Research on Written Composition* (1986). Later, these ideas were affirmed in *Standards for the English Language Arts,* by the IRA and the NCTE (1996), the twelve main principles of which appear in Chapter 3. For writing, the principles emphasize real audiences, students' own authentic purposes for writing, and the need for students to learn a wide range of writing strategies. These practices are elaborated in the NCTE's *Standards in Practice,* which describe primary, intermediate, middle school, and high school classrooms where writing was integrated into literacy education (Crafton 1996; Sierra-Perry 1996; Smagorinsky 1996; Wilhelm 1996). The principles have since been applied and elaborated by Nancie Atwell (2007), Lucy Calkins (2003, 2006), JoAnn Portalupi and Ralph Fletcher (2004), Regie Routman (2005), Tony Stead and Linda Hoyt (2011), Ruth Culham (2003) and many others.

The Common Core State Standards (CCSS) represent a somewhat different approach (CCSS Initiative 2010). From the start we should understand that these new standards were written as "outcomes," knowledge and skills that students are to demonstrate at each grade level. They are not intended to provide guidance on instruction or the processes by which students learn or produce such outcomes. Previous standards, such as those created by NCTE and IRA, were more explicit about the purposes for each item, along with ways for teachers to promote them and for students to learn and apply them. Educators might well be thankful that their professional work is not more tightly dictated, and in its introduction, the CCSS document claims this as a virtue. Good teachers will still be able to inspire and excite their students to strive for excellence and engage them in meaningful writing and learning.

What's new in these writing standards? The introduction describes a successful student as an independent learner, "engaged and open-minded—but discerning"—certainly a meaningful goal. The standards then address three types of writing: argument, informative/explanatory texts, and narratives of real or imagined experiences—a reasonable range, though clearly much more focused on nonfiction writing than many classrooms have been in the past. This will call for kids to think more extensively about the evidence they provide to support their ideas, and the information they gather to explain complex topics. Characteristics for each type of writing grow in sophistication up the grades. Separate language standards cover conventions, "knowledge of language," and vocabulary.

Along with elements of the various types of writing (i.e., introduction, logically ordered reasons or facts, transitions, conclusions), the standards include some important larger essentials. For example, experts (Graves, Calkins, Atwell, Fletcher) have stressed for decades that good writers think hard about the purpose and audience for their writing. So the Common Core Standard 4 for writing states that development, organization, and style must be "appropriate to task, purpose, and audience." Standard 5, on some elements of the writing process, introduces the needs of an audience, though only starting in seventh grade. And Standard 10 calls for "a range of discipline-specific tasks, purposes, and audiences." The standards are readily available online, so we won't attempt to describe them in greater detail.

The limitations. Along with many other experienced educators and researchers, however, we find several major limitations to these standards, and they fall into three main categories:

1. Lack of connection between the specific writing skills and structures listed in the standards and the larger communicative purposes they are meant to serve—resulting in a rather mechanical and unengaging picture of writing that is surprisingly like the isolated set of skills that has too often dominated writing instruction in schools.

2. Lack of recognition of the importance of voice and engagement in writing. Much communication in the wider world (except for documents like computer manuals, for example) depends on catching and holding a reader's attention. References to style and "reader interest" mentioned under "Effective Language Use" in the penultimate draft of the standards were eliminated for K–8 in the final version. And most of the elements of the types of writing describe rather bland, dutiful, and very traditionally organized products.

3. Absence of research-based understandings about the steps and stages students move through as they learn to write—resulting in the introduction of some skills too early, others too late; some at too low a level and others exceedingly unrealistic.

The first concern is reflected not in any one particular standard, but in the document's structure. Standard 4, for example, focuses on "clear and coherent writing in which the development and organization are appropriate to task, purpose, and audience"—recognizing larger purposes. But the standards outlining the characteristics of good argument, informational, and narrative writing make no explicit connection to that larger perspective. The various elements can certainly support such purposes, but standing alone they appear as absolutes, to be taught because an authority says they're important, rather than embedded in real communication that can make them relevant. Nowhere is it ever stated that writing should be created for and sent to any real audiences, or that student choice about these things matters.

The second concern is reflected in the very limited set of elements provided for each type of writing. For informative pieces at every grade level, the topic is to be neatly introduced and the direction of the essay clearly previewed. No surprises are contemplated, and no starting in the midst of a lively scene, though these are preferred strategies throughout much of the literate world. Instead, the requirement very much resembles the old five-paragraph theme pattern ("First I'm going to tell you about . . .") that persists in some schools but nowhere else in the universe of good written communication.

Finally, it's just not clear what model of language development guides the timing for various skills. Explicit attention to the needs of an audience, as we noted, first appears at seventh grade. In our experience, far younger students are able to think about and work on this issue, and Portalupi and Fletcher's *Non-fiction Craft Lessons* (2001) introduces it at the earliest grades. Or, for another example, why are fifth graders expected to use commas to separate items in a series, while fourth graders don't need to learn this yet? Generally, good teachers introduce these skills as they arise in the writing kids do, so that they are practiced and learned through actual, repeated use. What's important to avoid is a collection of disconnected grammar lessons that do not relate to the kinds of communication that students are attempting. Otherwise students simply do not internalize the skills.

As a result, the Common Core writing standards include much repetition from grade to grade, and some items are even starred, to be retaught in later grades. Of course, such reteaching has taken place year after year in many classrooms, eating up time that could otherwise be spent moving students further toward excellence. The standards do include charts showing a progression of skills—and these could provide the cornerstone for schoolwide planning, if they were made more central to the document.

What teachers can do. In sum, the Standards provide only a partial picture of good writing instruction. They focus on products we can see and measure, what the designers hope students can ultimately *do*. The one virtue of this is that too often, professional texts and staff development workshops have said more about what *teachers* should do than what *kids* actually accomplish. What these standards don't address, and what teachers can productively focus on, is the work of actually leading students to learn and produce good writing, and to carry their skills forward for "college and career readiness"—which is the standards' stated goal. Unfortunately, the standards are written in a way that seems to encourage the old skill-and-drill approach to writing instruction. But they needn't be used that way. Instead, we can make sure we don't simply march students mechanically through the various skills. We can build engaging, real-world activities that involve kids with the audiences and purposes for which they are writing, and connect the skills enumerated in the standards to these. We can teach brainstorming and drafting and revising techniques through which those writing skills and structures are created and strengthened. We can observe and confer with individual students, determine their stage of learning, and introduce the next appropriate challenge and skill. And we can support student choice among topics and genres, gradually guiding kids to widen their writing experience, so that all types of writing—including but not limited to those listed in the standards—are explored without turning them into empty exercises.

We can build engaging, real-world activities that involve kids with the audiences and purposes for which they are writing, and connect the skills enumerated in the standards to these.

These are things that Jessica Lopez-Rosario is doing in her classroom. She uses the standards as one aspect of her teaching, rather than being limited by them, observing her students' work for their progress on various standards and planning her instruction accordingly. As a result, the kids become enthusiastic, successful writers who score well on the tests. And this is what teachers can do as outlined in the standards for great writing instruction in this chapter.

As the standards efforts continue, two consortia are developing new computer-based assessments that reflect the standards and are intended to be used nationwide. Along with the U.S. Department of Education, the Gates Foundation has been funding the development of such tools, student assignments, and tests "to make higher standards real in classrooms" (Bill and Melinda Gates Foundation 2009). However, test designers themselves have warned that serious technical issues were being encountered, work had slowed, and truly revolutionary assessments probably will not be operational until several years after the planned 2014 rollout (*Education Week* April 20, 2011). Meanwhile, we're told that the high-stakes tests will continue to look very much like ones in use today. We'll see how this all unfolds. For now, teachers and districts can use the Common Core Standards judiciously, as indicators of some, but not all, of the aspects of writing that good writers need to learn. And educators should consult the many powerful research studies and professional texts developed over the past several decades for the strategies that actually guide students to learn to write well.

Qualities of Best Practice in Teaching Writing

Two major recent reports assembled the evidence from many studies (the research method called *meta-analysis*) on the strategies that improve students' writing. Sponsored by the Carnegie Corporation, these reports—*Writing Next*, by Steve Graham and Dolores Perin (2007), and *Writing to Read*, by Graham and Michael Hebert (2010)—confirm what good teachers and education experts have long known. *Writing Next* pinpoints a number of powerful teaching approaches that make a difference, including:

- Instructing students on planning, revising, and editing compositions.
- Engaging students in prewriting activities.
- Conducting inquiry activities that lead to writing.
- Having students write collaboratively.
- Having students read models for writing.
- Using writing for learning content.

Just about every one of these could be seen in the second-grade classroom we visited at the start of this chapter. *Writing to Read* further confirms that writing increases students' reading comprehension in three ways:

- writing about subject-area texts they read
- learning writing skills and processes that go into creating a published text
- increasing the amount of writing students do

The following qualities of Best Practice elaborate and add to these important lists.

All children can and should write. A preschooler recites a story from her "pretend" writing and later repeats it nearly word for word, as her parents admire her "cute" behavior. Recognizing constancy of meaning in written symbols shows that this child is already practicing literacy. Most children write long before they reach kindergarten. They make meaningful marks on paper, starting with drawings and moving through imitation writing to more conventional messages.

Children of all backgrounds bring to school extensive involvement in literacy, though the cultural patterns of language use vary widely—not just in grammar or pronunciation, but also in purposes and occasions for talk. Just as Jessica Lopez-Rosario starts her day with one-on-one conferences to help individual kids, teachers must build on children's strengths and then help widen their repertoires. It is vital to listen to children and learn their particular language abilities and needs, rather than assume that the teachers' own language styles and customs are universal.

Children of all backgrounds bring to school extensive involvement in literacy.

Writing should not wait for reading or grammar to develop first; as recent research has confirmed, generating written language is one of children's prime paths to reading achievement. So kids need sufficient time to complete and reflect on communicative tasks.

Help students find real purposes to write and real audiences to reach.

> In Alicia Rosenberg's third-grade bilingual classroom at McAuliffe School, the kids are researching and creating animal books as a project for their science unit on desert food chains. Alicia observes that some teachers think students in bilingual classes can't do much writing, but she finds that if she breaks the work down into more discrete steps using her writer's workshop mini-lessons, they dive right into it. Now they are reading their drafts aloud to each other, and the children say that this project is one of their favorites. We notice, too, that one of the charts on the wall lists strategies for identifying topics to write about, the most prominent being "things that matter to us."

When the topic matters, children work hard and invest time and effort in crafting their work. The best language learning occurs when students attempt actual communication and see how real listeners/readers react. Meaningful writing tasks bridge the cognitive demands of school and the issues of students' cultures and personalities. Further, arbitrarily assigned topics with no opportunity for choice deprive students of practice in a most crucial step of writing—making the first decision about what to write.

Publication of writing is vital for fulfilling these purposes: making bound books, cataloging student works in the school library, and displaying products in classrooms, school hallways, local libraries, neighborhood stores, and local dentists' waiting rooms. When the teacher is the only audience, students are robbed of the rich and diverse audience responses that build a writer's skills and motivation.

Help students exercise choice, take ownership, and assume responsibility. It's simple. The more choices teachers make, the fewer the responsibilities left for students. For a significant percentage of writing activities, students should choose their own topics. They can learn to look critically at their work, decide which pieces are worth continued effort, and set their own goals.

> **Yes, but . . .** *many students don't have enough knowledge about what makes good writing. Without this, how can they make good choices of their own?*

When students take ownership of their writing, there's actually much more teaching than before, but it's more focused on higher-level thinking, and on specific needs as these arise in their writing. Teaching techniques to promote real authorship and decision making include:

- modeling topic selection and self-evaluation processes using anonymous samples or the teacher's own writing

- brief one-to-one conferences in which the teacher asks questions that help both student and teacher understand what the student is trying to say, and then briefly teaching one skill most relevant to the writing—rather than the teacher taking over as an editor

- small-group collaborative work and peer responses, with students working together constructively, asking each other thoughtful questions about what the writer is trying to say—rather than acting as editors

Provide opportunities for students to experience the complete writing process. Many children never see skillful writers at work and are unaware that writing is a staged, craftlike process that competent authors typically break into manageable steps such as the following:

- selecting or becoming involved in a topic, finding a purpose for writing, and clarifying the audience

- prewriting—considering an approach, gathering thoughts or information, mapping plans, free-writing ideas

- drafting—organizing material and getting words down
- revising—further developing ideas and clarifying their expression
- editing—polishing meaning and proofreading for publication

Teachers can help children recognize that the process varies between individuals and between writing tasks. However, just as with other crafts, not all pieces are worth carrying through all stages, and children can learn by focusing on just one or two stages for a given piece. If they revise and edit just their best pieces, their work will more likely reflect real effort.

Help students get started. Support begins from the very start. Children can be helped to develop abundant ideas about self-chosen or teacher-assigned topics. Lists of topics and questions in students' folders or on wall charts help kids get started on their own. Skillful teachers conduct many kinds of prewriting activities:

- memory searches
- listing, charting, webbing, and clustering of raw ideas
- drawing and sketching
- group brainstorming
- free-writing (a specific process for probing thoughts)
- discussion in pairs, small groups, and the whole class
- reading and research on questions students generate

Guide students as they draft and revise. Jessica Lopez-Rosario taught her students about line breaks in poetry, helped them with that step in conferences, and then explored a further skill—"showing, not just telling"—through a read-aloud. For these second graders, revising writing is a regular activity. They've learned to ask each other lots of questions about the stage the writing is at and the help the writer seeks *before* discussing any possible revisions in a piece.

Successive stages in the writing process often are ignored in traditional approaches. But good writing usually is not created in one quick shot, so children need instruction in how to revise. Using role-plays, modeling, and group problem solving, teachers can introduce key revision processes:

- reviewing one's work and comparing what one has said to one's intended meaning
- seeing the words from the point of view of a reader, who may not know all that the writer knows about the topic
- studying examples from other writers to become aware of styles and strategies
- generating multiple options for expressing an idea and choosing what works best

Revision is about thinking and communication, not just fixing details. Simply telling how to fix an essay may achieve a better piece of writing, but doesn't teach the child how to revise.

Show students how writing is created. In conventional classrooms, teachers give writing assignments and prompts, which students are then required to fulfill. But we should make sure not to leave out a huge and important step here. Teachers need to *show* kids how to write using "write alouds." Whatever the grade level or subject area, teachers must regularly stand in front of the class and compose new text in front of their students, projecting their words and vocalizing their thinking process as they compose. "Hmmmn, now let me see, what's the best way to get my reader engaged from the beginning?" "Oops, I'm not sure I've got the just-right word here." "This section is getting kind of long, I better wrap it up." This vital "write-aloud" modeling process is just as key to writing instruction as think-alouds are to reading. For further expert modeling, teachers can help students find and study "mentor texts," fiction or nonfiction works by published authors that offer writing structures, patterns, or styles that young writers can emulate.

Lead students to learn the craft of writing. While children absorb a great deal about language through listening, talking, and reading, most also need to consciously focus on particular strategies for expressing ideas, ranging from generating ways to begin and end to options for organizing a piece, to identifying vivid details that bring ideas to life, to composing sentences clearly and with standard English conventions.

The craft of writing can be taught through brief mini-lessons focused on skills appropriate to particular writing tasks students are tackling, so the skills are practiced immediately in meaningful settings. The most effective mini-lessons will follow the Gradual Release of Responsibility model described in Chapter 2. As we observed there, this is one of the key structures effective teachers use to introduce new skills and strategies to their students. The key steps:

- Demonstration of a skill or strategy, using a write-aloud as described above, with the teacher's composition projected on a screen as she talks her thinking about it out loud, demonstrating a particular task or struggle the students have been engaged in.

- Shared writing in which the teacher still holds the pen, but invites students to help her compose text.

- Guided practice, in which students use the modeled writing strategy individually, but with teacher support. This may take place as part of the mini-lesson or in small groups or conferences as students turn to their own tasks.

- Independent practice—when kids take responsibility for developing their own pieces of writing from scratch. As preparation for this step, Lucy Calkins (2006) advises that the teacher emphasizes the link between the strategy demonstrated and the work the students will do next.

Confer with individual students on their writing. Just as important as whole-class mini-lessons are one-on-one conferences (see Chapter 2). Even when these are very brief, the individual attention makes a big impression on student learners. Moreover, they provide the best opportunity for teachers to differentiate instruction according to students' specific needs. Each student needs a folder to keep her writing, a list of goals, and a separate list of "can do" skills that she has mastered to guide both teacher and student in conferences and ensuing student work. This, of course, is a key strategy for addressing Response to Intervention (RTI) assessments of students' individual achievement levels and learning needs.

Teach grammar and mechanics in the context of actual writing. Grammar work is most appropriate in the later stages of the writing process and when it is connected with writing in which students are invested. When work that writers care about is going public, they want it to look good and to succeed. In contrast, research has shown for decades (see George Hillocks' classic *Research on Written Composition,* 1986) that isolated skill-and-drill grammar lessons do not transfer to writing performance. Beginning writers in primary grades can use invented spelling, so they'll develop fluency and not waste half the period waiting for the teacher to provide the correct spelling of a word.

Yes, but . . . *if kids' errors aren't all corrected promptly, won't they develop into bad writing habits?*

First of all, most teachers agree that traditional grammar instruction and heavy correction just doesn't work. It's very time consuming for teachers, reducing the amount of writing that can be assigned, and very discouraging for students, especially for struggling writers. It's much easier for a student to see patterns in her writing when she is asked to concentrate on just one element at a time. Focused lessons—either whole class or one-on-one—can be conducted during editing, when correctness is more relevant to the effort (if, that is, the writing has a real communicative purpose and destination) and doesn't interfere with motivation or the development of ideas. Specific grammar and mechanics lessons can then cover items appropriate to the task or to observed student needs. The aim is to develop writers, rather than just to achieve perfect products. The teacher should help kids acquire skills, and not act as an editor herself.

Approached this way, grammar needs far less reteaching than we think. For one thing, while mini-lessons applying grammar and usage to actual writing can be effective, teaching of formal grammar terms and parts of speech doesn't really translate into outcomes in children's work. Further, when children get lots of practice reading, writing, and polishing final drafts for a real audience, spelling gradually moves toward conventional forms, even without direct lessons. At the same time, teachers can promote student responsibility by having students keep lists in their writing folders of grammar and mechanics elements they've mastered, and then require that kids consult these as they proofread rather than wait for a teacher's markup after the fact. This way, the lessons and learning become cumulative.

Provide a classroom context of shared learning.

A teacher and three middle school writers listen to a fourth read her piece about children's challenges recuperating from injuries like a broken back. The author requests help with the ending and everyone makes weak suggestions. Finally, asked for more information about the experience described in the article, she declares, "The girl was never so happy as the day she went back to school—so I think it must take experiences like this to make kids appreciate what they have." The group cheers that she's found her conclusion— not through directives, but through supportive talk and listening.

Building a supportive context for working collaboratively is perhaps the most important step a teacher can take to promote writing growth (Nancy Steineke's *Reading and Writing Together: Collaborative Literacy in Action*, 2002, provides excellent strategies for this). In fact, if students don't find their classroom a safe place to try new approaches and to say what they believe, even the most up-to-date techniques can fall flat. On the other hand, when students hear one another's work in a positive setting, they're eager to try new topics and learn new strategies. Listening to each other's compositions, students discover what makes writing strong.

Teachers build this interactive learning context through lessons about listening and respecting other people's ideas, and through guided practice on working responsibly in small groups. The teacher must model respect and supportive questioning in her own conferences with students as well. Then young people readily learn to help each other critique themselves and figure out their own improvements. This approach yields much more learning than does direct advice about how to "fix" a piece, because the writer experiences the actual problem solving.

Support growth in writing for English language learners.

On a crisp fall morning in his Wisconsin elementary school, teacher Jeff Nielson tries something new. For the first time, he offers his third-grade students a chance to discuss a classroom topic by writing notes to a partner, rather than having to speak out loud. At lunchtime, Jeff is in the faculty lounge testifying: "I got more thinking and language out of my ELL kids in 20 minutes of writing that I have heard from them in last 20 days of school!"

Not only is it essential for students who are learning English to gain writing skills; they can also benefit greatly by using writing itself as a tool that helps them master the English language. Often with the assistance of fellow students and parents, new language learners can write their ideas and stories in both their first language and English, thereby building vocabulary by seeing the two versions side by side. Teachers like Alicia Rosenberg at McAuliffe School provide more structure on some aspects of kids' writing because they know that as the students write, they are putting a great deal of energy into using the new language skills they are acquiring, and cannot readily focus on all aspects of their writing at once. But these teachers still maintain core elements such as student choice, revising, and real audiences for writing. Bilingual and dual language experts tell us the strategies that work for our native English speakers are good for ELLs as well.

Use writing to support learning throughout the curriculum. Students value writing and use it more when it supports many learning activities. Writing is, in fact, one of the best tools for learning any material because it activates thinking. Brief, ungraded writing activities can activate prior knowledge, elicit questions, build comprehension, promote discussion, and help students reflect on ideas covered.

Writing in various subjects need not absorb large amounts of time or create an impossible paper load. Brief exploratory efforts that make learning more engaging and efficient include these techniques:

- First thoughts: Two- to three-minute free-writes at the start of a unit to surface students' knowledge about the subject.

- KWL charts: What students **k**now about a topic, what they **w**ant to know (questions or wonderings), and later, what they've **l**earned.

- Admit slips and exit slips: A few sentences on an index card handed in at the *start* of class, summarizing the previous day's work or reading; or a statement of something learned (or not understood) submitted at the *end* of class.

- Stop-N-Write: Brief pauses during teacher presentations or reading periods when students jot questions, responses to ideas, or predictions about what is coming next.

Teachers can read student responses to these activities quickly to learn whether concepts are understood. Students receive a "check" for credit or, better yet, an informal written response from the teacher. (For more on several of these writing-to-learn activities, see Chapter 2.)

Use evaluation constructively and efficiently. Masses of red marks on a page discourage children and don't teach revising or proofreading. Research indicates that writers grow more by praise and thoughtful questions about the topic than by criticism. (Again, George Hillocks' review of research made this clear many years ago.) Better strategies for evaluation include:

- focusing on one or two kinds of errors at a time
- brief conferences at various stages of the work
- portfolios or folder systems for evaluating writing improvement over time
- student involvement in goal setting, evaluation, and written reflection
- official grading only of selected, fully revised pieces
- along with more selective marking, a sheet in each child's folder listing skills and processes the child has learned, plus brief notes on broader aspects of growth

Such cumulative records enable individualization, help children reflect on their progress, focus on actual learning rather than just the written product, and yet maintain clear accountability for both students and teachers. Growth in writing means trying something new and probably making mistakes in the process. Students must feel trust in order to take that risk, and evaluation practices should support this necessary condition for learning.

Many schools and teachers use the "6+1 Traits of Writing" framework for evaluating writing. The 6+1 comprise ideas, organization, voice, word choice, sentence fluency, conventions, and presentation (Culham 2003). This can certainly help teachers identify and teach students the various aspects and qualities that make writing effective. It's important, of course, to teach and help students apply the various skills one at a time, to introduce each one when it relates most meaningfully to the specific writing task at hand, and to always take account of the strengths and needs of individual students. And then, once we have helped kids to practice a skill in isolation, we send them right back into what David Perkins calls the "whole-game," putting *all* their skills to use in creating complete pieces of writing, at their developmental level (Perkins 2010).

Yes, but ... *how can I possibly grade all these papers with kids writing so much?*

Students need to write a lot, so much that teachers couldn't possibly mark every error in every paper. However, we teachers don't need to monitor so heavily—just as a music teacher doesn't need to be present at her student's every practice session, but rather listens and comments in once-a-week lessons. And research strongly shows that traditional intensive marking of papers doesn't promote improvement in writing. It may be traditional, and it may be what parents expect, but

Research indicates that writers grow more by praise and thoughtful questions about the topic than by criticism.

is simply ineffective and a waste of teachers' precious time and energy. Instead, a brief conference, or marking a sample paragraph for just one type of problem, results in more real learning. The child then takes responsibility for making the improvements in the rest of the paper. Students can periodically submit their best revised pieces for in-depth evaluation. Thus, different types of evaluation—brief/informal versus extensive/formal—are employed to suit particular purposes. Good teachers aim for learning *within the child*, not just achieving a correct manuscript.

Writing in an Interdisciplinary High School Class

NEIL RIGLER AND KEN KRAMER

Deerfield High School, Deerfield, Illinois

"This is a journey of discovery for us as well as for you," Neil Rigler explains to the American studies class he teaches with social studies teacher Ken Kramer. The kids scatter around on the floor, spreading their index cards out in rows and swirls and little clusters. Each student is working with forty to fifty cards, half holding favorite one-sentence quotations they've individually chosen from books they've read over the semester, and half bearing quotations from their own personal journal entries on these books as well as on lessons and activities during that time. This is one part of their final project/exam for the year. Neil gives them their task:

> Group your cards into five or six categories, however they make sense to you, and then label the categories. The only groupings you CANNOT go by are the units that we've studied. You can have about twenty minutes for this. When you are finished, write a few sentences of your thoughts for each category.

The kids begin thinking hard about this task. The journal entries, and indeed the work over the year, have linked history, literature, and their own personal connections with the themes introduced by the readings, lectures, videos, and discussions. Now these are all coming together in their thoughts. One student's categories:

- good policy for internal American politics
- good policy for foreign countries
- the government's perspectives on war
- the soldiers' perspectives on war
- right policy as a goal

Another student's groupings:

- burdens
- ideas/questioning society

- consequences of time
- wants/hopes/dreams

Neil and Ken move around the room, looking over kids' shoulders and holding brief conferences with those who may be struggling. One girl moans, "I can't figure this out! Every time I put a card in one pile, I see how it also fits in another one." Coauthor Steve Zemelman, who was observing, comments, "Maybe you're thinking too hard about this," and she answers, "That's what I do with everything in my life!" Neil reassures her that however she completes it will be fine. The important thing is to be thinking about the connections and the big ideas. The student gets back to work.

When the kids are finished with this stage, Neil explains the next step. "OK, now label the cards with their category name so you can put them back in their groups later. Then shuffle them all together." As they shuffle their decks, he continues:

> Now you should rearrange your cards in a sequence, a kind of story line or a way to show how each idea leads to a next one. The only sequence you CANNOT use is chronology. When you're finished, write a journal entry about what your sequence means to you.

The kids are back on the floor, and again the cards begin to form lines and patterns. Neil notes that the shapes reveal kids' individual characteristics. Sure enough, a more compulsively organized student forms up in neat rows. A more divergent thinker's arrangement looks like a big question mark. One student explains how his sequence leads from American values to violence to slavery to World War II (when African Americans in the military began to experience more freedoms), to Vietnam, to questions of morality. Another arranges his cards to show the flow between individualism and more social and governmental obligations. When students read their reflections, everyone can see the variety of ways to think about what they've studied, and to appreciate the connections between the material and their own lives and struggles.

The students can't get enough of this class. It's more work than most of their other courses, they say. But they testify that they appreciate the lively experiences, the open-ended assignments, and the valuing of their own ideas, instead of just having to psych out "what the teacher wants to hear." "They helped me learn about critical thinking," one student explains. How did they do this? "By showing us how to connect the texts to our own ideas, and always pushing us to go one step further to make more connections." This instructional style works especially well for struggling students, because they experience more ways to learn the material and find it easier to request help from one or the other of their instructors. Yes, the class is team-taught, but it's larger than a standard class and both teachers are present for its double period, so their loads are about the same as everyone else's.

Neil learned the card strategy in his work with the Bard Institute for Writing and Thinking, though he and Ken adapted it to encompass the whole semester's work instead of focusing on just one book or issue. Much of the writing these teachers assign all year reflects a similar effort to make learning highly interactive, and to combine disciplined analysis with personal connections that bring the subject to life for adolescents. The teachers continually ask, "How does literature help you understand the history, and how does history help you understand the literature?" Instead of giving lectures or instructions about making connections, they use activities that simply enact the process. "Exploded imagery" is typical. The teachers first read a short passage aloud—the preamble to the U.S. Constitution, for example—and ask everyone to write an initial reaction. Then each student chooses a phrase from the passage as the start of a new piece of writing on the topic. Next, students write their own thoughts on it: Why did you choose this phrase? What are your personal connections with it? What does it say to you now? Finally, one of the teachers reads the passage again slowly. As students hear their phrases read, they stop the teacher and read what they've written. Voices pop up around the room, elaborating on each idea. For a final writing step, students compare their new, deeper understanding with their initial reactions. No wonder they told us they'd learned to analyze material more deeply.

About once per quarter, students write longer, more formal papers. Sometimes these are more creative. A research project, for example, is done as a blog, with entries on the various historical and literary materials they locate on their topic. They then pull these together into an online presentation that can include video clips and other multimedia materials, all linked in a package to the blog. Instead of boring periods in which students sit passively not listening to other people's presentations, everyone goes into the computer lab, browses through each other's online final products, and adds comments on the blog. The blogs are open to the public, so parents and friends can see and comment on them. The teachers especially value that the students are forced to think about this wider audience when they write. So now they have planned for students to maintain individual blogs all year, along with a class blog for which a different student provides an entry each day.

It's important to know that Neil and Ken are not lone wolves doing this kind of teaching. While there are no formal committees or grade-level team meetings at Deerfield High School, teachers share ideas regularly. In each department's teacher workspace, people hang out at their desks and talk about what they are doing, new resources they've found, new strategies they are trying. "Chaotic," Neil proudly describes it. Ken explains that history teachers' files of classroom ideas are open to all. While the teachers still see themselves individualistically, the sharing leads to much consistency across a department. Teachers credit each other when introducing something new in the classroom, so students recognize both the diversity and unity of the pedagogy that they experience in their school. This openness has been promoted by department chairs for many years, making it a permanent part of the professional culture of the school. While some schools need more of a structure to help teachers work together and build schoolwide impact, a professional culture like this is another way to expand Best Practice teaching and learning from isolated classrooms to a whole learning community.

Works Cited

Atwell, Nancie. 2007. *Lessons That Change Writers*. Portsmouth, NH: Heinemann.

Bill and Melinda Gates Foundation. 2009. *College Ready Education Plan*.

Calkins, Lucy McCormick. 2003. *Units of Study for Primary Writing*. Portsmouth, NH: Heinemann.

————. 2006. *Units of Study for Teaching Writing, Grades 3–5*. Portsmouth, NH: Heinemann.

Common Core State Standards Initiative. 2010. *Common Core State Standards, English Language Arts*. National Governors Association and Council of Chief State School Officers.

Crafton, Linda. 1996. *Standards in Practice: Grades K–2*. Urbana, IL: National Council of Teachers of English.

Culham, Ruth. 2003. *6 + 1 Traits of Writing: The Complete Guide, Grades 3 and Up*. New York: Scholastic.

Graham, Steve, and Michael Hebert. 2010. *Writing to Read: Evidence for How Writing Can Improve Reading*. New York: Carnegie Corporation.

Graham, Steve, and Dolores Perin. 2007. *Writing Next: Effective Strategies to Improve Writing of Adolescents in Middle and High Schools*. New York: Carnegie Corporation.

Hillocks, George. 1986. *Research on Written Composition: New Directions for Teaching.* Urbana, IL: National Council of Teachers of English.

International Reading Association and National Council of Teachers of English. 1996. *Standards for the English Language Arts.* Newark, DE, and Urbana, IL: International Reading Association and National Council of Teachers of English.

Perkins, David. 2010. *Making Learning Whole.* San Francisco, CA: Jossey Bass.

Portalupi, JoAnn, and Ralph Fletcher. 2001. *Nonfiction Craft Lessons.* Portland, ME: Stenhouse.

———. 2004. *Teaching the Qualities of Writing.* Portsmouth, NH: Heinemann.

Routman, Regie. 2005. *Writing Essentials: Raising Expectations and Results While Simplifying Teaching.* Portsmouth, NH: Heinemann.

Sierra-Perry, Martha. 1996. *Standards in Practice: Grades 3–5.* Urbana, IL: National Council of Teachers of English.

Smagorinsky, Peter. 1996. *Standards in Practice: Grades 9–12.* Urbana, IL: National Council of Teachers of English.

Sparks, Sarah. 2011. Experts See Hurdles Ahead for Common Core Tests. *Education Week* (April 11).

Stead, Tony and Linda Hoyt. 2011. *Explorations in Nonfiction Writing.* Portsmouth, NH: Heinemann.

Steineke, Nancy. 2002. *Reading and Writing Together: Collaborative Literacy in Action.* Portsmouth, NH: Heinemann.

Wilhelm, Jeffrey D. 1996. *Standards in Practice: Grades 6–8.* Urbana, IL: National Council of Teachers of English.

Suggested Further Readings

Anderson, Carl. 2008. *Strategic Writing Conferences: Smart Conversations That Move Young Writers Forward* (set of four books). Portsmouth, NH: Heinemann.

Anderson, Jeff. 2007. *Everyday Editing.* Portland, ME. Stenhouse.

Angelillo, Janet. 2005. *Writing to the Prompt: When Students Don't Have a Choice.* Portsmouth, NH: Heinemann.

Blachowicz, Camille, and Peter Fisher. 2009. *Teaching Vocabulary in All Classrooms* (4th edition). New York: Allyn and Bacon.

Daniels, Harvey, Steven Zemelman, and Nancy Steineke. 2007. *Content-Area Writing: Every Teacher's Guide.* Portsmouth, NH: Heinemann.

Dudley-Marling, Curt, and Patricia Paugh. 2009. *A Classroom Teacher's Guide to Struggling Writers.* Portsmouth, NH: Heinemann.

Fletcher, Ralph, and JoAnn Portalupi. 2001. *Writing Workshop: The Essential Guide.* Portsmouth, NH: Heinemann.

———. 2007. *Craft Lessons: Teaching Writing K–8* (2nd edition). Portland, ME: Stenhouse.

Fu, Danling. 2009. *Writing Between Languages: How English Language Learners Make the Transition to Fluency, Grades 4–12.* Portsmouth, NH: Heinemann.

Graham, Steven, and Karen Harris. 2005. *Writing Better: Effective Strategies for Teaching Students with Learning Disabilities.* Baltimore, MD: Brookes Publishing.

Graves, Donald. 1994. A *Fresh Look at Writing.* Portsmouth, NH: Heinemann.

Hicks, Troy. 2009. *The Digital Writing Workshop.* Portsmouth, NH: Heinemann.

Hill, Bonnie Campbell, Cynthia Ruptic, and Lisa Norwick. 1998. *Classroom-Based Assessment.* Available directly from www.bonniecampbellhill.com.

Macrorie, Ken. 1988. *The I-Search Paper.* Portsmouth, NH: Heinemann.

Vopat, Jim. 2009. *Writing Circles: Kids Revolutionize Workshop.* Portsmouth, NH: Heinemann.

Wilde, Sandra. 2007. *Spelling Strategies and Patterns.* Portsmouth, NH: Heinemann.

Writing Resources on the Internet

Ayres, Ruth, and Stacey Shubitz. Two Writing Teachers: Teaching Kids, Catching Minds, 565 Miles Apart.
http://twowritingteachers.wordpress.com

Bard College Institute for Writing and Thinking.
http://bard.edu/iwt/

Beach, Richard, Chris Anson, Lee-Ann Breuch, and Thom Swiss. Teaching Writing Using Blogs, Wikis, and Other Digital Tools.
http://digitalwriting.pbworks.com

Burke, Jim. English Companion Ning: Where English Teachers Go to Help Each Other.
http://englishcompanion.ning.com

George, Kristine O'Connell. Children's Poetry Corner. Promotes her poetry books, but also a good resource for teaching poetry.
www.kristinegeorge.com

Gregory, Mandy. Tips for Teachers. One teacher's ongoing effort to use writer's workshop and share the ideas she finds, borrows, or develops.
www.mandygregory.com

Hicks, Troy. Digital Writing, Digital Teaching: Integrating New Literacies into the Teaching of Writing.
http://hickstro.org

Inkspot Magazine, Lemont High School. Example of an online high school literary magazine.
www.lshinkspot.com

International Reading Association and the National Council of Teachers of English. ReadWriteThink. Extensive lessons on teaching writing.
www.readwritethink.org

Lesson Planet. Paid subscription site. Some lessons on writing are of good quality.
www.lessonplanet.com

National Board for Professional Teaching Standards.
www.nbpts.org

National Council of Teachers of English.
www.ncte.org

National Writing Project.
www.writingproject.org.

Northern Nevada Writing Project. WritingFix. Extensive lessons on teaching writing.
www.writingfix.com

Peha, Steve. Teaching That Makes Sense. Useful downloads on various aspects of
    teaching writing.
http://ttms.org

Teachers and Writers Collaborative. Subscription and membership site, but selected
    articles from their magazine available free.
www.twc.org

Teen Ink. Online and print magazine of high school writers.
www.teenink.com

21x20 Inc. Writing.com. For writers of all ages and interests; includes a "League of
    Young Writers" and a variety of writing activities, contests, blogs, etc.
www.writing.com

Recommendations on Teaching Writing

▲ INCREASE	▼ DECREASE
Student ownership and responsibility by: • helping students learn to choose their own topics and goals for improvement • holding brief teacher-student conferences • teaching students to reflect on their own progress	Teacher control of decision making by: • deciding all writing topics • suggesting improvements without student problem-solving effort first • setting learning objectives without student input • providing instruction only through whole-class activity
Class time on writing whole, original pieces through: • real purposes and audiences for writing • instruction and support for all stages of writing • prewriting, drafting, revising, editing	Time spent on isolated drills on "subskills" of grammar, vocabulary, spelling, etc. Writing assignments given briefly, with no context or purpose, completed in one step
Writing for real audiences, publishing for the class and wider communities	Finished pieces read only by the teacher
Teacher modeling of writing—"writing aloud" as a fellow author to demonstrate • drafting, revising, sharing • writing skills and processes	Teacher talks about writing but never writes or shares own work
Learning grammar and mechanics in context, at the editing stage, and as items are needed	Isolated grammar lessons, given in order determined by the textbook, before writing is begun
Making the classroom a supportive setting, using: • active exchange and valuing of students' ideas • collaborative small-group work • conferences and peer critiquing that give responsibility to authors	Devaluation of students' ideas: • students viewed as lacking knowledge and language abilities • sense of class as competing individuals • cooperation among students viewed as cheating, disruptive
Writing across the curriculum as a tool for learning	Writing taught only during "language arts" period
Constructive and efficient evaluation that involves: • brief informal oral responses as students work • focus on a few errors at a time • thorough grading of just a few of student-selected, polished pieces • cumulative view of growth and self-evaluation • encouragement of risk taking and honest expression	Evaluation as a negative burden for teacher and student by: • marking all papers heavily for all errors, making teacher a bottleneck • editing by teacher, and only after a paper is completed, rather than having the student make improvements • grading punitively, focused on errors, not growth

Best Practices—English Language Learners

Our classrooms are changing. Within fifteen years, one in four K–12 students will speak a language other than English, or will speak English with significant instructional implications. Although English language learners (ELLs) come from over four hundred different language backgrounds, 76 percent are born in the United States. However, 80 percent of their parents were born outside of the United States.

Spanish speakers represent 80 percent of ELLs. Spanish speakers in the United States tend to come from lower economic and educational backgrounds than other language-minority populations. The second-largest ELL group (8 percent) consists of speakers of Asian languages (e.g., Chinese, Korean, Vietnamese, Laotian). These families tend to come from higher income and education levels.

It is important to understand the difference between social and academic language. Jim Cummins refers to the language skills needed in social situations (conversations outside school or asking for help in the classroom) as Basic Interpersonal Communication Skills (BICS). These social interactions take place in a meaningful social context and are not necessarily cognitively demanding. These skills take between six months and two years to develop. Problems arise when teachers or administrators determine that a child is proficient in English based only on observations of the child's social interactions. (See "BICS and CALP" at http://iteachilearn.org/cummins/bicscalp.html.)

Cognitive Academic Language Proficiency (CALP) is the academic language needed when following directions, describing an event in a social studies lesson, or providing the names of concepts in a science class. Academic language is more cognitively demanding.

The development of academic language is the focus of the WIDA Standards (See *WIDA ELP Standards and Resource Guide, 2007 Edition*). These standards are based on ten guiding principles of language development:

1. Students' languages and cultures are valuable resources to be tapped and incorporated into schooling.
2. Students' home and community experiences influence their language development.
3. Students draw on their metacognitive, metalinguistic, and metacultural awareness to develop proficiency in additional languages.
4. Students' academic language development in their native language facilitates their academic language development in English. Conversely, students' academic

language development in English informs their academic language development in their native language.

5. Students learn language and culture through meaningful use and interaction.

6. Students use language in functional and communicative ways that vary according to context.

7. Students develop language proficiency in listening, speaking, reading, and writing interdependently, but at different rates and in different ways.

8. Students' development of academic language and academic content knowledge are interrelated processes.

9. Students' development of social, instructional, and academic language, a complex and long-term process, is the foundation for their success in school.

10. Students' access to instructional tasks requiring complex thinking is enhanced when linguistic complexity and instructional support match their levels of language proficiency.

Following are key suggestions for all teachers working with ELLs.

▶ **Get to know your ELLs.** Find out each child's level of proficiency in English, literacy skills, prior schooling, family background, and the similarity of home language and culture to that of the mainstream children.

▶ **Incorporate language development into your content lessons.**

- Become a language model. Speak clearly and consistently. Add gestures and actions that help to convey meaning. Repeat important words, and write or project them.

- Give ELLs plenty of opportunities to speak, read, and write in English. Do not let them sit silently just observing (unless they are newcomers). Set up activities through which they can interact and practice their skills in a safe, supporting environment.

- Plan for language practice in every lesson. ELLs need opportunities to try out new words and grammatical patterns as they learn new content.

► **Provide academic scaffolding to help ELLs access content.**

- Activate kids' background knowledge. ELLs benefit from explicit connections between new content and prior knowledge.
  - Brainstorm ideas.
  - Use KWL charts.
  - Think, pair, share.
- Repeat, review, summarize.
- Build background knowledge if you find gaps in an ELL's knowledge.
- Use peer tutors. If possible, select a student who is a step above the ELL's proficiency level.
- Use graphic organizers, maps, charts, and timelines to help students make visual associations.

► **Provide collaborative opportunities to construct knowledge.** Use cooperative learning strategies to promote social and academic language development. ELLs have access to more comprehensible input when they negotiate meaning with a partner. Some cooperative learning activities that work well with ELLs are:

- jigsaw reading
- numbered heads together
- partners

—Contributed by
Maria Teresa Garreton

Chapter 5

Best Practice *in*

Mathematics

Susan Friedlander teaches mathematics to sixth graders at Northbrook Junior High School in Northbrook, Illinois.

Susan tells her story about Chocolate Algebra. *Chocolate.* Smooth, velvety, rich luscious chocolate. *Algebra.* Structured, patterned, intensely functional algebra.

Art Hyde cooked up this investigation "in order to fully integrate the different representations, data tables, graphs (and equations for the older kids) within a real-life situation" (2006, 170). I had no idea how my students' excitement would continue to grow throughout every stage in this investigation.

Upon entering the room my sixth graders saw a large canister of Tootsie Rolls with a $1 price tag attached and a two-pound Hershey's bar with a $2 price tag attached. I handed each student the first Chocolate Algebra problem: "Suppose I have $10 to spend and I want to buy $1 Tootsie Rolls (TRs) and $2 Hershey Bars (HBs). I have to use all of my money. What combinations of chocolate goodies can I buy? Begin with a KWC."

The KWC is a metacognitive prompt, patterned after the KWL used to stimulate reading comprehension. In small groups of three or four, students are guided to ask three questions. **K:** What do I know for sure? **W:** What am I trying to figure (or find) out? **C:** Are there any special conditions? Through their discussion of the answers, they build understanding of the problem.

My sixth graders immediately began to work in their groups on the KWC. Within moments, many students were furiously raising their hands to write parts of their KWC on the board. As a result the context, question, and constraints were thoroughly discussed. I distributed a bundle of $1 and $2 bills in play money, so they'd be able to visualize solutions. We agreed that each $1 bill represented a Tootsie Roll and each $2 bill represented a Hershey Bar. I said, "Show me the money! Hold up an example of a possible purchase that I could make." In thirty seconds, each group was holding up a possible purchase.

As I walked around the groups, I announced what I saw each group was holding and asked the rest of the class to verify that each was a valid purchase. I noticed that not one group held up an amount that was either less than or greater than $10—all groups had obviously paid attention to the special condition listed in their KWC: all chocolate, no change.

I asked, "Are the examples you're holding up all of the possibilities?" "NO WAY!" they replied in unison. "How can we keep track of all this information in such a way that we'll be sure that we've found all possible cases?" Their response was, "A table!"

Before I sent them off in their groups to work on the table, I wanted to make sure that they all knew how to construct one for these data. They were accustomed to organizing information for a table by using the K and W from the KWC chart. We sketched on chart paper the outline for their first table in Chocolate Algebra (shown in Figure 5.1).

This modified T-table helps students focus on the relationship between the two variables (the number of each type of chocolate) while still keeping track of

Figure 5.1
Modified T-table

Figure 5.1
Modified T-table

their costs. The box in the right-hand corner of each cell allows students to enter the cost of the items in that cell. Students were given copies of this table to use.

"How can you be sure that you satisfy the special conditions in your table?" Several kids piped up, "Because the sum of the money in the boxes in each row should be exactly $10."

After ten minutes, I pulled the class back together and recorded their data in the table in no apparent order. "How can we be sure that we've got all the possible combinations of TRs and HBs?" Several kids commented, "Because we have zero to ten possible TRs up there." "So what does that mean?" I asked. One said, "Well, if you start with no TRs, then move slowly up by one, the price for each TR, then you keep going until you reach the maximum number of TRs, which is obviously ten because we only have $10 to spend. And Mrs. F., it would help if you ordered our table like that so that we could all keep track of the HBs and the TRs." And so we did. See Figure 5.2.

I then asked: "Using the technique of starting with the least number of TRs and moving through to the greatest number of TRs, what's happening to the HBs?" All of the students agreed that when the TRs went up, the HBs had to go down to make sure that we were only spending exactly $10. This marked the first real-world example that my students had with negative, or inverse, linear

$2 HBs		$1 TRs		total $10
5	$10	0	$0	✓
4	$8	2	$2	✓
3	$6	4	$4	✓
2	$4	6	$6	✓
1	$2	8	$8	✓
0	$0	10	$10	✓

Figure 5.2
Completed and reorganized T-table

relationships (when one quantity increases, the other decreases). The students had previously dealt with positive, or direct, linear relationships—that is, as one quantity increases, so does the other. I made a point of connecting our new investigation to previous ones.

Once I was confident that the students had a solid understanding of how to create the table and had a strategy to ensure that they found all possible combinations, I told them to work in their groups to generate a list of any patterns they observed in Chocolate Algebra. I compiled their observations on chart paper and we debriefed this session. In addition to seeing that the number of HBs went down while the number of TRs went up, they affirmed that the table in Figure 5.2 shows that, as HBs go down by one, TRs go up by two. I asked, "Why?" Although no one directly conceived of a ratio of 2 to 1 for the costs, several did note that when the HBs go down by one, the boxes in the corners of HB cells always go down by $2. And because you have to spend all your money, that means you must spend that $2 on TRs, adding two more TRs to your next row.

Another pattern that many spotted was that the total number of items increased by one as they went down the rows of the table from five to ten items. This made good sense to the kids because, as one observed, "It is like you're trading in one HB for two TRs."

Over the next five days, the kids created tables of six more chocolate problems where I varied the costs of two items and the amount of money they had to spend. They always had the special condition of "all chocolate, no change." They became quite adept at seeing patterns in the data tables. They also constructed first-quadrant graphs of the points that represented the solutions in the tables. It is critically important that the students know, for example, that the third row in Figure 5.2 has values of 3 and 4 that would be plotted as coordinates (3, 4) and that each of these were representations of the reality—three Hershey Bars and four Tootsie Rolls. The chocolate connections made the mathematics meaningful and enjoyable.

A LOOK AT THE MATHEMATICS STANDARDS

The highly interactive, energetic students in Susan's classes are doing mathematics, making connections, and creating representations as they solve problems. In many respects, these students are experiencing for themselves the Process Standards of the National Council of Teachers of Mathematics (NCTM 2000). But there is a new player in the math standards game (or what some have dubbed "the math wars"). The Common Core State Standards for Mathematics (CCSSM) were developed by the Council of Chief State School Officers and the National Governors Association for the purpose of creating "a set of expectations for student knowledge and skills that high school graduates need to master to succeed in college and careers" (CCSS Initiative 2011, i), with the inducement of billions of federal dollars from the "Race to the Top" sweepstakes. By 2011 forty-five of the fifty states had agreed to adopt the CCSSM in place of their own curriculum standards and frameworks.

Many educators found it curious that the authors of CCSSM didn't systematically build upon the work of NCTM, which has been extensive since the council published its landmark document: *Curriculum and Evaluation Standards for School Mathematics* (1989). The council followed it with *Professional Standards for Teaching Mathematics* (1991), *Assessment Standards for School Mathematics* (1995), and twenty-two addenda booklets that addressed mathematical topics at various grade levels. The NCTM standards and related materials offered a significantly broader view than ever before of the nature of mathematics, what it means to know mathematics, how students learn mathematics, and what kinds of teaching practices best foster this learning. This body of work stimulated the National Science Foundation (NSF) to fund the development of more than a dozen new curriculum programs that embodied the NCTM standards.

The history. Before addressing the new Common Core math standards, let's back up to see how we arrived at the present mixture of programs. In attempting to change some fundamental societal beliefs about math teaching and learning, NCTM met with considerable inertia from schools as well as fierce resistance from a group of parents and a number of mathematicians and scientists who formed an organization called Mathematically Correct. With the help of the Internet, they organized opposition to NCTM and the NSF-funded curricula across the United States. In letters to the editor and over the Internet, they have posted horror stories of bad math teaching, attributed to the NCTM standards. Their website has a hundred "papers"—an amazing collection of half-truths, misconceptions, and rhetoric. These folks refer to themselves as traditionalists and criticize NCTM's work as "fuzzy math" and the "new-new math."

In 2000, NCTM released a revision of its standards that synthesized their previous documents and articulated five content standards and five process standards for grades pre-K–12 (see *Principles and Standards for School Mathematics*). The standards are initially explained in a global fashion and then examined in detail in four grade-level bands (pre-K–2, 3–5, 6–8, and 9–12). The five content standards address the familiar branches of school mathematics: number and operations, algebra, geometry, measurement, and data analysis and probability. The five process standards describe the interrelated aspects of cognition that build understanding of mathematics: problem solving, reasoning and proof, communication, connections, and representations. To supplement these standards, NCTM has provided an extensive set of booklets, the *Navigation* series.

In 2006, NCTM produced *Curriculum Focal Points for Prekindergarten Through Grade 8 Mathematics: A Quest for Coherence*, which states: "Curriculum focal points are important mathematical topics for each grade level, pre-K–8. [They are] areas of instructional emphasis [and] core structures that lay a conceptual foundation . . . [that serve] to organize content, connecting and bringing coherence to multiple concepts and processes taught at and across grade levels" (NCTM 2006, 5). In the wake of the No Child Left Behind Act of 2001, school districts were faced with a dizzying array of expectations and objectives in mathematics that varied dramatically from state to state. NCTM's focal points were presented as one way to build coherence into each grade level, quite differently than their prior grade-level bands. There were fewer topics to be emphasized in the focal points than had been in the "mile wide and inch deep" 700-page textbooks.

As an important support for the NCTM approach, meanwhile, the National Research Council has produced several major volumes synthesizing research on human cognition and conceptual understanding in content areas of the curriculum: *How People Learn: Brain, Mind, Experience, and School* (Bransford et al. 2000); *Adding It Up: Helping Children Learn Mathematics* (Kilpatrick et al. 2001); and *How Students Learn: History, Mathematics, and Science in the Classroom* (Donovan and Bransford 2005). Collectively they provide strong testimony to the validity of NCTM's assertions and to what we espouse as Best Practice.

The CCSSM approach. What, then, is the basis of the Common Core State Standards for Mathematics? The authors' core argument is this: "For over a decade, research studies of mathematics education in high-performance countries have pointed to the conclusion that the mathematics curriculum in the United States must become substantially more focused and coherent in order to improve mathematics achievement in this country" (CCSS Initiative 2011, 3). International comparisons for the scope and sequence of standards played a major role in the authors' thinking.

So now let's look at the Common Core math standards and how they differ from the NCTM version. The CCSSM at each grade level "define what students should understand and be able to do" (5). The document attempts to illustrate connections among math concepts by grouping related standards into clusters and then into larger groups called *domains* (see Figure 5.3).

Kindergarten	1	2	3	4	5	6	7	8	High School
Counting and Cardinality									Number and Quantity
Number and Operations in Base Ten						Ratios and Proportional Relationships			
			Number and Operations: Fractions			The Number System			

Operations and Algebraic Thinking	Expressions and Equations	Algebra
	Functions	Functions

Geometry	Geometry	Geometry

Measurement and Data	Statistics and Probability	Statistics and Probability

Figure 5.3

The Common Core State Standards domains and conceptual categories for mathematics

This curricular organization contrasts with the NCTM content standards, which took five strands of mathematics (number and operations, algebra, geometry, measurement, data analysis and probability) and illustrated how each would flow from kindergarten through grade 12. The CCSSM use that pattern only for geometry. For other domains, one would need a road map to interpret the flow of connected ideas. In fact, their high school domain of modeling is not a separate entity: "Modeling is best interpreted not as a collection of isolated topics, but rather in relation to other standards . . . Specific modeling standards appear throughout the high school standards indicated by a star symbol" (CCSS Initiative 2011, 73).

The biggest difference between the Common Core and the NCTM standards can be seen in the Common Core "practices" versus NCTM "processes." NCTM devoted 135 pages, over one-third of its 400-page book (NCTM 2000), to explaining the cognitive processes in which students need to meaningfully engage in order to understand and learn the math content *and* what teachers need to do to help their students enact these processes. The CCSSM offer two paragraphs on page 4 on understanding mathematics and three pages (6–8) on the standards of mathematical practice. In addition, and even more significantly, the CCSSM do *not* provide a developmental progression of building understanding across the grades.

The Common Core developers avoided the controversies that plagued NCTM by not addressing teaching strategies or instructional methods. It is significantly easier to suggest that teachers address a new topic than to help them change their teaching methods from stand and deliver to discuss and debrief. Teaching routines are notoriously difficult to change.

The CCSSM developers state that their mathematical practices are based on the NCTM process standards and the strands of mathematical proficiency from the National Research Council's *Adding It Up*. So perhaps one way for teachers to follow the Common Core effectively is for them also to draw on the crucial thinking and learning processes that NCTM so clearly describes. Therefore, we have organized the CCSSM practices plus the NCTM processes and proficiencies of NRC's *Adding It Up* into four clusters that would likely illustrate their similarities and differences and provide a context for *interpreting* the CCSSM practices. We kept the original language and coded each by its source: CCSSM, NCTM, and NRC. The eight major CCSSM practices are highlighted in gray. The additional CCSSM practices not highlighted are clarifying statements in the math practices standards.

▶ *Mathematical Process, Proficiencies, and Practices*

CONNECTIONS (NCTM)

Teachers should enable all students to:

- ▶ recognize and use connections among mathematical ideas (NCTM)
- ▶ understand how mathematical ideas interconnect and build on one another to produce a coherent whole (NCTM)
- ▶ recognize and apply mathematics in contexts outside of mathematics (NCTM)
- ▶ look for and make use of structure (CCSSM)
- ▶ develop a deep understanding requiring that learners connect pieces of knowledge, so that they can use what they know productively in solving problems (NRC)
- ▶ comprehend mathematical concepts, operations, and relations (NRC)
- ▶ carry out procedures flexibly, accurately, efficiently, and appropriately (NRC)
- ▶ see mathematics as sensible, useful, and worthwhile, coupled with a belief in diligence and one's own efficacy (NRC)
- ▶ become motivated to develop a productive disposition (NRC)

PROBLEM SOLVING (NCTM)

Teachers should enable all students to:

▶ build mathematical knowledge through problem solving (NCTM)

▶ solve problems that arise in mathematics or in other contexts (NCTM)

▶ apply and adapt a variety of appropriate strategies to solve problems (NCTM)

▶ monitor and reflect on the process of mathematical problem solving (NCTM)

▶ make sense of problems and persevere in solving them (CCSSM)

▶ start by explaining to themselves the meaning of a problem and looking for entry points to its solution (CCSSM)

▶ analyze givens, constraints, relationships, and goals (CCSSM)

▶ develop strategic competence (the ability to formulate, represent, and solve mathematical problems) (NRC)

▶ develop adaptive expertise and metacognition (knowledge about one's own thinking and ability to monitor one's own understanding in a problem-solving activity) (NRC)

▶ create mathematical models by applying the mathematics they know to solve problems arising in everyday life, society, and the workplace (CCSSM)

▶ use appropriate tools strategically (consider the available tools when solving a mathematical problem) (CCSSM)

▶ create and use representations to organize, record, and communicate mathematical ideas (NCTM)

▶ select, apply, and translate among mathematical representations to solve problems (NCTM)

▶ use representations to model and interpret physical, social, and mathematical phenomena (NCTM)

REASONING AND PROOF (NCTM)

Teachers should enable all students to:

▶ recognize reasoning and proof as fundamental aspects of mathematics (NCTM)

▶ make and investigate mathematical conjectures (NCTM)

▶ develop and evaluate mathematical arguments and proofs (NCTM)

▶ select and use various types of reasoning and methods of proof (NCTM)

▶ reason abstractly and quantitatively, making sense of quantities and their relationships in problem situations (CCSSM)

▶ construct viable arguments and critique the reasoning of others (CCSSM)

▶ look for and express regularity in repeated reasoning (CCSSM)

▶ notice if calculations are repeated, and look both for general methods and for short-cuts (CCSSM)

▶ develop adaptive reasoning (the capacity for logical thought, reflection, explanation, and justification) (NRC)

Although all these items are a lot to assimilate, they provide guidance on interpreting the eight CCSSM practices.

QUALITIES OF BEST PRACTICE IN TEACHING MATHEMATICS

The CCSSM for both mathematical practice and content must be interpreted within a context of related meaning. Fortunately, many of the CCSS math standards use the term *understand*, by which the authors appeal to a higher cognitive function than *recall* or *remember*. However, they have explicitly avoided addressing methods of teaching. So what we offer now are guidelines for powerful and meaningful instruction that can enable students to meet and readily exceed the content standards, whether these are from NCTM or CCSSM. Generally, as research shows and as we shall see, this cannot be accomplished by traditional means.

Help all students understand that mathematics is a dynamic, coherent, interconnected set of ideas. To see mathematics as a coherent whole, one must realize that, although numbers and computation are an important part of mathematics, they are only one part. Mathematics is the science of patterns. Mathematical concepts describe patterns and relationships. A concept is an abstract idea that explains and organizes information. Mathematicians look for relations among ideas and try to see patterns in these relationships. Every branch of mathematics (e.g., geometry, probability) has its own patterns. Expert mathematicians use abstract, symbolic notation to describe the patterns they conceive. Big ideas, such as *pattern, dimension, quantity, uncertainty, shape,* and *change,* anchor the important concepts of mathematics. Teachers can promote coherence by emphasizing big ideas and helping students see the connections among concepts.

Unfortunately, few of us experienced mathematics this way when we were students. Most people see mathematics as a bunch of unrelated topics, theorems, procedures, and facts. Study after study for the past thirty years has found the mathematics curriculum of the United States to be narrowly focused on procedures and facts, not concepts; highly repetitive, with significant overlap and review from year to year, and often covering a topic in the same superficial manner for four years in a row.

The CCSSM were written to counteract these tendencies by emulating the curricula of countries whose students scored highest in the Third International Mathematics and Science Study (TIMSS), respectively, Singapore, Korea, Chinese Taipei, Hong Kong, and Japan. TIMSS revealed that these countries focused more on reasoning and understanding concepts while the United States spent more time on procedures and facts. The curricula of high-scoring countries had more in-depth study of fewer topics each year (e.g., in Japan, ten) compared to the United States, which had superficial coverage of thirty to thirty-five topics.

Mathematical thinking is a normal part of everyone's mental ability, and not confined to a gifted few.

Support all students to understand and use mathematical concepts powerfully. Students should develop true understanding of mathematical concepts and their related procedures. They must come to see and believe that mathematics makes sense, that it is understandable and useful to them. They can become more confident in their own use of mathematics. Teachers and students alike must come to recognize that mathematical thinking is a normal part of everyone's mental ability, and not confined to a gifted few.

Yes, but . . . *what about the differences in mathematical ability that students bring to the classroom?*

Many more students are capable of learning and understanding much more mathematics than previous generations ever thought possible. Conceptual understanding does not come from a teacher telling students what a concept is. Concepts are built by each person. Understanding is created. Students have to explore many examples and talk about what they see and think, as well as hear explanations from the teacher and other students. This kind of teaching raises the bar for everyone. But this guidance is happening too rarely in American schools. TIMSS researchers videotaped random samples of a hundred eighth-grade math teachers in Japan and the United States. Analyses of these classrooms were startling. More than half (54 percent) of the problems in Japanese classrooms emphasized making connections among several mathematical concepts, versus only 17 percent in the United States. Two-thirds of the problems in the U.S. classes emphasized procedural skills. When challenging problems were addressed, the Japanese teachers required students to discuss solutions to make connections; *none* of the American teachers in the study did so. In fact, a third of the time the American teachers just gave the answer.

Focus instruction on enabling students to successfully engage in critical cognitive processes. Making connections, problem solving, representational strategies, and communicating mathematical ideas are four powerful tools for developing understanding.

1. *Making connections.* Help students make connections to their prior mathematical knowledge, between related mathematical concepts, and between concepts and procedures. Help them build bridges between situations or contexts that may appear different but are examples of the same concept. Students can realize the connections between different representations of a problem, which is especially important in moving from concrete to more abstract representations. A skillful teacher is always juggling examples and explanations. For students to see patterns or to develop true conceptual understanding, they will need many more examples than are provided in the textbook. Presentation of an explanation, no matter how brilliantly worded, will not connect ideas unless students have had ample opportunities to wrestle with examples. An explanation must connect to something. Provide experiences so that students can make and investigate mathematical conjectures, select and use various types of reasoning (e.g., inductive pattern finding and deductive logic), and develop and evaluate mathematical arguments and proofs. Reasoning mathematically is essentially a habit; it is developed by use in a variety of situations and contexts.

2. *Problem solving.* Traditionally, problem solving has been seen as an application of skills *after* mastery. Instead, we now know that problem solving can be a means to build mathematical knowledge. Choose worthwhile mathematical problems or tasks for students to work on. How to solve these problems should not be obvious; students should have to *think*. The best problems are authentic, challenging, intriguing, mathematically rich, and even counterintuitive. Susan Friedlander's Chocolate Algebra activity at the start of this chapter is an excellent example of this. Look at it again in this light and notice how students are learning concepts *as they are solving the problem*. With help to apply and adapt good problem-solving strategies, the students can attack problems and develop understanding. Guide students to become metacognitively aware of their own problem-solving processes, monitoring their progress and reflecting on their own thinking.

3. *Representational strategies.* We can ensure that students gain experience with a variety of strategies and are able to decide when to use which one. With the most powerful strategies, students create their own representations. The common strategies of *look for a pattern* and *use logical reasoning* are overarching *metastrategies*, essential to doing

mathematics. Students must be encouraged to look for patterns and to use logical reasoning in *every* problem. But at a more specific level, students should develop capability with five critical strategies that are based on creating representations:

- Discuss the problem in small groups (language representations).
- Use manipulatives (concrete, physical representations and tactile sense).
- Act it out (representations of sequential actions and bodily kinesthetic sense).
- Draw a picture, diagram, or graph (visual, pictorial representations)
- Make a list or table (symbolic representations).

These representations build understanding of the problem (and often find a solution) because in creating them, students are developing different mental models of the problem or phenomena. In worthwhile tasks, students may use several of these representations, moving from one to another to figure out more about the problem. Later they might draw on supplementary strategies (e.g., guess and check, work backward, simplify the problem), but these cannot be used effectively unless one understands the problem. As students become more mathematically sophisticated, they are able to use more abstract and symbolic strategies (e.g., make an equation, use proportional reasoning, apply a formula.)

Students often need help moving back and forth between representations with the realization of how they are related and how each reveals something different. Notice how Susan Friedlander shifts from tables to graphs once the students are ready to understand this. Flexibility of translating between representations and realizing the value of each are good indicators of true understanding.

4. ***Communicating mathematical ideas.*** In mathematics, students should be encouraged and helped to communicate their ideas by using a full range of language representations—speaking, writing, reading, and listening. Communication and reflection go hand in hand. Even though symbols are used to represent the most abstract aspects of mathematics, the symbols represent ideas that are developed and expressed through language. Oral language—discussing, verbalizing thoughts, "talking mathematics"—for most students, most of the time, greatly facilitates their understanding. Of course, we must build a safe environment in our classrooms where students believe they can freely express their ideas without negative consequences for mistakes.

Math journals provide another opportunity for students to express and justify their reasoning and ideas. They can describe how they solved a problem, why they used this approach or strategy, what assumptions they made, and so forth. When they have to explain a mathematics concept in their own words, they have to think and rethink what is really important. With feedback from the teacher, learners begin to move from the specifics of each activity to more general and abstract conceptions, expressed precisely in mathematical language. Eventually, students' mathematical language, oral and written, becomes a powerful tool for thinking, helping them create models, mental maps to organize their world, solve problems, and explore relationships.

Help students understand and use counting strategies, number concepts, operations, and computational procedures. It is vital to children's later work in mathematics that they have a strong foundation in number concepts upon which to build. The traditional practice of reviewing and reteaching the same arithmetic skills, algorithms, and procedures in the same manner year after year is dysfunctional. There are far better ways.

> Children enter the world prepared to notice number as a feature of their environment. Much of what preschool children know about number is bound up in their developing understanding of counting. Counting a set of objects is a complex task involving thinking, perception, and movement, with much of its complexity obscured by familiarity. (Kilpatrick et al. 2001, 159)

Just as in language acquisition, awareness of number is universal in normally developing children. However, environmental influences play a key role in their rate of development (Donovan and Bransford 2005, 219). There appears to be a three-year range in the early number knowledge levels among children four years of age entering preschool. This difference between low-attaining and average or able students increases during schooling, and after ten years, a seven-year difference can be seen (Wright, Martland, and Stafford 2006, 2). The good news is that early intervention of the right kind closes the gap before too much failure locks the children into a pattern of math anxiety or hopelessness.

The highly successful Math Recovery Program provides assessments of specific knowledge needed by low-attaining first graders and intensive individualized and group teaching so that they can progress to a level at which they can succeed in a regular class setting. Developed in Australia, the program is now widely used in the U.K. and the United States. Thoroughly researched and based on sound theory, it is guided by the Learning Framework in Number (LFIN), which reflects the developmental learning progression of children's early numerical knowledge (Wright, Martland, and Stafford 2006, 19–28):

1. early arithmetical strategies

2. base-ten arithmetical strategies

3. forward number word sequences and the number word after

4. backward number word sequences and the number word before

5. numerical identification

6. combining and partitioning

7. spatial patterns and subitizing (immediate recognition of the number of items in a small set without counting)

8. temporal sequences

9. finger patterns

10. five-based strategies (using five as a privileged number)

11. multiplication and division

The Math Recovery Program and its LFIN incorporate the critical organized knowledge needed for a comprehensive understanding of whole number counting, relationships, decomposing and recomposing quantities, structuring numbers in base ten, conceptual understanding of the meaning of the four operations, and strategies for working with them with high proficiency. This deep and thorough grounding in the way numbers work is critical for future success in mathematical learning.

Yes, but . . . *is this for every child? Can't most kids just learn their number facts the traditional way?*

Developing conceptual understanding and the relationship between concepts and procedures is critically important for all children. The eleven aspects of LFIN are major pieces of the puzzle that traditionally have been underemphasized or even overlooked. Many teachers have assumed that if children can orally produce the string of the whole numbers in order, then they "know" how to count. Not true. There are many more aspects to counting.

The gaps in students' math knowledge often don't get recognized by classroom teachers until middle school. When teachers administer Math Recovery assessments to their middle school students, they are often shocked by the mistakes their students make. The teachers have assumed that students have knowledge that they do not. One can trace the origins of students' misconceptions to the traditional approaches used in the elementary schools, including premature symbolization and emphasis on procedures that lacked meaningfulness.

Liping Ma (1999) investigated Chinese and U.S. elementary school teachers in their knowledge of mathematics (especially arithmetic) and the ways that they teach. She found serious gaps in the U.S. teachers' conceptual and procedural knowledge. Ma describes how Chinese teachers teach algorithms much more conceptually than American teachers. Using the students' knowledge of number relationships as well as their deep understanding of place value, equivalence, and expanded notation, the Chinese teachers help them understand underlying concepts and procedures of computation.

The genesis of Asian students' knowledge and understanding is in their language. Asian languages are structured very differently from English and most other Indo-European languages. For instance, English speakers will count "ten, eleven, twelve, . . . twenty," whereas Asian speakers will count "ten, ten-one, ten-two, . . . two-tens." Asian languages introduce and support the base ten place value thinking from a children's earliest oral counting experiences *before starting school.* This language feature greatly facilitates regrouping and renaming in computation (Miura 2001). Chinese teachers build on this base-ten language by using different thinking strategies than Americans do to help students learn basic facts (Sun and Zhang 2001). The moral of this story is that American teachers must emphasize the full range of strategies in the LFIN to make up for the valuable numerical thinking that Asian-speaking students receive from birth.

Give all students opportunities to engage in doing algebra and reasoning algebraically throughout their K–12 school years. Algebra is a way of thinking with various representations that become increasingly more symbolic and abstract. Historically in the United States, Algebra I has been a "gatekeeper course" consisting of generalized arithmetic; a relatively narrow range of paper-and-pencil skills for transforming, simplifying, and solving equations; and "problems" that might have provided real-life contexts a hundred years ago, but are barely imaginable today. This model should not be mandated for all students. Under the rationale of adding more "rigor" to the math curriculum, many districts moved the traditional Algebra I course from ninth grade to eighth grade as a required course. The result was predictable. Students' failure rates skyrocketed.

For more than a decade, NCTM has advocated the creation of an algebra strand in the elementary school mathematics curriculum that engages all students in context-based problems, using tables, graphs, and equations (especially functions) that mathematically model situations and quantitative relationships (see Greenes 2008). Again, this is what we see Susan Friedlander doing in her Chocolate Algebra lesson. With full understanding, students should be able to flexibly move back and forth between different representations. They must understand that each is a different way of representing the same thing, but each allows one to perceive different aspects of the phenomenon. The CCSSM include the domains of Operations and Algebra K–5, Ratios and Proportional Reasoning 6–7, and Expressions and Equations 6–8, leading up to Algebra in High School. These standards focus on the algebraic thinking that encourages students to generalize about various number concepts. Recent research strongly suggests that this approach should be taken very broadly. Patterns and "regularities, emerging naturally from children's work, become the foundation not only for exploration for generalizations about number and operations but also of the practices of formulating, testing, and proving such generalizations" (Schifter et al. 2008).

Other researchers and developers have different conceptions of early algebra K–5. Blanton (2008, 5) emphasizes functional thinking, which "draws on a different skill set than does generalized arithmetic." In functional thinking children must pay attention to change and growth, "looking for patterns in how quantities vary in relation to each other." Fosnot and Jacobs (2010) have investigated how various realistic contexts and representational models can support children's development of algebra concepts. They write: "Contexts that have the potential to suggest comparing quantities provide students opportunities to develop pre-algebraic abilities, such as reasoning with unknown quantities, using and generalizing relations, and developing notation to support such reasoning" (130).

Problems that come from rich contexts (such as Chocolate Algebra) can help students build an understanding of the big ideas of algebra: change, variable, equality/equation, function, rate of change, linearity/nonlinearity. Students need to understand how to use these ideas and related tools to describe patterns in real-world contexts around them. They do have to learn how to represent and model using equations and in the process of doing so, learn the rules of the game for balancing equations, simplifying radicals, rationalizing denominators, and factoring polynomials. These symbol manipulation skills can best be learned when they are embedded within a meaningful context that gives students a good reason for learning these skills—they want to find the answers to the real problems. Speaking of meaningful contexts . . .

Problems that come from rich contexts can help students build an understanding of the big ideas of algebra.

To build understanding of mathematical concepts in geometry, measurement, data, statistics, and probability, use real-world, realistic, authentic contexts that are inherently meaningful to students. Although each of these domains of mathematics has qualitatively different concepts, they share the common ground of usefulness in science and social studies. Each domain developed out of human endeavors to understand the forces of nature or the nature of humans. The big ideas of shape and dimension appear in the standards of geometry and measurement. Some geometric concepts students do not measure (e.g., symmetry, similarity, spatial visualization); other concepts one might call geometric measurement (i.e., angles, length, area, volume, which correspond to dimensions 1, 2, and 3). There are attributes one measures that are not geometric (e.g., capacity, mass/weight, temperature, time, money). Students should develop a deep understanding of the attributes being measured (e.g., compare and contrast volume and capacity). However, traditional chapters in geometry and measurement textbooks are a game of memorizing definitions, plugging in values for variables in formulas, and converting units between metric and English systems.

Students must understand geometric concepts, characteristics and properties of two- and three-dimensional shapes, coordinate geometry to represent relationships, and units of measure. Such understanding can be accomplished best through *hands-on manipulation of concrete materials.* All students must have extensive experience handling real three-dimensional objects—determining, comparing, and measuring their attributes. They must work with individual attributes to build understanding before working with rates and derived measures that require understanding the relationship between two measures. These experiences must precede the more abstract work with symbols and formulas.

One definition of data is "numbers with a context." We should provide challenging tasks in which students formulate questions and design their own studies that can be addressed with data that they collect, organize, and analyze. Students need to understand a variety of statistical methods and when to use them. Some of them fit hand in glove with algebraic concepts such as variables, tables, graphs, and mathematical modeling. We are now seeing a strong interest in data modeling in mathematics and science for students K–12. This work is always embedded in real contexts of authentic inquiry. Students are highly motivated to argue for their inferences from data-based evidence (Lehrer and Schauble 2002).

Probability has a host of slippery concepts that should be addressed inductively via probability experiments. We should exercise caution in pushing theoretical probability too early. When the ideas are grounded in extensive data collection to build understanding, theoretical ideas take hold. The language of probability helps us; children's questions often have answers such as "maybe," "perhaps," and "probably," appropriately dealing with the big idea of uncertainty.

Use assessment that provides an understanding of what students know and guides meaningful decisions about teaching and learning activities. A variety of formative assessment methods should be used to assess individual students, including written, oral, and demonstration formats. There are multiple purposes for formative assessment: (1) to allow students to show the teacher what they know and can do, (2) to reveal misconceptions, (3) to accurately pinpoint the places where students are stuck, and (4) to guide the teacher in planning what to focus on for intervention, continued development, or enrichment.

The assessment procedures for the CCSSM will be put in place in 2014–2015, and prior to that schools will see examples of the structure and format of assessment that will be used. Developers of the assessments have said that their instruments will assess the standards of both content and practices. For a decade, Illinois has included in its state assessment of mathematics one or two "extended response problems." Broader in scope than the traditional multiple choice questions, these problems are scored with an analytical rubric composed of three scales: knowledge of the concepts in the problem, use of appropriate strategies to solve, and ability to explain what one did and why. Fifteen minutes per problem are allowed. States that have included similar extended-response problems should have less concern about assessing students' mathematical practices than states with only multiple-choice questions in their state assessments. Excellent resources for performance assessment tasks and open-ended problems are available. (See the Internet resource list for sample tasks and problems.)

Introducing Multiplication to Third and Fourth Graders in a Title I Math Lab

SUSAN HILDEBRAND

Jenks East Elementary School, Jenks, Oklahoma

After teaching special education and first grade, I accepted the challenge to work with students who qualified for the Title I math lab program. These students are traditionally behind their peers two or more years in math. In addition, many are English language learners. I found that helping these students keep up with their peers while redoing workbook pages and giving timed math fact tests didn't produce mathematical thinkers. They continued to lack the deep understanding of number sense. How could they be taught two- and three-digit multiplication when they could not partition the number ten?

While listening to a professional development consultant describe strategies used for teaching reading comprehension, the thought occurred to me to use the same strategy to unwrap "word problems" for the Title I math students. Students are often overwhelmed with the thought of a "word problem." Could they use the same reading strategies (asking questions, making connections, visualization, communicating with peers) to help understand math problems?

I began a journey to develop a different format for the Title I math lab program. I needed to go deeper into conceptual learning, to give students time to think, time to talk and communicate their thinking, time to show proof, and time to write their thoughts. We started "projects" that had real-world content while introducing students to mathematical concepts.

▶ *The Different Math Lab*

As you walk down the hall toward my classroom, you see brightly decorated magic pots displaying a student's personal in/out function machine. These were from a lesson based on a recent NCTM journal article using the children's picture book *Two of Everything* (Hong 1993), in which a magic pot creates a double of anything put inside it. Step up to the classroom door, and view the photographs of smiling students working on math projects. Inside the math lab, you notice cubbies filled with student notebooks crammed with handwritten notes, drawings of their representations, and paragraphs written to record personal thoughts. There are no drill worksheets!

While looking around the classroom, you'll find bookcases full of plastic tubs containing traditional and nontraditional manipulatives and project supplies. Charts (large Post-it posters) completed by each group during their "math huddle" or debriefing time are in full view. This room is not a quiet place; rather, it is filled with mathematical conversations like these: "I got it!" "Let's try six, five doesn't work," and "I just know there is another way." Quite often students are searching through their notebooks or the charts that line the walls for that missing piece of data they had seen before to formulate a mathematical idea to share with their classmates.

A bulletin board displays the student's "Brain Explosions," handwritten notes describing their mathematical thoughts that connect either math to self, math to world, or math to math for all to see. Recently, after Brittany had explained two math-to-math connections one after another, Robbie asked her, "Does your brain hurt from all of that thinking?" She answered with excitement, "I think it does!"

▶ *The Horse Ranch Project*

The students arrive at the math room with excitement because today they will begin a new "project." Nonfiction and fiction books about horses and ranches are nestled in a tub along with a bucket of pattern blocks and a set of dominoes on the check-in table, providing a preview of the project. As students gather around the table, I tell them: "Our new project begins with a story." I show a picture to study and think about. "What do you see?" Josh is first to say, "I see horses." "Has anyone ever touched a horse?" Hands are raised. "What color was the horse?" Emily pauses and then blurts out, "It is black." The students have much to share since they are familiar with horses from books, television, and visits to the state fair or to a nearby ranch. Susan shares a story about the horse she once owned with details of the blaze on its face and the black-and-white color of the tail. (We'd obviously use a different story if this class were located in an urban setting, since connection to the students' prior knowledge is important.)

The students are intrigued as the new story begins: "Imagine you work on a horse ranch with twenty-four horses." I tell them, "We can use one of our reading strategies to help us think about our story. Let's use visualization with our story. That's when we see pictures in our brain. Remember, it's like we have a 'movie in our mind.' Think about what those horses look like. Are your twenty-four horses lined up in a row, or nose to tail? What color are they? Are they all black?"

Everyone has an idea of what the horses look like. Corrie describes in great detail, "Ten of mine are white with brown spots, the other ten are babies brown with black spots and other four are white newborns." She is able to unitize her counting of twenty-four. I guide the students throughout the project, give them the "gift of time," and encourage them to communicate their thinking.

Students are engaged and listen as I tell the story once again, "Imagine you work on a horse ranch that has twenty-four horses. The owner of the ranch tells you that you must put all of the horses in corrals." After a pause, I ask, "Does anyone know what corrals are?"

I get several answers: "They are little ranches with gates that you put around horses so they don't get out." They're "made out of wood," and "I saw a picture of one in that book over there." I continue the story. "You can fence off the corrals many different ways. The owner says you must put the same number of horses in each corral. What is one way you might do this? How many different ways to do this can you find?"

"Josh and Luke are new to our math group and have never used a KWC chart before, so today let's work together to complete the KWC." This will help the others in the group to become more secure and independent with the chart. The KWC chart pulls out elements of the problem while using the "asking questions" reading strategy. "Let's do our KWC now."

Emily speaks up: "**K** is for know, what do you know for sure!" I reread the story quickly and say, "We are going to look at **K**; what is something you know for sure from the story?" The list begins: work on a horse ranch, twenty-four horses, there are corrals. "What about **W**—what are we trying to find out?" Corrie raises her hand and stands up to answer, "You are trying to figure out how many numbers to put in the corrals." I repeat what she just said, emphasizing the word *number*. The students interrupt to say, "Horses in each corral!"

"Let's look at **C**," I prompt. "Are there any special conditions? What do we know for sure to solve this problem?" Emily tells us, "We need twenty-four horses." After Corrie says we need corrals, she adds, "I figured out something about corrals, it has a part of my name in it, CORRA!" "Same number of horses in each corral," adds Josh.

Placing a plastic tub on the table, I explain: "Today in our project, we have twenty-four Unifix cubes and some corrals that are made out of Popsicle sticks. What do you think the Unifix cubes represent if we have twenty-four cubes?" "The horses!" exclaims Emily. While still at the table, I ask the students to show me one way that they could put the horses in corrals. As they turn and talk to their partner, I hear Josh say, "I got it! We are trying to make all fours."

Wanting to understand his thought, I ask, "What does that look like?" Josh moves the Unifix cubes in and out of the corrals and decides he needs more than two corrals to finish the solution. On the other side of the table, Emily and Corrie are busy counting out six cubes each. "I'll put six here, and put another six in the same corral. Oh, that's twelve and put these twelve cubes over here. Twelve and twelve, that's twenty-four!"

Since Emily wants to make sure they have used all twenty-four cubes, she recounts the cubes by twos. Listening to their conversation, I ask: "What are you thinking about? So, how does that relate to the corrals?" While pointing to two corrals, Corrie explains that each cube represents a horse and we put six and six in each corral, which uses all twenty-four cubes or horses. Luke adds, "I knew that there would be two corrals because twelve plus twelve equals twenty-four."

"This is how we solved the problem using pictures, numbers, or words. You did a great job corralling the horses, but now you need to fill in a sentence strip that describes your corrals and horses." Holding up a sentence strip that reads "____ corrals with ____ horses in each corral," I ask, "Emily, what would you write in the blanks?" Emily completes the sentence strip as 2 corrals with 12 horses in each corral. "Glue your sentence strip into your math notebook and make a simple drawing of your cubes and corrals."

I emphasize internalizing the work. I want kids to repeat back the instructions for added reinforcement. I release math partners to work on the carpet or at the table with their project tub, notebook, pencils, and glue sticks.

As I drop in on students' mathematical conversations, they discuss, predict, and process their data. When a student or small group hits a roadblock, I ask simple questions such as, "What does that look like? Can you prove that? What are our special conditions?" The questions help the students revise their thinking in order to further develop understanding. With my notebook in hand, I record what they've said and done—formative assessments that I'll review later.

As I regroup the students in our math huddle for debriefing, they share their solutions, which are then listed on a T-chart in a random manner. A second T-chart reorganizes the data in numerical order. The students discover patterns on the second T-chart: "I see 1, 2, 3, 4, here and 4, 3, 2, 1 there." "The numbers become larger as they go down the list." "All of the ways make twenty-four." "They are turn-around facts." "The top half of numbers look like the bottom half but just flipped around."

As these connections are being made, Luke blurts out, "We are doing times!" After a long pause, Grace tells the class, "The T-chart [reorganized] reminds me of the time line I just made in my classroom about Benjamin Franklin." After continued discussion, I ask the students if they would like to do another project. The response: "It's fun!" "Can we do one now?"

I describe the task: "Write a letter to me about what you learned from this project. Be sure to include any new vocabulary and any connections you made. Explain why you should have another project kit." Writing in their notebooks cements together all of the elements of the project: the thinking, language, maneuvering of the manipulatives, hand-drawn representations, and use of symbolic representations. I support the students by frontloading the task, giving them meaningful and rich text, open-ended problems, and manipulatives (some that are real to life), so they become engaged and take ownership of the problem.

After a few days, I introduce several new projects that follow the same pattern of the Horse Ranch Project by giving the students multiple contexts to develop and deepen their conceptual understanding and mathematical thinking. Before releasing the students with each new kit, we take time to develop the story as we did with the Horse Ranch Project. When creating a project, I have to design a "story" that has engaging, real-world texts and situations so that the students become an integral part of the solution. The students may recognize the name of a friend or teacher or school club that's purposely placed in the story. Each project has two versions of the story printed on card stock (4¼ x 5½ inches) using appropriate clip art to visually enhance the problem. The first story contains a specific number of items while in the second story, the number of items is left blank. This allows for quick differentiation of the students' needs.

Vary the context for the same concept. Vary the names, vary the quantities, and vary the types of numbers (composites, primes, squares). Vary the representations. Vary the debriefing questions. Require that students *think*. And they will!

Works Cited

Blanton, Maria. 2008. *Algebra in the Elementary Classroom: Transforming Thinking, Transforming Practice.* Portsmouth, NH: Heinemann.

Bransford, John, Ann Brown, and Rodney Cocking, eds. 2000. *How People Learn: Brain, Mind, Experience, and School* (expanded edition). Washington, DC: National Research Council, National Academies Press.

Common Core State Standards Initiative. 2011. *Common Core State Standards for Mathematics.* National Governors Council and Council of Chief State School Officers. www.corestandards.org/.

Donovan, M. Suzanne, and John Bransford, eds. 2005. *How Students Learn: History, Mathematics, and Science in the Classroom.* Washington, DC: National Research Council, National Academies Press.

Fosnot, Catherine Twomey, and Bill Jacobs. 2010. *Young Mathematicians at Work: Constructing Algebra.* Portsmouth, NH: Heinemann.

Greenes, Carole, ed. 2008. *Algebra and Algebraic Thinking in School Mathematics.* Reston, VA: National Council of Teachers of Mathematics.

Hong, Lily Toy. 1993. *Two of Everything.* Park Ridge, IL: Albert Whitman.

Hyde, Arthur. 2006. *Comprehending Math: Adapting Reading Strategies to Teach Mathematics, K–6.* Portsmouth, NH: Heinemann.

Hyde, Arthur, with Susan Friedlander, Cheryl Heck, and Lynn Pittner. 2009. *Understanding Middle School Math: Cool Problems to Get Students Thinking and Connecting.* Portsmouth, NH: Heinemann.

Kilpatrick, J., Jane Swafford, and Bradford Findell, eds. 2001. *Adding It Up: Helping Children Learn Mathematics.* Washington, DC: National Research Council, National Academies Press.

Lehrer, R., and L. Schauble, eds. 2002. *Investigating Real Data in the Classroom: Expanding Children's Understanding of Math And Science.* New York: Teachers College Press.

Ma, Liping. 1999. *Knowing and Teaching Elementary Mathematics: Teachers' Understanding of Fundamental Mathematics in China and the United States.* Mahwah, NJ: Lawrence Erlbaum Associates.

Miura, I. 2001. The Influence of Language on Mathematical Representations. In Albert A. Cuoco, ed., *The Role of Representation in School Mathematics.* Reston, VA: National Council of Teachers of Mathematics.

National Council of Teachers of Mathematics. 1989. *Curriculum and Evaluation Standards for School Mathematics.* Reston, VA: National Council of Teachers of Mathematics.

———. 1991. *Professional Standards for Teaching Mathematics.* Reston, VA: National Council of Teachers of Mathematics.

———. 1995. *Assessment Standards for School Mathematics.* Reston, VA: National Council of Teachers of Mathematics.

———. 2000. *Principles and Standards for School Mathematics.* Reston, VA: National Council of Teachers of Mathematics.

———. 2006. *Curriculum Focal Points for Prekindergarten Through Grade 8 Mathematics: A Quest for Coherence.* Reston, VA: National Council of Teachers of Mathematics.

Schifter, Deborah, Virginia Barnstable, Susan Jo Russell, Lisa Seyferth, and Margaret Riddle. 2008. Algebra in Grades K–5 Classroom: Opportunities for Students and Teachers. In Carole Greenes, ed., *Algebra and Algebraic Thinking in School Mathematics.* Reston, VA: National Council of Teachers of Mathematics.

Sun, W., and J. Y. Zhang. September 2001. Teaching Addition and Subtraction Facts: A Chinese Perspective. *Teaching Children Mathematics*, 28–31.

Wright, Robert, James Martland, and Ann Stafford. 2006. *Early Numeracy: Assessments for Teaching and Intervention* (2nd edition). London: Paul Chapman Publishing.

Suggested Further Readings

Fosnot, Catherine Twomey, and Maarten Dolk. 2001. *Young Mathematicians at Work: Constructing Number Sense, Addition, and Subtraction.* Portsmouth, NH: Heinemann.

———. 2001. *Young Mathematicians at Work: Constructing Multiplication and Division.* Portsmouth, NH: Heinemann.

———. 2002. *Young Mathematicians at Work: Constructing Fractions, Decimals, and Percents.* Portsmouth, NH: Heinemann.

Murray, Miki, with Jenny Jorgensen. 2007. *The Differentiated Math Curriculum.* Portsmouth, NH: Heinemann.

Wright, Robert, Jim Martland, Ann Stafford, and Garry Stanger. 2002. *Teaching Number: Advancing Children's Skills and Strategies*. London: Paul Chapman Publishing.

Wright, Robert, Garry Stanger, Ann Stafford, and James Martland. 2006. *Teaching Number in the Classroom with 4–8 Year-Olds*. London: Paul Chapman Publishing.

Mathematics Resources on the Internet

The National Council of Teachers of Mathematics is the premier source of math education materials for teachers in grades K–12. Note their *Illuminations*.
www.nctm.org

Excellent performance assessments and open-ended problems by grade level with specific rubrics can be found at
www.exemplars.com and http://balancedassessment.concord.org

The CSMC conducts scholarly inquiry and professional development on issues concerning the K–12 mathematics curriculum.
www.mathcurriculumcenter.org

Of the hundreds of websites for supplementary mathematics materials, a short list of the very best would include:

Cynthia Lanius' Math Projects
http://math.rice.edu/~lanius/Lessons/

Ask Dr. Math and the Math Forum
http://mathforum.org/dr.math/ and http://mathforum.org

Aunty Math
www.dupagechildrensmuseum.org/aunty/index.html

The Shodor Educational Foundation
www.shodor.org

Mega Math
www.ccs3.lanl.gov/mega-math/

National Library of Virtual Manipulatives
http://matti.usu.edu/nlvm/nav/vlibrary.html

Recommendations on Teaching Mathematics

▲ INCREASE	▼ DECREASE
Problem Solving • Word problems with a variety of structures and solution paths • Open-ended problems and extended problem-solving projects • Investigating and formulating questions from problem situations	**Problem Solving** • Use of cue words to determine operation to be used • Practicing routine, one-step problems
Creating Representations • Creating one's own representations that make sense • Creating multiple representations of the same problem or situation • Using representations to make the abstract ideas more concrete • Using representations to build understanding of concepts through reflection • Sharing representations to communicate ideas	**Creating Representations** • Copying conventional representations without understanding • Reliance on a few representations • Premature introduction of highly abstract representations • Forms of representations as an end product or goal
Communicating Math Ideas • Discussing mathematics • Reading mathematics • Writing mathematics	**Communicating Math Ideas** • Doing fill-in-the-blank worksheets • Answering questions that need only yes or no or numerical responses
Reasoning and Proof • Justifying answers and solution processes • Reasoning inductively and deductively	**Reasoning and Proof** • Relying on authorities (teacher, answer key)
Making Connections • Connecting mathematics to other subjects and to the real world • Connecting topics within mathematics	**Making Connections** • Learning isolated topics • Developing skills out of context
Numbers/Operations/Computation • Developing number and operation sense • Understanding the meaning of key concepts • Using calculators for complex calculations	**Numbers/Operations/Computation** • Early use of symbolic notation • Memorizing rules and procedures without understanding • Complex and tedious paper-and-pencil computations
Geometry/Measurement • Using geometry in problem solving • Developing spatial sense using objects • Measuring and exploring the concepts related to units of measure	**Geometry/Measurement** • Memorizing facts and formulas • Memorizing equivalencies between units of measure
Statistics/Probability • Collecting and organizing data • Using statistical methods to describe, analyze, evaluate, and make decisions	**Statistics/Probability** • Memorizing formulas
Algebra • Recognizing and describing patterns • Identifying and using functional relationships • Developing and using tables, graphs, and rules to describe situations • Using variables to express relationships	**Algebra** • Manipulating symbols • Memorizing procedures
Assessment • Making assessment an integral part of teaching • Assessing a broad range of mathematical tasks • Using multiple assessment formats, including written, oral, and demonstration	**Assessment** • Using assessment only to assign grades • Focusing on a large number of isolated skills • Using only written tests

Special Education

Does Best Practice teaching also "work" for students with special needs, with identified learning problems, or with individualized educational plans? Absolutely. In fact, Best Practice teaching is not a *problem* for kids with special needs—it is a very important part of the *solution.* The traditional model of sitting thirty students in rows and then "teaching to the middle of the class" (which usually means *talking*) never worked very well for anyone—but it especially shortchanged kids with learning issues. Best Practice classrooms, on the other hand, are highly decentralized; they emphasize active, experiential learning and offer students real choices and responsibilities. Their fluid structure opens many more pathways for kids who think differently, who need extra support, or who operate on different timetables.

In true Best Practice classrooms, we don't need (or want) to label, track, or level *anyone.* Instead, teachers provide individually appropriate work, materials, and choices for *everyone.* In a workshop environment (see Chapter 2), teachers address every child's needs by creating a variety of temporary student groups, holding individual conferences, and using assessment tools sensitive to different learning styles. Contrary to the old "sit 'n' git" model, sophisticated and adjustable Best Practice classrooms allow true individualization to happen. This climate welcomes a much wider range of learning styles, personality types, and work habits; kids can try multiple entry points into subject matter; and there are many ways for young people to show what they know. Further, the classroom workshop provides a natural setting for "push-in" special educators to work seamlessly with identified kids—as well as provide help for other students along the way.

We three authors have raised some children with "special needs" ourselves, and we feel pretty passionate on this subject. We've learned much from our colleague Patrick Schwarz, chairman of the Department of Diversity in Learning and Development at National-Louis University in Chicago. In his work, Schwarz is developing a new paradigm of special education called "possibility studies" (see *From Disability to Possibility: The Power of Inclusive Classrooms,* 2006). This approach begins with a quite different set of assumptions and baseline procedures about students with "disabilities."

Assumptions

▶ Each of us has, or during our lifespan will develop, a "disability" (e.g., old age).

▶ Differences are normal.

▶ Diversity is an asset; we learn more from people who are different from us.

▶ Every classroom is diverse.

- ► All teachers are special educators.
- ► School structures and procedures cause some "disabilities" (e.g., rules requiring absolute silence or stillness).

Practices

- ► The only acceptable label is a student's name.
- ► We should "normalize difference" by incorporating students into classroom life instead of sending them away.
- ► Kids should not have to "earn" their way into a regular education classroom; instead, it should be the home of all students, whenever possible.
- ► All kids can meet the same educational standards, but not in the same way or at the same time.
- ► Classrooms should support effort-based learning.
- ► Community building is key; successful learning requires strong relationships.
- ► Caring is OK; pity is not.
- ► All students deserve the dignity of taking risks and doing challenging work.
- ► No child should ever be moved out of the regular classroom unless there is a written plan to bring her back in.
- ► Medication should be the last, not the first, resort.

While our book is not expressly aimed at special educators, Best Practice teaching is deeply harmonious with these progressive ideas about working with students with special needs. When you set up a decentralized classroom with high individualization, plenty of hands-on activity, genuine choices for students, and a strongly supportive social climate, then a much broader range of learners can not only feel at home, but thrive and excel.

Chapter 6

Best Practice *in*

Science

Brad Buhrow, a second-grade teacher at Columbine Elementary School in Boulder, Colorado, starts his kids off thinking like entomologists, scientists who study insects in the following activity.

Brad explains. Studying bugs and insects any time of year is exciting for kids as well as the many specialists who study them as their lifelong passion. My team and I decided a great time would be late spring, so our second graders could walk outside and scoot up close to see and hear the insects. We wanted the kids to embrace a culture of scientific thinking by doing the real work of a scientist. To begin, we framed our unit around essential questions related to insects.

What is an insect? How do insects affect people? Are insects dangerous? Why do people study insects? The kids and I wrote these questions big and posted them on the wall to help us remember them along our journey and, if possible, answer them. To ascertain the kids' background knowledge, I had them talk, draw, and write their thinking about these questions on Post-its. We then posted their thinking on an anchor chart titled "What We Think We Know About Insects."

Earlier in the year I gathered picture books so we could learn specifically about scientists and what scientists do. The texts I gathered were all written from a kid's perspective and offered us a glimpse into the lives of renowned specialists. As we read, we focused on two big questions: What is a scientist? Why become a scientist? We read *The Boy Who Drew Birds: A Story of John James Audubon*; *Snowflake Bentley*, about William, who became a snowflake specialist; *Summer Birds: The Butterflies of Mary Merian*, a story about a girl who contests the theory of spontaneous generation by observing the life cycle of butterflies and moths; and *Rare Treasure: Mary Anning and Her Remarkable Discoveries*, about Mary's lifelong study of fossils.

These are all picture books that document the curiosity these scientists felt when they were young, along with the scientific methods they used. We learned what these young scientists did as they studied their passions. We learned about how they made observations, asked questions, planned and completed investigations, and gathered information with drawings, photographs, notes, and artifacts. We also learned that they taught others with presentations and published work. Our goal was to do the same with our study of insects (Heisey and Kucan 2010).

Online sources provide a wide choice of insects that can be ordered for observation. We ordered butterfly larvae to observe their life cycle up close, take notes, draw, and talk about it. Each morning the kids rushed to check how their larvae were changing. The second graders huddled up close to the butterfly net and, in keeping with the spirit of scientific observation, had their small notebooks in hand, drawing, sketching, and writing to record what they noticed (see Figure 6.1). As the kids talked, I listened in, wrote any content-specific vocabulary that came up on Post-its, and stuck them on the butterfly net. This helped them use new vocabulary in their notes. Later the kids peeled the content words off the net and placed them on a chart. I read and commented on the kids' observations—when I came across a spelling or conceptual approximation, I drew a line over the word and wrote the standard spelling above, like this.

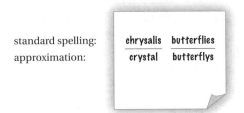

In the spirit of inquiry I took notice of kids' questions and misconceptions and later attempted to guide them to answers and conceptual understandings with other texts—or by talking to a real specialist!

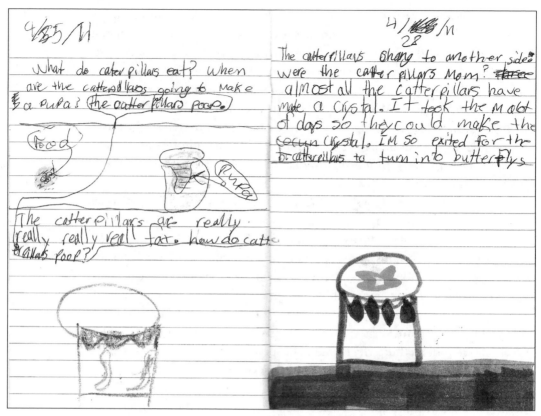

Figure 6.1
A science notebook (Courtesy of Brad Buhrow)

▶ *I Wonder*

Listening in on kids' questions guides us and leads our investigations in directions that are sometimes unpredictable. During our butterfly observation one student, Lucia, developed a great passion for ladybugs. At home Lucia wrote down everything she was wondering about them. Her questions eventually led her to investigate and understand big concepts about our world.

I wonder if ladybugs have antennas to hear?

I wonder if ladybugs have a brain?

I wonder why ladybugs have spots?

I wonder do ladybugs have ears and a nose?

I wonder how ladybugs can eat?

I wonder . . . do ladybugs dance?

I wonder why they have 6 legs?

I wonder why ladybugs have 2 antennae?

I wonder do ladybugs fight?

I wonder . . . do ladybugs have a mouth?

I wonder why they hide their wings?	I wonder where do they live in Winter?
I wonder what they eat in Summer and Winter?	I wonder why ladybugs come in Summer?
I wonder . . . do ladybugs play?	I wonder why ladybugs protect their wings?
I wonder if ladybugs are poisonous?	

Kids' questions help us understand the depth of their knowledge base about a topic or issue. Lucia's questions related to concepts of migration, adaptation, survival, and anatomy that we would explore in more depth.

▶ Preview

Lucia's eagerness and curiosity led me to introduce a thinking routine, collaborative annotations (Harvey and Goudvis 2007), which gets kids active by viewing images, reading, talking, sketching, and writing with the goal of determining importance. I began this thinking routine by finding some insects in the news, and there always seem to be plenty! From nytimes.com, "*The South Endures the Buzz of the Latest Cicada Year.*" An npr.com headline: "*Study: Honeybees Might Have Feelings, Too.*" The one I chose was "*Where to Find the World's Most Wicked Bugs,*" containing a recent interview with the science writer Amy Stewart, along with transcripts and vibrant insect images. After firing up our LCD projector and computer, we opened up the website to view insect images from the article, up close and big. Visuals are priceless to grab kids' attention and with our goal of learning content-specific information, viewing is a must! When I clicked on the image of an Asian giant hornet, the kids immediately reacted with *Whoa! Wow! What is that? That's scary looking! Is that its head?* To get everyone involved, I left the images on the screen so we could turn and talk about them.

▶ Turn and Talk

What is that? What do you see? We first practiced by using language frames. We post these frames on large chart paper so the kids can reference them when they turn and talk. I say, "Let's quickly practice what turning and talking looks and sounds like." We turn our bodies to face each other, sitting close enough to hear easily. Usually we are on the rug so it's easy for us to move around.

Student 1: Would you like go first?

Student 2: Yes, thank you.

Student 1:   What do you see?

Student 2:   I see ____.

Student 1:   Say more. What else do you see?

Student 2:   I also see ____.

Student 2:   What do you see ____?

Student 1:   I see ____.

Student 2:   Say more about that.

Student 1:   I think ____.

This was a group of culturally and linguistically diverse second graders whose heritage languages included Hindi, Nepalese, Spanish, and English. "Let's all try this now. Find someone next to you," I announced. To use our other languages as a bridge to understanding, I reminded them, "Remember, you can talk in Spanish, Hindi, and Nepalese too."

As soon as I said turn and talk, the room erupted with the beautiful sound of language!

With this kind of metascript, the kids quickly internalize how to initiate and extend a conversation about a topic. I know it's working when the room is full of kids talking. I listen in. If the kids go silent, I nudge kids to say more, or participate in their discussions. "You can ask your partner some of these questions here," I say, pointing to the language frames.

So as the kids were talking, I quickly jotted down their comments and questions to gauge their interests and background knowledge. I then clicked through the online images, stopping on each one to let the kids turn and talk. Compelling images, models, and real-life objects top my list of how to get kids excited and engaged.

▶ Engage

After a few minutes we came back as a group so we could annotate together. I'd made a big printout of the online article. I held up our iPad to help kids remember the term *online*. The kids gathered up close to the article while sitting on the carpet. The print was large enough for them to see and read with me. In my hand I held a few brightly colored markers for writing on the text. Alongside the article I had a printout of our sources, so, I pointed out, "we know where our information is coming from." I read our goals, which I had written on a large sheet of paper.

"Let's think about some codes to put with our thinking," I said. The kids quickly chimed in and we decided to use these codes:

T = Think (brown)

? = I wonder (green)

L = Learned (orange)

! = Wow (red)

I explained, "I'm going to start with the title." I pointed to the title and then to the photograph of the Japanese hornet I had placed below it. The image was posted in color to bring it to life.

Where to Find the World's Most Wicked Bugs

"What an attention-grabbing title! I for sure want to read more. I'm going to quickly write what I think this is about." The kids naturally started talking, either with a friend or with me. I overheard, "I think it's about different kinds of insects!" and "I think that it's about bugs people are afraid of or are poisonous!" At this point everyone started chiming in. When this kind of instructional conversation happens, I try to guide the kids to look and talk to one another rather than to me. This way the conversation involves everyone rather than just the adult and the student.

I grabbed the brown marker and talked out loud as I wrote on the chart paper, "We think it's about different kinds of insects" and "We think this is about bugs people are afraid of or are poisonous!" I drew an arrow connecting these statements to the title and wrote T with a circle around it for our code. "Let's start reading and see if what we inferred is true." As I began reading the first sentence, some kids chose to read with me.

Japan is home to the world's largest and most painful hornet.

"I learned something." I grabbed an orange marker. I wrote, "Japan is home to the largest hornet" and coded it L for *I learned,* but before I finished the kids were interrupting. "What is a hornet? How big is it? What do they eat?" I was handed the markers and chose the green to write the questions I overheard.

I connected the questions with arrows and mentioned, "Look what we're doing. We are creating a line of questioning, that's what scientists do!" We kept reading, stopping to talk, then to write and code what we were thinking. As we kept reading, we came across words like *neurotoxin* and *entomologist.* I grabbed the brown marker, drew a line to the word, and wrote what I thought the word meant, modeling the use of my background knowledge to help me infer the meaning. I said out loud, "I know toxin is bad for you. Have you heard of poison?" A few kids said yes. So I wrote, "I think it's poisonous."

I continued to read, then stopped at the word *entomologist*. Thinking aloud, I said, "What does that mean?" I seized the moment to bring attention to the morphology of the word. "I know that *-ologist*, like biologist, geologist, means a person who studies something. So I think an entomologist is someone who studies insects. I'm going to write that." I did and drew an arrow connecting my thinking to the word in the article. Peeling off a Post-it note, I wrote the *-ologist* words to create a content-specific mini-word wall. At this point the kids were extremely eager to investigate some other insects.

At home that night I created some simple leveled reading materials for the kids to read and annotate the next day. Some were compelling close-up photographs with a simple paragraph that I had written, and others had more complex and longer text I'd grabbed off the web. The kids could choose which piece they wanted to work with. On this day I let the kids self-select their groups. I placed the texts on large posters so they could make their writing and drawing big. I also gave each group a sheet of poster board to place beneath their text so they had what I called a giant clipboard. Once in their groups with a box of new colorful markers, the kids began reading together.

Some groups began by making up their own codes; others used the same ones I had with the whole group. Kids also wrote from language frames we have posted around the room on small charts: "I learned _____. I wonder _____? I think _____. Amazing _____! I never knew _____!" As the kids worked I helped them with the reading, modeling to stop and write and draw when they had a reaction. The kids responded and wrote their new learning with things like, "Yuck!! It stings brains." They also wrote questions with inferential answers—for example, when they came across the new term *parasite*, they wrote, "What's a parasite? I think it sucks blood!" See Figure 6.2.

As I was sitting and participating with one group of kids who were intrigued with their learning, Tara exclaimed, "When can we share this because it's so amazing!" After asking her to say more, she explained that she wanted to share their thinking with the rest of the class and teach them what they had learned. As the other groups agreed, it was clear the sentiments were the same—all wanted to take their thinking public!

▶ *Students Sharing and Teaching*

Later that day and the next morning, I scheduled time for groups to first review, then share what they had learned, and to offer a synthesis of their learning with their posters. The kids took their roles of facilitator seriously and had fun, too.

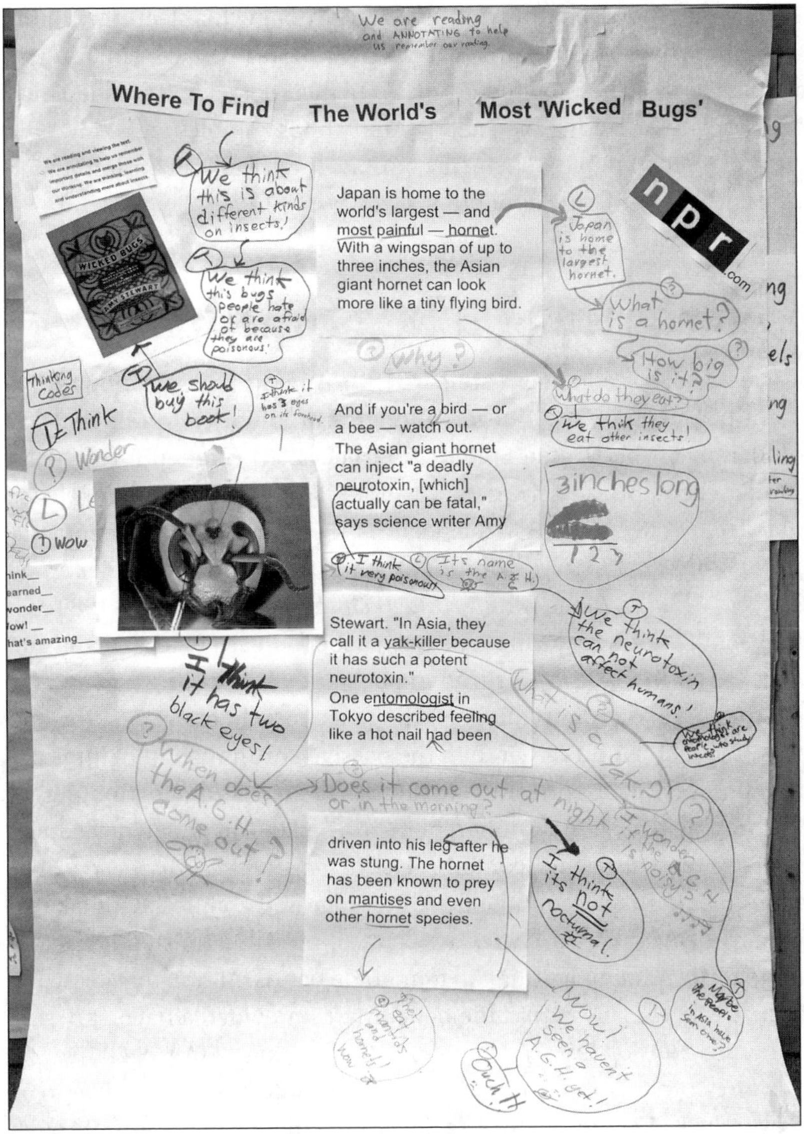

Figure 6.2.
*Wicked Bugs chart
(Photograph courtesy
of Brad Buhrow)*

Each group taped their poster on the easel and with pointing sticks in hand, summarized what they had read and viewed, along the way discussing and explaining their writing and drawings. Rather than wave our hands in the air, Alma instructed us to use our thumbs as a signal for having something to say.

To demonstrate how their thinking changed after reading, each group used the language frame, "I used to think _____, but now I know _____." As the first group presented, they also, on their own, decided to stop and have the class turn and talk about what they were thinking so far. They knew that lecturing to the group was boring. They also knew that getting their peers involved with talk was fun. To my surprise, they pointed to the bottom of their poster and finished their presentation by singing a song they had written about zombie bugs! Now who would have predicted that! We went on to continue the collaborative annotation routine with other current articles about insects.

A LOOK AT THE SCIENCE STANDARDS

In 1986, the year Halley's comet last appeared, the American Association for the Advancement of Science (AAAS) began a long-term initiative to reform K–12 science education in the United States. In Project 2061, named for the year Halley's comet will reappear, scientists set out to identify the basic knowledge and skills needed by U.S. students in the sciences, mathematics, and technology. Their landmark document, *Science for All Americans: A Project 2061 Report on Literacy Goals in Science, Mathematics, and Technology,* came out in 1989 and signaled that significant transformations were needed in science curricula and teaching. *Science for All Americans* set an important tone in calling for students to experience science as an intriguing, exciting, active search for meaning and understanding of their world rather than the passive accumulation of information from lectures or the memorization of unconnected facts and definitions.

The vision of science literacy inherent in Project 2061 included developing a comprehensive map of science content. *Science for All Americans* gave teachers and schools a narrative account of the knowledge and abilities that make up science literacy. *Benchmarks for Science Literacy* (AAAS 1993) listed ideas and skills as the goals for student learning in four grade bands. Although lacking the vitality of *Science for All Americans,* the benchmarks provided a necessary step in developing the *Atlas of Science Literacy, Volumes 1 and 2* (AAAS 2007). The *Atlas* took the benchmarks and wove a rich tapestry of interconnected ideas to be developed over the K–12 grades. The *Atlas* illustrated these connections through nearly a hundred "strand maps," graphical representations of the development of students' understandings of both science concepts and scientific thinking.

The National Research Council (NRC), in collaboration with the National Science Teachers Association (NSTA) and AAAS, created the *National Science Education Standards* (1996), a far-reaching document outlining standards in four areas of science education: teaching, professional development of teachers, assessment, and science content knowledge. This document amplified the vibrant portrayal of teaching and learning begun in *Science for All Americans.*

These new standards made it clear that the content of science should no longer be studying disciplines (physical, life, earth, and space sciences) simply for their own sake. Rather, our concern must be for learning these disciplines via a few fundamental, unifying science concepts in the context of inquiry, technology, personal and social perspectives, and the history and nature of science.

Inquiry and the National Science Education Standards: A Guide for Teaching and Learning (NRC 2000) drew heavily upon Bransford, Brown, and Cocking's (2000) cognitive science research to support its recommended practices. *Inquiry* presented a description of what teachers should do in their classrooms to help students understand science concepts through the process of inquiry.

Several influential reports by the NRC emerged since 2000: *How Students Learn History, Mathematics, and Science* (NRC 2005); *America's Lab Report: Investigations in High School Science* (NRC 2006); *Taking Science to School: Learning and Teaching Science K–8* (NRC 2007); *Ready, Set, Science: Putting Research to Work in K–8 Science Classrooms* (NRC 2008); and *Surrounded by Science: Learning Science in Informal Environments* (NRC 2009). These reports led scientists and science educators to begin to reconceive K–12 science standards. Supported by the Carnegie Foundation, NRC's Board on Science Education appointed a committee to create a "framework" to guide those who would develop the science standards for the "next generation." The framework was drafted and available for review in 2010. After some significant changes, the final version was published in July 2011. The actual standards will be written by Achieve, a private educational firm, again supported by Carnegie.

Adding engineering. The framework (NRC 2011) is a remarkable document, different in several ways from, yet building on, the work of the AAAS's benchmarks and NRC's prior standards. Perhaps the most prominent difference is the incorporation of engineering education into the science framework. This goes along with the emergence of the STEM approach: signifying the importance of science, technology, engineering, and mathematics as vital disciplines. The NRC created a committee to develop a set of core concepts for engineering education K–12 that might be used (NAE and NRC 2009). The committee wrote, "Engineering is a discipline that uses scientific principles to design and build useful tools and technologies, and to respond to real-world challenges and design opportunities." The NRC commissioned another panel of experts to determine whether separate standards should be developed for engineering education K–12. The experts said no, largely because the United States did not have a sufficient number of teachers capable of teaching engineering concepts. Instead, they recommended "mapping" engineering concepts onto a new set of science standards.

Our concern must be for learning these disciplines via a few fundamental, unifying science concepts.

Therefore, the framework addresses the development of goals for K–12 science and engineering education.

The framework is organized into three dimensions, none of which should come as a surprise to those following the work of the AAAS and NRC. They are:

1. Practices—used by scientists as they build models and theories about the world and by engineers as they design and build systems. Also, the term *practices* was used to "better specify what is meant by inquiry in science and the range of cognitive, social, and physical practices it requires" (NRC 2011, 2–5).

2. Cross-cutting elements—major ideas that have application across all four science domains: the physical sciences, the life sciences, the earth and space sciences, and engineering and technology.

3. Disciplinary ideas in those four domains—science education K–12 should not attempt to teach all the facts, but rather prepare students with enough core knowledge to develop their ability to interpret claims and evidence. Students need knowledge of central concepts so they can fit new information into a well-structured set of understandings.

The framework emphasizes the importance of students "doing science" in Dimension 1, science and engineering practices. It strongly urges educators not to create a dichotomy, separating content and process, or knowledge and skills, so prevalent in science education. Rather, we are urged to instill in students the conception of "science as both a body of knowledge and an evidence-based, model-building enterprise that continually extends, refines, and revises knowledge" (NRC 2008, 17). Students must engage in these practices, not merely hear about them secondhand, in order to fully appreciate "the wide range of approaches used to investigate, model, and explain the world" (NRC 2011, 3-1).

The framework lists eight practices in which students should be appropriately immersed in grades K–12 and explores why are they central to science and engineering (NRC 2011, 3-5, 3-6):

---

1. Asking questions (science) and defining problems (engineering).
2. Developing and using models.
3. Planning and carrying out investigations.
4. Analyzing and interpreting data.
5. Using mathematics, information and computer technology, and computational thinking.
6. Constructing explanations (for science) and designing solutions (for engineering).
7. Engaging in argument for evidence.
8. Obtaining, evaluating, and communicating information.

It is important to note that these eight practices are broader than skills, and are not a linear sequence of steps. They are done iteratively and in combination. They can also be enacted in the earliest grades, as we saw in Brad Buhrow's classroom, at the start of this chapter. Later in the framework, there is a discussion of four strands of scientific proficiency that shows how the eight practices fit together in a coherent fashion (see NRC 2011, Chapter 10). Although the framework stops short of prescribing teaching methods, the four strands are based on a synthesis of research on science learning, examined in detail in NRC 2007 and NRC 2008. These strands are (NRC 2011, 10-7):

1. Knowing, using, and interpreting scientific explanations of the natural world.
2. Generating and evaluating scientific evidence and explanations.
3. Understanding the nature and development of scientific knowledge.
4. Participating productively in scientific practices and discourse.

We elaborate these ideas in the next section on the qualities of best practice in teaching science.

Dimension 2, on cross-cutting scientific concepts, in fact addresses the unifying concepts and processes of the prior *National Science Education Standards* (NRC 1996) and the common themes of the AAAS benchmarks (AAAS 1993):

▶ Patterns.
▶ Cause and effect: mechanism and explanation.
▶ Scale, proportion, and quantity.
▶ Systems and system models.
▶ Energy and matter: flows, cycles and conservation.
▶ Structure and function.
▶ Stability and change.

These concepts bridge disciplinary borders, have great explanatory power in both science and engineering, and provide students with "an organizational framework for connecting knowledge from the various disciplines into a coherent and scientifically based view of the world" (NRC 2011, 4-1).

Many scientists and science educators have argued for decades that the explosion of scientific knowledge has been so rapid that teaching facts is an outmoded approach. So Dimension 3 calls for focusing on a small number of "core ideas" in each scientific domain. A core idea for K–12 science instruction should (NRC 2011, 2-6):

• Have broad importance across multiple science or engineering disciplines or be a key organizing principle of a single discipline.
• Provide a key tool for understanding or investigating more complex ideas and solving problems.

- Relate to the interests and life experiences of students or be connected to societal or personal concerns that require scientific or technological knowledge.

- Be teachable and learnable over multiple grades at increasing levels of depth and sophistication. That is, the idea can be made accessible to younger students but is broad enough to sustain continued investigation over years.

The framework uses these criteria to identify a small number of core ideas from each of the four disciplines (NRC 2011, ES-3):

Physical Sciences

    PS 1. Matter and its interactions

    PS 2. Motion and stability; Forces and interactions

    PS 3. Energy

    PS 4. Waves and their applications in technologies for information transfer

Life Sciences

    LS 1. From molecules to organisms: Structures and processes

    LS 2. Ecosystems: Interactions, energy, and dynamics

    LS 3. Heredity: Inheritance and variations of traits

    LS 4. Biological evolution: Unity and diversity

Earth and Space Sciences

    ESS 1. Earth's place in the universe

    ESS 2. Earth's systems

    ESS 3. Earth and human activity

Engineering, Technology, and the Applications of Science

    ETS 1. Engineering design

    ETS 2. Links among engineering, technology, science, and society

---

To assist in the development of the new science standards, the framework includes guiding questions for each core idea. Then there are more focused ideas under each core idea with their own guiding questions. Finally, for each focused idea, there are grade band endpoints that explain the knowledge and understanding expected by the end of grades 2, 5, 8, and 12.

Another major difference in the new standards proposed by the framework is that they follow the logic of *learning progressions* for practices, concepts, and ideas. One can see this approach emerging from the strand maps of the *Atlas*. Progressions would begin using the intuitive ideas of children and build increasingly sophisticated understandings in each grade. The framework includes several examples of learning progressions to guide the developers of the new science standards. The qualities for Best Practice science instruction that follow can enable teachers to promote the kind of learning that this new standards effort has defined for us.

Qualities of Best Practice in Teaching Science

Build on students' innate curiosity about the natural forces of the world. Young children are in a state of perpetual inquisitiveness. They ask anyone who will listen a dazzling array of questions. Why is the sky blue? Where do the squirrels go at night? How did the snow get up in the sky? They try to make sense of their world, to *construct* for themselves their own explanations of what they observe and experience. Recall Brad Buhrow's class and that curious second grader's long list of "I wonder" questions about ladybugs.

In science, with its countless amazing phenomena, you can harness this innate curiosity of children and encourage a passion for exploring mysteries. The extent to which students experience the awe and wonder of confronting natural phenomena determines their future willingness to seek out those moments of profound insight into life's mysteries. When you exude a passion for knowing why and invite students to share the power and beauty of scientific understanding, you can nourish the wonder already present in their minds.

The extent students experience the awe of confronting natural phenomena determines their future willingness to seek out moments of insight into life's mysteries.

Yes, but . . . *don't students vary in their aptitude and interest in science?*

Not all will choose to become scientists, but teachers should foster in *all* students the awareness of science as a dynamic, creative interplay of questions and evidence, data and ideas, predictions and explanations. We must enable all students to experience the exhilaration of the search for answers and the satisfaction of putting together the pieces of a great puzzle. We have seen that the excitement of these experiences will sustain them through the hard work of sifting through mounds of information, trying to make sense of it. If they have never experienced the power and joy of playing scientist, they have no way of knowing that the time spent in tedium is worth it. And as citizens they will need a good understanding of scientific evidence when evaluating challenges in our natural world and the policies that respond to them. When taught well, science has enormous power to attract and motivate.

Do more than merely cover topics; help students immerse themselves in doing science. There is a broad consensus about how people learn and develop true understanding of concepts. Research from child development and cognitive psychology strongly supports the teaching practices advocated by the science and engineering framework. Conversely, direct instruction dominated by science lectures, front-of-the-class demonstrations, and rote memorization of isolated facts, definitions, or explanations does not build deep or enduring conceptual understanding. But what does it mean to immerse oneself in doing science? As we've pointed out, the framework explains this through a description of four strands of proficiency (NRC 2011, 10-7), which in turn draws upon NRC 2007 and NRC 2008. So again, these strands involve the following processes (NRC 2011, 10-7):

---

1. Knowing, using, and interpreting scientific explanations of the natural world.
2. Generating and evaluating scientific evidence and explanations.
3. Understanding the nature and development of scientific knowledge.
4. Participating productively in scientific practices and discourse.

These represent a broad sense of what scientists do and what students need to know and do. They clarify what we mean by *inquiry*. Next, we elaborate on these four strands, addressing them separately, while acknowledging that they are inextricably woven together.

Enable students to know, use, and interpret scientific explanations of the natural world. Scientific explanations include facts, concepts, principles, laws, theories, and models of science. This knowledge must be organized around core ideas that assist students in the retrieval and use of relevant information. These powerful explanatory core ideas are what will enable students to construct their own explanations of other novel situations, phenomena, or cases that are not exactly like their previous experiences. The information cannot simply be covered in lectures and textbook readings, however. As Brad Buhrow's insect project illustrated, it can be gathered through activity and engaged inquiry.

Enable students to generate and evaluate scientific evidence and explanations. This practice covers a tremendous amount of territory. Science is an evidence-based discipline. Help students develop their knowledge and thinking to:

- build and refine models and explanations (conceptual, computational, and mechanistic)

- design and analyze empirical investigations and observations (asking questions; deciding what to measure; developing and using measurement instruments and tools; collecting data from those measures; structuring, interpreting, and evaluating the data; and using the empirical results to develop and refine arguments)

- construct, defend, and critique arguments with empirical evidence

Unfortunately, students are rarely challenged by a provocative question (e.g., Where do we find the world's most wicked bugs?) and the need for examining evidence; too often, they get just a lecture or a textbook with information, devoid of a spark that might ignite interest. This concern for a scientific question and good evidence is not just for older or more capable students; it is for all students. Obviously, younger students will require more guidance from the teacher. But even at grades K–2, students must learn how to evaluate evidence and determine the quality of the data used to make explanations. They begin this process in their early years and become increasingly sophisticated over time.

Yes, but . . . *aren't scientific explanations very abstract and beyond the developmental level of young children? Why not just teach facts that are concrete and real to the young students and provide the scientific explanations when they are developmentally ready?*

There has been a predominant assumption among science educators that elementary school children must develop their logical reasoning capability "naturally" through maturation and they will go through various "stages" with little intervention from adults. However, there is now quite a body of research that questions the validity of such assumptions. "Virtually all contemporary cognitive developmentalists agree that cognitive development is not as general stage-like or as grand stage-like as Piaget and the rest of the field once thought" (Flavell 1994, 574, as cited in NRC 2007).

Stage-like conceptions of development tend to ignore the powerful support and guidance that knowledgeable adults and peers can provide. Development of conceptual frameworks and core ideas in science do not come from memorizing definitions, but rather from knowledgeable others acting as catalysts and mediators of the students' experiences. As expressed in NRC 2008: "Children are more competent and capable science learners that we once thought. Their capabilities and knowledge are a resource that can and should be assessed and built upon during science instruction" (15).

In the past decade the research on preschoolers' conceptions of science phenomena has exploded, revealing that they cannot be conceived as "blank slates" at all, but rather beings who bring to school a host of intuitive conceptions (and misconceptions) of the simple mechanics of solid objects (permanence and solidity), psychological agents (intentionality, cause and effect), the actions and organization of living things, and the makeup of substances and materials. These are important building blocks for science learning in place as students enter school. See NRC 2007, 53–83, for a full treatment of this research.

Enable students to understand the nature and development of scientific knowledge. Science is a way of knowing. Students need to reflect on all of the things they are doing to generate and evaluate scientific evidence and explanations. Doing science includes much more than experimentation. Students need to understand what it means to create a scientific model, conduct systematic observations, and follow the historical development of the core ideas. They need to realize that there may be multiple and even competing interpretations of the same phenomena (e.g., the wave theory versus the particle theory of light).

Enable students to participate productively in scientific practices and discourse. Thinking about Brad's second graders as a model of a scientific community can give us a flavor of what this practice is all about. Even at their young age, they emulated entomologists in research mode: asking questions, relying on systematic observation, drawing pictures, taking notes, testing their ideas, sharing, discussing, and pondering the meaning of data. These youngsters were practicing the habits of mind that typify good science. If this approach to science teaching continues each year, imagine what these children will be able to do with their knowledge when they are in high school.

The teacher gives more guidance and direction in the early grades and students assume more responsibility for their practices in later grades. In middle and high school, student investigations should be far more flexible than the rigid, lock-step procedures of the familiar lab manual. They should require imagination, inquisitiveness, and inventiveness, especially in creating models, which may be physical but are just as likely to be visual, mathematical, or conceptual.

Even in the elementary grades, we should expect students to formulate and revise scientific explanations and models. Science educators urge us to help students engage in the key practices of modeling, generalizing, and justifying (Carpenter and Romberg 2004). An emphasis on modeling can help teaching be more like the authentic practices of scientists. Modeling with real data, students can use increasingly sophisticated mathematics in describing natural phenomena. See examples of elementary school classes modeling with data in Lehrer and Schauble (2002). Also see the Exemplary Instruction story of Olivia Jones' multi-age middle school class at the end of this chapter.

Integrate engineering and science so that students have experience with the knowledge and practices of both areas. Engineering addresses problems of human adaptation in the environment, while science attempts to answer questions about the natural world. And each, of course, influences the other. Fifteen years ago, the *National Science Education Standards* (1996) urged that we give students opportunities to engage in "technological design" (sometimes called "design science"). The framework now urges that we fully integrate technology and engineering with science.

Design is the approach engineers use to solve problems, such as determining the optimal way to make a device or create a process for a specific purpose, given certain specifications and constraints. The design process is systematic and iterative. Each version of the design is tested and then modified according to specific criteria. Learning this process adds a rich dimension to students' scientific thinking.

Build on students' prior knowledge, while recognizing the different types of conceptual change that may be needed. Recent research has refined our ideas about misconceptions that students have: "What we call misconceptions may be necessary stepping-stones on a path toward more accurate knowledge" (NRC 2008, 44). The easiest form of conceptual change is elaborating on an already existing conceptual structure, extending it with new evidence, knowledge, or experiences. More challenging would be thinking about a preexisting set of concepts in new ways. For example, changing one's conception of "air as nothing" requires changing thinking about both air and matter. A third very challenging type of conceptual change is achieving a deeper level of understanding or explanation of some phenomena. As stated in NRC 2008, "Learners have to break out of the familiar frame and reorganize a body of knowledge, often in ways that draw on unfamiliar ideas" (43). For example, to truly understand the concept of matter, students would have to grapple with atomic-molecular theory, wherein concepts of atoms and molecules are not accessible through their everyday sensory experience. Deep understanding requires knowledge reorganization. This change cannot be accomplished by either teacher telling or simple discovery by the students, since the necessary experiments aren't readily available in classrooms. Researchers have found metacognition to be a key component. Excellent resources for connecting students with information and concepts about a topic like atomic theory are available at websites like MSP2 Middle School Portal (www.msteacher.org). For this topic, for example, students can synthesize new understandings by viewing electron microscope images, learning how an electron microscope works, hearing a materials scientist talk about his work, engaging in activities that show how scientists make inferences about unseeable phenomena, and more.

Students' metacognitive abilities are critical to fundamental conceptual change. By detecting and monitoring incongruities in their existing conceptions, learners alert themselves to potential conceptual problems. Metacognition also can direct productive *reflection* in which students seek possible reasons for the incongruity (e.g., faulty data, outliers, incorrect hypothesis, limited explanatory theory). The teacher selects activities and questions (metacognitive prompts)

"What we call misconceptions may be necessary stepping-stones on a path toward more accurate knowledge"

that "make students aware of their initial ideas and that there may be a conceptual problem that needs to be solved" (NRC 2007, 112). Researchers are now finding that significant conceptual change requires "reflective classroom discourse that is structured around explicit argumentation" (NRC 2007, 117).

Balance individual learning and collaborative group work. Saying that learners construct their own knowledge does not mean they do so alone. Research indicates that learners benefit from opportunities to express their ideas to others, challenge each other's ideas, and, in doing so, reconstruct their own ideas. This kind of discourse and argumentation is often done in small groups initially and then debriefed with the whole class.

Real-world scientists frequently work in groups.

Real-world scientists frequently work in groups, and science educators stress the importance of group work in school. Discussion promotes thinking and problem solving by leading students to compare alternative ideas and solutions. When differences of opinion occur in a group, the students are naturally forced to elaborate their explanations and reasoning, making their ideas more explicit and testing them against opposing arguments. From this process, students think through scientific explanations instead of just memorizing them. They are motivated to seek answers from the text or the teacher because they desire to settle the passionate arguments that develop. As a result, they also remember a lot more of what they've studied.

Help students become increasingly self-directed in their learning. Especially in the classroom inquiry they conduct, teachers should help students become less dependent on them for guidance and increasingly self-reliant during the school year and over many years. Students need to become more metacognitive, more able to monitor their own processes of doing inquiry. They must learn to recognize when they do not understand and to seek more information. They need to realize when they should ask questions, such as, "What evidence would convince me that these explanations are probably true?" Research underscores the value of self-assessment in developing students' understanding of science concepts as well as their abilities to reason and think critically (Bransford, Brown, and Cocking 2000, 140; NRC 2000, 119).

Use meaningful assessment of students' learning in science to promote inquiry. Since assessment influences curriculum, if we don't assess the *doing* of science, our schools won't teach it. Testing in science classrooms often focuses on a particular body of knowledge, rather than the thinking and investigative processes or attitudes a student should acquire. To promote experiential work and thinking skills in science, assessment should stress these as well.

Instead of checking whether students have memorized specific information, assessments need to probe for students' understanding, reasoning, and ability to use knowledge. We need more authentic assessments such as portfolios, interviews, performance tasks, and self-assessment. While it is difficult for formal pencil-and-paper tests to assess attitudes and thinking skills, informal but structured assessment based on teacher monitoring of group investigations can accomplish this purpose. Teachers can use checklists to guide their observations, have students fill out self-evaluation forms, and in brief conferences, ask questions about why individuals or groups are proceeding in a particular way. Even written tests can be designed so that they focus on the process of finding an answer, rather than just the answer itself. Some questions can be designed to have more than one right answer, so as to recognize creative thinking and problem solving.

The Role of Heat Transfer in Understanding Plate Tectonics

OLIVIA JONES

Lincoln Prairie School, Hoffman Estates, Illinois

My middle-level science class, a heterogeneously mixed, multiaged class of students from grades 6, 7, and 8, recently completed a geology unit on plate tectonics. Having an understanding of plate tectonics enables students to understand the occurrence of earthquakes, volcanoes, tsunamis, and mountain-building processes. These happenings are part of daily media reports because such events affect people's lives around the world.

During their studies, students learned about the movement of tectonic plates, which comprise the cracked surface of the lithosphere. According to the theory of plate tectonics, these plates are underneath the surface of the planet and move on top of the asthenosphere. Students read in their text and on the Internet about these parts of the earth, but I wanted them to "experience" these concepts (without the terror of really experiencing natural disasters!). To understand a key attribute of the asthenosphere, that some solids can behave like a fluid, students concocted "gluep," a non-Newtonian fluid.

There are various recipes for creating gluep, but the one that I asked my students to make begins with measuring 10 milliliters of white glue into a small clear plastic cup and then mixing in 10 milliliters of water. Students used a wooden stick to stir the mixture until it had a consistent texture. Next, a 4 percent borax solution must be added (borax is available in grocery stores in the laundry section), and this is the tricky part. Only a few drops can be added at a time while constantly stirring. I had the students work with partners. They followed this process, drop by drop, stirring until the mixture became a semisolid lump. At this point students took the gluep lump out of the cup and kneaded it into a ball. This can be messy, so I provided paper towels at all workstations to help with cleanup. Students didn't mind the mess and did their best to keep things in order—after all, this is a science lab!

Students love gluep no matter how many times they have been exposed to this activity. It certainly is fun, yet each time a student works with the gluep, he or she learns something new. In this case it was to model a portion of the earth's structure.

As the students continued to knead the gluep, they noticed that the substance acted like a solid when pressed or squeezed, snapped or broke like a solid when pulled and stretched quickly, but started to flow around the edges and flatten like a fluid if set down. We discussed how this surprising behavior was similar to the asthenosphere. The solid rock of the asthenosphere is flexible and plastic-like, causing it to flow very slowly. It is this characteristic layer within Earth's mantle that is able to rise and sink due to the exchange of thermal energy from within the Earth. One of the theories to explain what drives the tectonic plates is that convection below Earth's mantle pushes the plates apart.

Thus, the next step for students to understand the movement of the tectonic plates was to learn about the presence of convection currents in Earth's mantle. We needed an experiment that would address the question, how does thermal energy flow in a system? The sequence that I describe here took approximately four days.

I wanted my students to answer these essential questions: How is heat transferred? What causes convection currents? What causes convection currents within Earth's mantle? The intent of the lessons was not to present a thermal energy unit of study but to connect science content that would enrich the understanding of plate tectonics. In planning, I utilized the BSCS 5-E Instructional Model (see www.bscs.org/curriculumdevelopment/features/bscs5es.html). The five phases of learning for this model are engagement, exploration, explanation, elaboration, and evaluation.

The purpose of this series of investigations was for students to understand the movement of tectonic plates within the Earth's mantle.

▶ Engagement

To elicit prior knowledge, I asked the students how various methods of heat transfer occur in everyday living. I administered a formative assessment to discover students' ideas on how thermal energy flows by using a glass of tea to which we added ice cubes. Students sketched their ideas as we discussed what was happening to the temperature of the tea. A common misconception that many students had was that cold moves from the ice to the tea. I asked them to review the particle theory of matter, previously studied. It states that the particles within a substance having the higher temperature have the faster speed.

▶ Exploration

To identify the three methods of heat transfer (convection, radiation, and conduction), the "exploration" hands-on activity involved using a candle and a nail. I emphasized safety guidelines when using an open flame. I reviewed why long hair must be tied back and loose clothing avoided when working with fire. Convection: Working in pairs, the students first put a hand high above the lit candle flame and then lowered it until they felt warm air. Radiation: I asked each student to move a hand to the side of the candle flame and stop when they sensed warmth. Conduction: The third activity involved holding a nail at its head and putting its point in the flame for fifteen seconds. Then they pulled it out from the candle and counted until they sensed warmth. I strongly emphasized that they should leave the nail in the flame for only fifteen seconds.

Each short activity illustrated one of the methods of heat transfer. Through these activities, students obtained a common base of experiences enabling them to compare and contrast the three methods of heat transfer. These three activities may seem simple, but students were amazed at the results. They were surprised at how high the heat energy travels by convection above the candle flame and even a bit disappointed at the closeness needed to sense heat transfer by radiation. I reminded them that radiation is occurring in all directions from the flame, though not easily sensed. We discussed the importance of radiation as a method of heat transfer from the sun. The third activity is the one that surprised students the most. They were surprised that when they initially pulled the nail out of the flame, they felt no warmth. Then they were startled when, still holding the nail, they began to feel heat! They believed that once they removed the nail from the flame, it could not get warm. The metal conducted the heat slowly but inexorably throughout the nail. They thoroughly debriefed these experiences.

▶ Explanation

The explanation phase provided students with the opportunity to summarize their thoughts. Students constructed a three-tab, three-dimensional graphic organizer, called a "Foldable," for their notes and additional material acquired from their text and Internet resources such as definitions and examples. After recording the additional information on their Foldable, students stored it in their interactive science journal. We use this journal for organizing all testable materials and for displaying students' creativity as they illustrate and put down their thoughts.

▶ Elaboration

After defining heat energy and learning to identify, compare, and contrast the three methods of heat transfer, students embarked upon the "elaboration" phase with a guided-inquiry lesson. This was not an open-inquiry lesson because the problem was given to the students. The purpose of the activity was for the students to create a model that would help them connect what they'd learned about the flow of heat energy with their gluep activity to understand the nature of movement within Earth's mantle.

Rather than just march these young learners through a set of steps, I required the class to formulate the procedures themselves for a heat transfer experiment. This would involve two containers of water at different temperatures and a means for transferring heat between them. The students would discover that as the water in one cup cools, the other heats up. But first we needed to establish procedures for the experiment. Writing procedures can be difficult, but it is an important part of understanding scientific practices. I instructed my students to use the "cookbook" method for procedure writing, where every step begins with a verb. Each group decided on its controlled variables—how much water to put in each container, timing intervals, and the length of the activity. Through our discussion, students became aware that while there may be more than one set of steps that can be used to complete the same task, the steps still need to follow some logical order.

Students also constructed their own data tables based on the procedures and the variables that they were investigating. I instructed students that the independent variable is the labeled and completed part of their data table at the start—the time intervals, in this case. The dependent variables—the temperature of the water in each cup—are labeled but left blank, to be filled in as the students observe during the experiment. When students graph their data, the independent variable goes along the x-axis and the dependent variable goes along the y-axis. Based on their data tables, students can prepare their graphs beforehand with everything except the interval and numbers for the dependent variable! Students then hypothesized their expected outcome based on the problem "How does thermal energy flow in a system?" Their guesses varied quite a bit—would the water in the cooler cup heat up? How quickly? Faster at the start? And what did they expect to happen to the water in the hotter cup?

Working in teams of four, they took two calorimeters (Styrofoam cups with thermometers attached inside) and connected them to each other with an aluminum U-bar. This equipment is obtainable through various science supply companies. (The U-bar can also be made with rolls of aluminum foil if you can't afford the aluminum ones.) One calorimeter was partially filled with room-temperature water; the other contained an equal amount of hot water. Students recorded temperature data in each cup every minute for twenty minutes. The data collected was then used to construct a graph, which the students interpreted in order to analyze their results and to form a conclusion.

The equipment we had available to measure temperature was the TI-84 Plus calculator with a Vernier Easy-Link and attached stainless steel temperature probe. Students have prior knowledge and experience reading a regular thermometer temperature scale from their elementary grades, but using the digitized thermometer is actually easier and the smaller changes in temperature are easily detected. Students used the graphing calculator to construct their graphs.

Students then constructed and presented their graphs to the class. They reviewed proper components of a graph along with what they discovered about heat flow. With both their graph and data tables for reference, students practiced discussing and writing their conclusions, appropriately supporting their ideas. Students often associate graphing only with their mathematics studies, so I reminded them that math is the language through which much of science is communicated.

After formulating a conclusion that could be quantitatively supported, each group reviewed its original predictions and stated whether or not the conclusion was supported by the data. Having students write a proper conclusion that refers back to their data is an ongoing skill that is practiced and reviewed throughout the course of the year. We discussed how scientists not only work as team members but also organize and interpret data to communicate their findings to others.

As students discussed their analysis questions, I asked them to identify the occurrence of all three methods of heat transfer, not just conduction, which was the most obvious because students could touch the aluminum bar and feel that it was hot. This kinesthetic reinforcement supported the concept that heat moves, not the cold. I also wanted students to use their graphs to predict what eventually happens to the thermal energy and to come up with a generalization to describe the direction of heat flow in relation to temperatures.

Scientists not only work as team members but also organize and interpret data to communicate their findings to others.

▶ Evaluation

The final step in this inquiry process was for me to demonstrate a model of how heat is transferred within Earth's mantle, applying all that we had learned. This demonstration involved using a Pyrex glass pan with water in it, two Styrofoam blocks floating in the water, and a heat source—a gas burner held underneath the pan. I first asked the students to predict what would happen to the blocks as the water above the heat source heated up. Then, as the students observed the block movement, I asked them to draw an illustration that could represent the asthenosphere and the tectonic plates. In addition, they were to sketch the movement of the water and explain what type of energy transfer was taking place. What they observed, of course, was that by varying the position of the heat source, the blocks would move in different directions.

The first figure (Figure 6.3) illustrates a diverging plate boundary where the plates are moving apart as they are carried upon the asthenosphere. The second figure (Figure 6.4) illustrates a converging plate boundary where a plate moves toward another.

The final step in this science learning process was for each student to write a summary of what they had learned about the theory of plate tectonics. The many steps in this set of experiments obviously took a good deal of class time, and we science teachers are always pressed to cover a lot of material. But these kids had

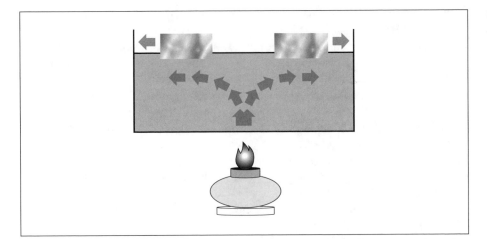

Figure 6.3
Heat transfer experiment

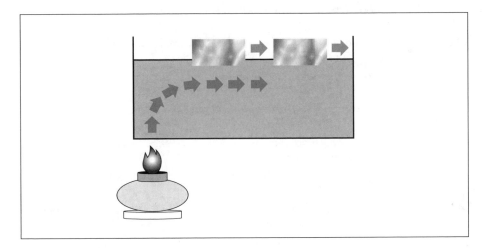

Figure 6.4
Heat transfer experiment

a lot to say about all they had learned, and they realized how valuable it was to understand the powerful forces beneath their feet that could gradually move continents or create mountains, as well as cause the destructive earthquakes and tsunamis they'd all heard about.

Works Cited

American Association for the Advancement of Science. 1989. *Science for All Americans: A Project 2061 Report on Literacy Goals in Science, Mathematics, and Technology.* Washington, DC: AAAS.

———. 1993. *Benchmarks for Science Literacy.* New York: Oxford University Press.

———. 2007. *Atlas of Science Literacy, Volumes 1 and 2.* Washington, DC: AAAS.

Bransford, J., A. Brown, and R. R. Cocking. 2000. *How People Learn: Brain, Mind, Experience, and School* (expanded edition). Washington, DC: National Academies Press.

BSCS—A Science Education Curriculum Study, www.bscs.org/curriculumdevelopment/features/bscs5es.html.

Carpenter, T. P., and T. A. Romberg. 2004. *Powerful Practices in Mathematics and Science.* Madison, WI: National Center for Improving Student Learning and Achievement in Mathematics and Science.

Harvey, Stephanie, and Harvey Daniels. 2009. *Comprehension and Collaboration.* Portsmouth, NH: Heinemann.

Harvey, Stephanie, and Anne Goudvis. 2007. *Strategies That Work.* Portland, ME: Stenhouse.

Heisey, Natalie, and Linda Kucan. 2010. Introducing Science Concepts to Primary Students Through Read Alouds: Interaction and Multiple Texts Make the Difference. *Reading Teacher* 63(8): 666–676.

Lehrer, R., and L. Schauble, eds. 2002. *Investigating Real Data in the Classroom.* New York: Teachers College Press.

National Academy of Engineering and National Research Council. 2009. *Engineering in K–12 Education: Understanding the Status and Improving the Prospects.* Washington, DC: National Academies Press.

National Research Council. 1996. *National Science Education Standards.* Washington, DC: National Academies Press.

———. 2000. *Inquiry and the National Science Education Standards: A Guide for Teaching and Learning.* Washington, DC: National Academies Press.

———. 2005. *How Students Learn History, Mathematics, and Science.* Washington, DC: National Academies Press.

———. 2006. *America's Lab Report: Investigations in High School Science.* Washington, DC: National Academies Press.

———. 2007. *Taking Science to School: Learning and Teaching Science K–8.* Washington, DC: National Academies Press.

———. 2008. *Ready, Set, Science: Putting Research to Work in K–8 Science Classrooms.* Washington, DC: National Academies Press.

———. 2009. *Surrounded by Science: Learning Science in Informal Environments.* Washington, DC: National Academies Press.

———. 2011. *A Framework for K–12 Science Standards: Practices, Crosscutting Concepts, and Core Ideas.* Washington, DC: National Academies Press.

Ohio State University. *MSP2 Middle School Portal.* www.msteacher.org.

Suggested Further Readings

Buhrow, Brad, and Anne Upczak Garcia. 2006. *Ladybugs, Tornadoes and Swirling Galaxies: English Language Learners Discover Their World Through Inquiry.* Portland, ME: Stenhouse.

Hand, Brian, Lori Norton-Meier, Jay Staker, and Jody Bintz. 2009. *Negotiating Science: The Critical Role of Argument in Student Inquiry.* Portsmouth, NH: Heinemann.

Hoffer, Wendy Ward. 2009. *Science as Thinking: The Constants and Variables of Inquiry Teaching.* Portsmouth, NH: Heinemann.

Norton-Meier, Lori, Brian Hand, Lynn Hockenberry, and Kim Wise. 2008. *Questions, Claims, and Evidence: The Important Place of Argument in Children's Science Writing.* Portsmouth, NH: Heinemann.

Worth, Karen, Jeff Winokur, Sally Crissman, and Martha Heller-Winokur with Martha Davis. 2009. *The Essentials of Science and Literacy: A Guide for Teachers.* Portsmouth, NH: Heinemann.

———. 2009. *Science and Literacy, A Natural Fit: A Guide for Professional Development Leaders.* Portsmouth, NH: Heinemann.

Science Resources on the Internet

The website of Project 2061 of the American Association for the Advancement of Science features the Center for Curriculum Materials in Science, professional development workshops, books, and online tools.

www.project2061.org

The Annenberg Foundation has excellent curriculum materials and many videos for students and teachers.

www.learner.org

The Exploratorium Institute for Inquiry provides elementary science educators with excellent experiences with inquiry through workshops, online resources, follow-up opportunities, and networking.

www.exploratorium.edu/IFI/resources/websites.html

Lawrence Hall of Science at the University of California, Berkeley, is probably the premier source of science resources. It offers programs, workshops, and publications.

www.lawrencehallofscience.org/

Massachusetts Institute of Technology includes on its website a section with an incredible amount of information on inventors, inventions, and discoveries.

http://web.mit.edu/invent

National Science Teachers Association offers teachers excellent professional development programs, tons of resources for all grade levels, books, materials, and guides.

www.nsta.org

NOVA is a great resource for videos.

www.pbs.org/wgbh/nova/teachers/ and www.pbs.org/wgbh/nova/sciencenow/

Science NetLinks provides lesson plans and reviewed Internet resources for K–12 science educators.

www.sciencenetlinks.com

Accomplished teachers who are ready to seek national certification can learn about the rigorous one-year process, find out the benefits of a successful review in their own state, and find a support group at the website of the National Board for Professional Teaching Standards.

www.nbpts.org

Recommendations on Teaching Science

▲ INCREASE	▼ DECREASE
ADAPTING THE CURRICULUM • Selecting and adapting curriculum • Curriculum with a variety of components emphasizing active and extended scientific inquiry • Learning disciplines (physical, life, earth sciences) in the context of inquiry, technology, personal and social perspectives, history and nature of science • Curriculum that includes natural phenomena and science-related social issues that students encounter in everyday life • Studying a few fundamental, unifying science concepts • Understanding scientific concepts and developing abilities of inquiry • Integrating all aspects of doing science • Connecting science to other school subjects	**ADAPTING THE CURRICULUM** • Rigidly following curriculum • Curriculum dominated by presentations of scientific knowledge through lecture, text, and demonstration • Studying disciplines (physical, life, earth sciences) for their own sake • Broad coverage of unconnected factual information • Covering many disconnected science topics • Memorizing scientific facts and information • Separating science knowledge and science process • Treating science as a subject isolated from other school subjects
BUILDING UNDERSTANDING • Providing challenging opportunities for all students to learn science • Focusing on student understanding and use of scientific knowledge, ideas, and inquiry processes • Building on students' prior knowledge to foster conceptual change • Sharing responsibility for learning with students • Supporting a classroom community with cooperation, shared responsibility, and respect • Providing opportunities for scientific discussion and debate among students • Understanding and responding to individual student's interests, strengths, experiences, and needs	**BUILDING UNDERSTANDING** • Providing science learning opportunities that favor one group of students • Focusing on student acquisition of information • Providing direct instruction irrespective of prior knowledge • Teacher maintaining responsibility and authority • Supporting competition • Asking for recitation of acquired knowledge • Treating all students alike and responding to the group as a whole

▲ INCREASE	▼ DECREASE
PROMOTING INQUIRY • Implementing inquiry as instructional strategies, abilities, and ideas to be learned • Activities that investigate and analyze science questions over extended periods of time • Emphasizing multiple process skills (manipulation, cognitive, procedural) in context • Using evidence and strategies for developing or revising an explanation • Science as argument and explanation • Communicating science explanations • Student collaborative groups defending conclusions, analyzing and synthesizing data • Doing more investigations in order to develop understanding, ability, values of inquiry, and knowledge of science content • Applying the results of experiments to scientific arguments and explanations • Public communication of student ideas and work to classmates	**PROMOTING INQUIRY** • Implementing inquiry as a set of processes • Activities that demonstrate and verify science content and investigations confined to one class period • Emphasizing individual process skills (e.g., observation or inference) out of context • Getting an answer • Science as exploration without purpose and experiment based on recipes • Providing answers to questions about science content • Individuals and groups of students analyzing and synthesizing data without defending a conclusion • Doing few investigations in order to leave time to cover large amounts of content • Concluding inquiries with the result of the experiment • Private communication of student ideas and conclusions to teacher
ASSESSING SCIENCE LITERACY • Continuously assessing student understanding with students engaged in ongoing assessment of their work • Assessing to learn what students do understand • Assessing what is most highly valued: rich, well-structured knowledge as well as scientific reasoning and conceptual change	**ASSESSING SCIENCE LITERACY** • Testing students for factual information at the end of the unit, chapter, or term • Assessing to learn what students do not know • Assessing what is easily measured: discrete, scientific knowledge

The Arts: Visual Art, Music, Dance, Drama

There's an old puzzle that goes: "What part of the blanket keeps you warm at night?" The correct answer is, "the part that hangs over the side." Get it? Most people immediately assume that the part that keeps you warm is the part that's directly covering you. But what happens if your blanket is just the size of the top of your bed? It slides off, right? And then you're freezing. In other words, it is the "extra" part of the blanket that makes the whole thing work.

If you haven't heard this little parable, that's because it is most frequently told by arts educators, and no one is listening to them these days.

The arts have long led a marginal existence in American schools, but today their role in our children's education is more tenuous than ever. During especially hard times of budget cuts and focus on tests in "core" content areas, art can all but disappear from some schools, treated as an unnecessary frill—just like all that "wasted" blanket hanging over the bed.

As we explain in our section on representing learning, students urgently need opportunities to think about subject matter in a wide variety of modes—and they also need many ways to show what they have learned, later on. The arts provide a grand toolbox of ways for both building knowledge and sharing it. Here are some of the key principles.

Let Kids Do Art

From the earliest preschool years, children have a powerful urge to make art. We don't have to "assign" children to draw with markers, chant jump-rope rhymes, share dramatic monologues, make theatrical faces, or dance. Artistic expression seems to be wired into children's genes. Therefore, the first job of teachers and other adults is to get out of the way and let kids express and experiment. We need to provide tools, materials, equipment, models, examples, coaching, and plenty of time.

Integrate the Arts Across the Curriculum

There are infinite opportunities for weaving artistic thinking and expression into all subject areas. Students who are reading a novel can show their understanding by illustrating critical scenes, acting them out, translating them into movement and dance, or creating background music for them. Ideally, the arts take a central place in broad, integrative projects that teachers and students plan together and that extend over long chunks of time. In every subject, the arts can provide new ways of exploring and expressing ideas about practically anything—the Civil War, triangles, photosynthesis, or To Kill a Mockingbird.

Use the Arts to Advance Thinking

Students should regularly use art as a tool for the exploration of ideas. These informal, tentative, exploratory applications can help kids engage and grapple with ideas in any subject area. For example, teachers often ask students to keep a learning log in which they write notes about their learning. Instead, teachers can have students keep a sketchbook, where they can still jot words—*or* sketch pictures, make diagrams, map ideas, or create unique combinations of words and graphic elements in response to class activities.

Bring Artists into the Classroom

There's something special and different about people who make their livelihoods as musicians, videomakers, dancers, actors, sculptors, artists, poets, web game designers, storytellers, or painters. They can make unique, sometimes magical, connections with young people and provide knowledge, motivation, and inspiration to growing artists. Therefore, children need chances to meet, observe, and work with adult artists in their school. While one-shot performances and traditional residencies are helpful, even better are genuine long-term partnerships between the school and community arts organizations, providing sustained, intensive arts experiences for children, coplanned with the regular teachers and integrated into the school's overall curriculum. This model transforms the artist from a transient celebrity to a long-term consultant and deeply involves the classroom teacher as a coartist as well.

Chapter 7

Best Practice *in*

Social Studies

Debra Henderson's seventh- and eighth-grade social studies classes at Clissold School on Chicago's far South Side love their projects. Having finished one on Chicago's high-profile mayoral race as the election itself ended, they launched into another—on protest movements in the Middle East. Although the historic upheavals in that region were filling the news headlines, Debra knew her kids would have little idea about the countries or the causes for their turmoil. But she also knew that a research project on these dramatic events offered a great opportunity to help students acquire important social studies knowledge, concepts, and skills. They'd explore geography, learn about other cultures, hone investigative skills, and do some good subject-area reading.

Debra organized the kids into inquiry groups (very much like those described in Harvey's and Daniels' *Comprehension and Collaboration*) (2009)each focused on a country of their choice—Algeria, Egypt, Tunisia, Libya, or Tunisia. Students also selected roles within their groups—discussion director, word interpreter, camera specialist, fact finder, FBI agent (i.e., investigator about important people). She provided news summaries, put up chart paper, and handed out sticky notes and laptops from the computer cart. By the late winter date of this project, the kids were completely accustomed to their small-group inquiry process and got right to work. Camera specialists searched on the web for pictures of important political figures as well as geographic features of their country. The FBI agents looked on the web for information about those people. Fact finders catalogued basic data about their countries. Word interpreters checked out definitions and usage of vocabulary found in the news articles—*escalation, defection, besieged, brainwashing, monsoon, corruption*—and entered them into a vocabulary file box and onto the class word wall. Discussion directors read and searched along with the others, and then identified the big, critical questions that the group needed to debate before reaching final conclusions.

The kids were accustomed to small-group inquiry and got right to work.

As kids worked in country-centered teams, Debra rotated around the room, coaching, especially some of the students with special needs she knew might struggle. After time on research, each group added sticky notes about their country onto posters hung along one wall. Then Debra jigsawed everyone, grouping all the students with the same role together to compare their countries. Finally, every student wrote a short summary of all that he or she had learned about a country. Once the summaries were finished and added to their posters, everyone studied the posters to learn about each other's countries in more depth.

Clissold social studies classes are scheduled so each grade-level meets for a double period for five weeks, and then cycles off for five. This provides the extended work time Debra needs for her in-depth projects without detracting from other subjects. A smart strategy, just when we might have doubted there was any way to get more flexibility out of a school schedule.

Debra also feels fortunate to have obtained an endorsement in reading, so she comes to social studies armed with a great repertoire of teaching strategies. She herself had difficulties learning to read as a child but was mentored by a teacher neighbor who, took Debra under her wing. Debra not only introduces reading strategies in her social studies classes but also talks with the students about how they're applying these in other courses. She also earned an administrative certificate—not to become a principal, she says, but to gain a wider perspective on the work of education. It's from teachers like Debra Henderson that we've learned about many of the principles that we'll outline in this chapter—studying topics in depth, having students exercise choice and responsibility, inviting them to think and explore, promoting both individual and cooperative learning, connecting learning to the real world.

What standards do Debra Henderson and her fellow social studies teachers at Clissold School follow? Interestingly, she balances the Illinois state standards with standards and project ideas from the humanities portion of the International Baccalaureate Middle Years program. The humanities materials in this program are actually quite applicable to any middle school classroom, and provide excellent in-depth study projects that would be engaging for any middle school students. They feature interdisciplinary learning, a wide range of resources, and what the program calls "international-mindedness." Fundamental concepts in the program: intercultural awareness, holistic learning, and communication. It's worth keeping these in mind as we survey the various standards for social studies currently in use.

A Look at Social Studies Standards

The history of social studies standards is a checkered one. In 1994 the National Center for History in the Schools published a set of history standards, perhaps the first for this field. It was forward-looking and promoted thinking and active student participation, along with essential factual knowledge. The document was intensely attacked by the far right as "anti-American," however, especially because it dwelt too much, in the critics' view, on the decimation of Native American populations and other dark aspects of American history. The document was actually condemned by the U.S. Senate in 1996 just as a revised edition was being issued, after which it faded from view. Around the same time, the National Council for the Social Studies (NCSS) developed and published *Expectations of Excellence: Curriculum Standards for Social Studies* in 1994 and followed up with *National Standards for Social Studies Teachers* in 1997 (updated in 2007). The NCSS approach was highly conceptual but less controversial, and perhaps just less noticed. It emphasized ten thematic strands:

- Culture
- Time, Continuity, and Change
- People, Places, and Environments
- Individual Development and Identity
- Individuals, Groups, and Institutions
- Power, Authority, and Governance
- Production, Distribution, and Consumption
- Science, Technology, and Society
- Global Connections
- Civic Ideals and Practices

The document outlines four perspectives for approaching these themes: personal, academic, pluralist, and global. Four learning skills are called for: (1) acquiring information and manipulating data; (2) developing and presenting policies, arguments, and stories; (3) constructing new knowledge; and (4) participating in groups. The authors then list principles for teaching and learning intended to make social studies meaningful, integrative, value-based, challenging, and active. Clearly, the NCSS aimed to make social studies engaging for students, central to the development of citizenship, and focused on higher-level thinking.

Thirteen years later these standards have been revised, maintaining the same ten thematic categories and skills, but offering a sharper focus, adding the following curricular elements:

- Purposes
- Questions for exploration
- Knowledge: what learners need to understand
- Processes: what learners will be capable of doing
- Products: how learners demonstrate understanding

At the same time, the NCSS has collaborated on a very different kind of standards project with a whole new twist, working with the Partnership for 21st Century Skills and a number of other education organizations. Founded in 2002 by a group of major communications and computer businesses, this effort has been endorsed by fourteen states, though it's not clear that they've actually incorporated the guidelines into their standards. Along with knowledge in core subjects like English, math, science, and history, the 21st Century Skills focus on "Four Cs:"

- Critical thinking and problem solving
- Communication
- Collaboration
- Creativity and innovation

Also stressed are media and technology skills, which tend to be just barely mentioned in most state and national standards. And compared to the fairly traditional approaches to learning in so many of the state and national standards, these are focused on what leading businesspeople believe are the skills Americans will need to be successful and thoughtful as workers and citizens—skills that are also needed to keep companies globally competitive. Some educators are wary of this business-backed movement, fearing that its main intention is to pawn its own job-training costs off on the public schools. Decide for yourself, but learn more at www.p21.org . All things considered, the 2010 NCSS standards plus some version of 21st Century Skills probably make the best guides available for meaningful social studies teaching and learning to date.

Actually, the Common Core State Standards do include social studies and science in the reading and writing standards, though mainly to emphasize the importance of literacy in the study of these subjects. And now a group of states and professional teachers' organizations have been meeting to begin developing a new set of social studies standards and are working on a conceptual framework for it. In January 2010, NCSS and the Civic Mission of Schools (CMS) convened a meeting of national organizations in civics, economics, geography, and history to discuss working together on common social studies standards. They agreed on a common definition of social studies that includes the individual disciplines and the "literacies" outlined by the Partnership for 21st Century Skills, stating, "The social studies is an interdisciplinary exploration of the social sciences and humanities, including civics, history, economics, and geography in order to develop responsible, informed and engaged citizens and to foster civic, global, historical, geographic, and economic literacy" (*National Council for the Social Studies*, 2010).

In October 2010, a coalition of fifteen states and fifteen professional organizations met to begin exploring the development of common state standards in social studies. These groups convened again in February 2011 to work on a conceptual framework and criteria for the standards. Eighteen states are now involved. There will be more to come, obviously, and so we will all need to watch and see whether this new initiative brings us still better and more thoughtful guidance.

Meanwhile, states have, over the years, developed their own social studies standards, curriculum guidelines, and tests, though all, including the NCSS standards, are thoroughly overshadowed by the national focus on literacy and math—overshadowed despite the assertion in the preambles of many of the documents that citizens' knowledge of history and civic responsibility are essential to a functioning democracy. So now we take a quick look at a few individual states' standards. Perhaps in these examples, you'll recognize some features (or pitfalls) of your own state's approach to social studies.

California. The California standards in social studies consist of three components published by the California Department of Education:

1. a document called *History–Social Science Framework for California Public Schools, Kindergarten Through Grade Twelve* (updated 2001a)

2. *History–Social Science Content Standards* (2001b), which lists the expectations for each grade

3. the social science portions of the California Standards Tests (2009)

The *Framework* is an extremely ambitious document that presents broad principles and outlines coursework for each grade level. It begins with a set of seventeen principles that set very high, laudable aims for content knowledge, development of citizenship, active application of learning, and in-depth thinking. Many sound similar to those provided by the NCSS, though the *Framework* is so sharply centered on the chronological study of history that other social studies areas are pushed to the side. Some of the key principles, briefly (California Department of Education 2001a, 4–8):

- History should be viewed "as a story well told."
- The study of history should be enriched with literature, "both literature *of* the period and literature *about* the period."
- A richer and broader curriculum (than has been customary) is needed for the early grades (K–3).
- Major historical events and periods should be studied "in depth as opposed to superficial skimming of enormous amounts of material."
- A multicultural perspective should be incorporated throughout the social studies curriculum.
- "Ethical understanding and civic virtue" should guide thinking about public affairs.
- Civic and democratic values should be developed "as an integral element of good citizenship."
- Teachers should "present controversial issues honestly and accurately within their historical or contemporary context."
- Critical thinking skills should "be included at every grade level."
- A variety of content-appropriate teaching methods must be supported to "engage students actively in the learning process."
- Students should participate "in school and community service programs and activities."

A noble and thoughtful set of goals. The *Framework* goes on to elaborate these in terms of broad ideas, critical thinking, and students' personal development.

If only California had just stopped right there! The actual standards are composed entirely of lists of historic events, people, and social developments. Sixth grade, for example, must cover prehistoric development, Egypt and Mesopotamia, ancient Hebrews, ancient Greece, ancient India, early Chinese civilization, and ancient Rome. Considering the limited time available during the year, this becomes the very "forced march across many centuries and continents" that the *Framework* specifically warns against.

The sixth-grade curriculum, for example, does meet some larger aims of the *Framework*. It's multicultural. It allows for integrating other social sciences—archaeology, geography, political science, comparative religion. It's open to critical thinking and a variety of teaching methods. But it doesn't address students' active participation in school or community service, or real-world application of democratic values, items that do not appear until high school senior year.

The picture gets still more troubling when we look at the tests (California Department of Education 2009). Social science is not tested until eighth grade, but that test covers material from all three middle school grades. And the questions are almost entirely focused on factual recall. Questions released from the 2003–2008 history–social science tests, for example, ask about the topic of a speech by Horace Greeley, the source through which papermaking was introduced to Europe, and the geographic center of Incan civilization. One sample question: "What was the main contribution of Emperor Shi Haungdi to China?" OK, well-educated adult readers, answer that one without Googling it first. (So, we looked, and he was indeed important—the first ruler to unify China, who in the process started the Great Wall and commissioned the famous Terracotta Warriors for his tomb. But how many competent college grads know this?) Some questions can be answered by logical guessing. But thinking skills, citizenship, exploration of controversial issues as called for in the *Framework*? Gone. Caring "deeply about the quality of life in their community, their nation, and their world"? Not a hint.

So what can a California teacher do to prepare students for such questions? Obviously, memorizing Emperor Shi Haungdi's accomplishments won't work—that question won't reappear on the next year's test. Instead, wide reading and memorable in-depth study projects (like the one we saw in Debra Henderson's eighth-grade class), in the spirit of the *Framework* introduction, will prepare kids to deal with questions intelligently, whatever is thrown at them.

Pennsylvania. This state offers a fascinating alternative. The Pennsylvania Board of Education's "Education Hub" website includes a section called the "standards aligned system" (the URL is a long one, so search for "Pennsylvania social studies standards" to get to the full program). Social studies are divided into four areas—civics, economics, geography, and history—with major subtopics for each. Click on a subtopic to get to a page where you select a grade level and see a series of buttons:

- Clear Standards
- Fair Assessments
- Curriculum Framework
- Instruction
- Materials & Resources
- Interventions

The actual standards for U.S. history include few lists of events or places or names, but instead ask students to analyze broad historical patterns, such as social class differences, women's rights, or immigration. The subitems under "Curriculum Framework" include Big Ideas, Concepts, Competencies, Essential Questions, Vocabulary, and Exemplars. And while some other educational materials list mere topic headings as if they were "essential questions," this document does a creditable job when actual questions are posed. One of the questions under U.S. history for ninth graders, for example: "How can the story of another American, past or present, influence your life?" This system clearly aims for larger learning goals, rather than simply lists of names and dates to memorize.

South Carolina. The South Carolina standards for the most part offer the usual march of topics, requiring students to "summarize," "explain," or "compare" various events, historical developments, people, concepts. However, appended to each document is a set of tables that organize the various kinds of material to be taught according to a revised version of Bloom's Taxonomy—so that teachers are advised to engage students in the full range of thinking activities, from distinguishing important elements to critiquing, to inventing new ways to solve a problem. Another appendix lists the types of social studies "literacies" that students should learn. Most of these are procedural—creating and using time lines and maps, for example. However, several call for more student initiative and deeper thought (South Carolina Department of Education 2005):

- Demonstrate responsible citizenship within the school community and the local and national communities.
- Use texts, photographs, and documents to observe and interpret social studies trends and relationships.

Teachers and district curriculum coordinators should be sure to read all the way to the end of these documents. There they may find, tucked away in appendices like those for South Carolina, support for the thinking skills, active learning, and preparation for citizenship that were initially announced as the real objectives for social studies instruction.

▲ ▲ ▲

We could continue with more states, but the story is usually similar—dry lists of facts to learn, juxtaposed on occasion with higher-level goals and thinking skills. Wherever teachers face standards that require them to "cover" interminable lists of topics, we need to recognize that students won't learn much from just marching through the items. Anyway, preparing students for specific items that just might be on the state test will be hit or miss. Instead, students need to read widely and deeply. And in-depth inquiry activities will help them make meaning from the information they encounter. That way, they'll remember the material because it's part of something larger, something important. It's easy to panic when you see a long list of content items or a parade of factual test questions from previous years. But smart teachers know that the larger principles outlined

In-depth inquiry activities will help students make meaning from information they encounter on tests.

in documents like the introduction to the California *Framework* are good ones, and if we stick to them, our kids will do just fine. We needn't let a weak standards design derail us from good teaching.

QUALITIES OF BEST PRACTICE IN TEACHING SOCIAL STUDIES

Whatever set of state standards or new common standards teachers may be aiming to meet, the following qualities of instructional practice will lead students toward achieving them.

Provide regular opportunities to investigate social studies topics in depth.
Complete "coverage" in social studies inevitably results in superficial and unengaging teaching, like painting a room—covering plenty of square feet but only one-thousandth of an inch thick. That's certainly not what we saw in Debra Henderson's Middle East Protest Movements project. All the national reports and even some state standards recognize that real learning involves in-depth understanding of the complexities of human existence. The *National Curriculum Standards for Social Studies* highlights this need:

> Key concepts and themes are developed in depth. The most effective teachers do not diffuse their efforts by covering too many topics superficially. Breadth is important, but deep and thoughtful understanding is essential to prepare students for the issues of twenty-first century citizenship. (NCSS 2010, 170)

Yet with so many social studies fields—history, geography, sociology, anthropology, psychology—each including many topics, teachers must accept that under *either* approach—thin coverage on everything or depth for a few areas—students won't learn it all in twelve years of school. Covering less in more depth, however, not only ensures better understanding but increases the likelihood that students will learn how social scientists *think*, and entices them to pursue further inquiry on their own.

Create opportunities for students to exercise choice and responsibility for their own inquiry topics. Particularly because learning in social studies is meant to prepare students for *democratic* citizenship, student initiative is necessary in the classroom. It sends a mixed message to *talk* about making intelligent choices as a citizen but never to allow kids to practice doing so. Debra Henderson at Clissold School clearly understood this when she let her students choose which country to study and which roles to play in their groups. But student choice need not mean chaos or avoidance of important content. Good teachers provide lists of significant topics, give mini-lessons on how to thoughtfully choose a topic for writing or a research project, and conduct brief individual conferences to give students guidance. This not only increases engagement, but teaches an important skill needed for research projects in the upper grades and college—how to judiciously choose topics for meaningful reports and papers.

Choice allows for differentiation, which is at the core of implementing Response to Intervention (RTI) in the classroom. Once students' particular needs are identified, the teacher can use brief individual student conferences to help students choose inquiry topics and readings that are at their specific developmental levels. Choice is also especially valuable for English language learners, enabling them to draw on and share specific cultural and geographic knowledge that other students in the class may not possess.

Explore open questions that challenge students' thinking. Any study of human social existence brings up meaningful and often controversial questions—the pull between community and individual freedoms, abundance and scarcity of resources, particularity of local regions versus interrelatedness in a larger world. Ask questions that invite discussion, rather than merely check for memorized facts. Then help students to examine both problematic and positive historical events honestly and to analyze their meaning.

This open approach requires effective management of small-group learning. Assigning brief learning-log entries and small-group tasks prepares students to contribute to class discussion. Climate-setting activities are also essential, helping students respect one another's opinions and trust that their ideas will not be ridiculed (see Chapter 2). After a good discussion, students' follow-up journal entries, reports, and wall charts—or at the very least, end-of-class reflections—solidify learning so ideas do not evaporate when class is over.

Yes, but . . . *how can a teacher find time to prepare if individuals or groups of students are working on different issues?*

Planning projects around exploration of large, open questions requires some work. But increasingly, fascinating and useful units and inquiry projects are available on the Internet. "History Lab" at http://hlab.tielab.org, for example (run by the Technology in Education Laboratory), features projects using primary sources, which are themselves viewable online. "Best of History Websites" (www.besthistorysites.net) can connect teachers to hundreds of web resources—but it's well organized so a teacher or student needn't be overwhelmed with information. A thematic approach, as outlined in Tarry Lindquist's *Seeing the Whole Through Social Studies* (2002), makes student participation easier to include in the curriculum. Many strategies are described in Janet Alleman and Jere Brophy's set of three books, *Social Studies Excursions, K–3* (2001–2003), and Laurel Schmidt's *Social Studies That Sticks: How to Bring Content and Concepts to Life* (2007). When teachers teach with themes, they find that many of the items in their social studies curriculum guides are automatically covered.

To make concepts real, promote students' active participation in the classroom and the wider community. Real-world involvement is crucial for imparting the values of civic involvement and responsibility in our society. Our colleague, the noted reading educator Stephanie Harvey (2011), simply says that the final stage of reading comprehension is *taking action*—that kids haven't fully understood a text until they carry out some behavior that shows what knowledge they have built. That may mean something as subtle as internally changing an attitude, explaining an issue to others, or continuing to investigate a topic—or it may be as outward and concrete as raising money to save endangered species or petitioning for an important environmental improvement around school. The best of the standards documents and research studies emphasize such real-life connections and investigations, collaborative learning, and increased individual responsibility for learning. In spite of overstuffed curriculum guides, the task need not be overwhelming. Aspects of sociology, economics, and politics can always be found right in the school building. Children of most ages can debate an issue, draft letters and proposals, propose changes in classroom procedures, or set up committees to accomplish some new goal. Student participation in these matters will, as an additional benefit, contribute to the social health of the school (Apple and Beane 2007). Active involvement can easily reach outside the school walls as well. Representatives of many social and governmental organizations happily visit classrooms. Parents who work in relevant fields are great resources. Genuine responses from community leaders to students' letters, proposals on community projects, and real advocacy are long remembered by students. And they are especially motivating for students who may be struggling academically or who feel culturally marginalized in the classroom.

Involve students in both independent inquiry and collaborative learning. To build skills and habits for lifelong, responsible learning, students must learn how to work with others. Inexperienced kids will need training to use collaborative learning well, but this in itself is an important skill for use in school as well as their adult lives, as the 21st Century Skills site points out. At the same time, it is wise to balance individual and group work, since students need their own time for processing new ideas. A classroom workshop structure, in which students research individually chosen topics while the teacher holds brief one-to-one conferences, is a highly efficient way of immersing children in such individual study. These two organizational structures—collaborative groups and classroom workshop—are also essential tools for making a heterogeneous classroom work to serve students at many different achievement levels, as individual student needs are identified through RTI assessments (see Chapter 2 for descriptions of collaborative groups and classroom workshop).

Include reading of a variety of engaging, real-world documents, not just textbooks. Textbooks present many limitations for effective learning. They are difficult to read, stuffed with facts but lacking exploration of concepts in any depth. They're boring. And especially problematic, they generally present just one view of events, compared with the many intense and engaging controversies that surround so many social studies topics. Primary sources, in contrast, bring history to life. Articles from newspapers, magazines, and collections on the Internet abound, and since various publications aim at differing complexity levels, a teacher can choose a range of options to meet students' needs. An excellent example of quality reading is *Making Freedom: African Americans in U.S. History* (Primary Source 2004), a five-volume set of primary documents and materials. Websites on this topic, such as "In Motion: The African American Migration Experience" (www.inmotionaame.org) make still more resources available. The reading of images that are connected to various significant topics can add still another dimension to students' thinking and literacy, and can reach students who might otherwise not become engaged in the material. This can be a great tool for supporting the learning of special education students as well. To ensure that kids become lifelong readers, able to evaluate many points of view on topics important to their lives, we must get them well into the habit of reading widely in school.

Engage students in writing, observing, discussing, and debating activities to ensure they internalize important ideas that are new to them. Teachers often picture writing, discussion, or group work as time-consuming add-ons. We imagine essays that take days for kids to write and nights for us to grade. But activities can be brief and informal—taking only moments to help individual students focus, consider a problem, or reflect on the material. Students can write for two minutes at the beginning of the period to recollect main points covered the day before. They can stop in the middle of the class to talk for two minutes in pairs or threes about solutions to a problem. At the end of class, they can reflect on a note card about what they've learned or don't understand. The Common Core Speaking and Listening standards explicitly call for students to frequently engage in just such whole-class and peer group discussions.

Writing, drawing, and other forms of expression help students create new understandings for themselves. As the *National Curriculum Standards for Social Studies* describes its vision for an active classroom:

> Active lessons require students to process and think about what they are learning. There is a profound difference between learning about the actions and conclusions of others and reasoning one's way toward those conclusions. Active learning is not just "hands-on," it is "minds-on." . . . Powerful social studies teachers develop and/or expand repertoires of engaging, thoughtful teaching strategies for lessons that allow students to analyze content in a variety of learning modes. (NCSS 2010, 171)

Build social studies learning on students' prior knowledge of their lives and communities, rather than assuming they know nothing about the subject. News reporters love to bash kids and education by recounting the geography or history bloopers written on quizzes. Yet children listen far more closely to adult conversation than we like to acknowledge, and they sense issues and paradoxes in their community, school, and families much more sharply than we realize. By drawing out and building on this prior knowledge, we show how social studies concepts are relevant to children's lives, and not just abstract words.

This is especially important for English language learners, who can easily experience a wide gap between the world of school and their home lives. Drawing on students' knowledge about their own cultures not only strengthens this connection between home and school; it also helps students to learn academic concepts because it provides them with concrete examples that enable them to grasp the more school-oriented materials; for example, when history teacher Andy Pascarella (whom we will read about at the end of this chapter) teaches his students about drawing inferences from, and evaluating the limitations of, evidence, he starts by asking them to write about objects in their own homes and what an outsider might think they reveal about the kids' lives.

Of course, students grasp more complexities as they move up the grades and grow more aware of the wider world and social interactions around them. Traditional social studies curricula have followed an "expanding environments" formula for elementary grades, starting with the family and working outward. More recently, however, educators have found ways to introduce young children more effectively to history, geography, and other topics by connecting their own experience with the larger social studies themes, thus building more of a knowledge base, but in a meaningful way. Janet Alleman and Jere Brophy's book set, *Social Studies Excursions, K–3* (2001–2003), and *Doing History: Investigating with Children in Elementary and Middle Schools*, Fourth Edition by Linda Levstik and

Drawing on students' knowledge about their own cultures strengthens the connection between home and school and helps students to learn academic concepts.

Keith Barton (2010), provide detailed guidance for elementary and middle school teachers to involve children in active historical inquiry.

Help students explore the full variety of cultures found in America, including their own backgrounds as well as others'. The acrimonious debate over "our common heritage" versus study of individual ethnic groups has sadly obscured much of the real value in both these perspectives. First, minority children are not the only ones who have been cut off from their own history. Most students in any age group or social stratum know little of the historical and political developments that affected their families and forebears. History, politics, economics, culture, folklore—all become more meaningful to students through interviews with parents, grandparents, neighbors, and other adults (Zemelman et al. 2000).

Nevertheless, children of minority backgrounds in particular tend to see school as disconnected from their own lives. English language learners especially need both to value and understand more about their own heritage in order to feel confirmed as members of the larger community. However, once we've helped them connect school subjects like history with their own lives, students are eager to learn about other cultural groups and appreciate both their rich particularity and their common struggles and aspirations. Far from engendering divisiveness, this approach helps eradicate it.

What is crucial is *how* these things are studied. We've observed children endure profound boredom when required to memorize the principal grain crops of African countries. Such activities do not connect children with history but further alienate them. In contrast, when students make choices, discover facts that they find significant in their own family backgrounds, and share them with mutual respect, they not only feel pride in their heritages, but also become more excited about history and geography and culture in general—and perhaps even learn to critique and evaluate aspects of their own past, as well as to honor them.

At the school level, avoid tracking for social studies so as to provide everyone with knowledge essential to citizenship. As more educators contemplate the social and racial implications of ability grouping, they realize the need for alternatives. Research indicates that tracked classes do not even benefit high-track students as much as once claimed, but they do discourage the lower-achieving ones. Particularly in social studies, students of various backgrounds and achievement levels benefit greatly by hearing from one another (Wynne and Malcolm 1999). This understanding strongly supports RTI approaches, which focus on providing the support students need within regular heterogeneous classrooms as much as possible.

One answer is to rethink how the classroom is organized. Traditional lectures and quizzes are least adaptable to heterogeneous grouping, offering only one version of the material for everyone. Small-group work is much more successful, as long as children are trained to take an active role. When kids talk through and argue over ideas, more learning happens. The teaching that stronger students provide for the less prepared benefits them both—the old saw being quite true, that the teacher of a subject often learns more than her students. When clusters of students need particular kinds of support, the teacher can form temporary ad hoc groups but needn't employ permanent divisions that label and segregate kids.

The other effective structure for a part of each day or week in a nontracked setting is the classroom workshop. As we describe in Chapter 2, students individually or as a group choose topics they are interested to learn about, within the content of the unit or subject. They work independently while the teacher circulates for *brief* one-to-one sessions where, rather than giving answers, the teacher leads students to take responsibility and solve problems themselves. In brief mini-lessons, usually at the beginning of a session, particular concepts or processes are taught, based on the curriculum or observed student needs. Near the end of the period, one or two individuals may share something they've written or created on the web, and every few weeks everyone turns in a final product.

This structure requires training for both teachers and kids. But it uses time efficiently, allows students to work at their own levels and to make choices according to their interests, and teaches responsibility, something often missing from traditional classrooms. Teachers at all grade levels, in every socioeconomic setting, have found classroom workshop highly effective.

Evaluate students' thinking and responsible citizenship, rather than focusing on decontextualized facts. Since the goal of social studies education in the national standards and many state documents is not just acquisition of information, but preparation for democratic citizenship, evaluation in social studies should relentlessly support that goal. Yes, we can ask students to show they have specific knowledge of a subject. But evaluation should also include larger questions; for example, what in the students' view constitutes a good historian (or history book, or observer of folk traditions)? How well do students gather and winnow information, take positions and build arguments, make a logical case for their interpretations? We should ask students to reflect on *how* they've learned about families or economic systems. Students should analyze the significance, implications, and human issues within the material studied. Then answers should be valued by extending discussion, rather than simply graded and forgotten.

However, for students to feel free to speak their minds, we must have many occasions when their ideas are *not* evaluated. Students should be able to express their thoughts with a sense of safety and respect. One way to balance this with assessment is to have students select the writings they will submit for evaluation out of a larger portfolio, to maintain a zone of safety for expression that is risky, tentative, or unresolved.

Finally, to mirror the democracy for which we are preparing them, students can participate in setting the standards by talking together about what makes a good paper/answer/project and how to evaluate it. In fact, the issue of meaningful evaluation of students' education is a worthy social studies topic in itself.

Asking Good Questions in U.S. History

ANDREW PASCARELLA

Juarez High School, Chicago, Illinois

Andy Pascarella leans over his smoothie at the Jumping Bean coffee shop, a long-time fixture in the Pilsen neighborhood of Chicago, a locale inhabited mostly by Mexican American families. He talks about how he views his history teaching at nearby Juarez High School: "I love it there. These kids are the future of the American dream. And I have a tremendous responsibility to the families to help their children achieve it." We'll describe his teaching in a minute, but it's important to understand not only what an inspiring classroom looks like but also what attitudes and professional knowledge it is built on. In his work, Andy uses—and also provides professional development on—the Document-Based Question approach developed by Phil Roden and Chip Brady (see www.dbqproject.com). In DBQ activities, students study original materials and artifacts to consider large questions raised by major historical events. An example of such a question in American history: "How revolutionary was the American Revolution?"

Visiting Pascarella's Latin American history class at Juarez High School, what might one see? Early in the year, he helps students understand the elusive nature of historical fact by having them list information, documents, and artifacts available about their own lives. Then the exercise poses these questions: "Once they are assembled and examined, could these sources of information be used to write a complete history of your life? Could two people use the same information about your life to write different stories? Could the two interpretations differ and still be valid?" Students begin to realize that the historical information about events hundreds of years ago is likely to be quite incomplete and open to many alternative ways of understanding it.

The next day, kids arrive in class to find a variety of artifacts around the room—a bowl-like object made from a gourd, a thickly twisted strand of rope with a loop at one end, a small metal spoon, a rough blanket with a slit in the middle, and so on. In groups, students rotate around the room, jotting conjectures about what these objects are, their use, and what civilization they belonged to. In fact, they are (or are replicas of) objects used by the ancient Bolivian Incas that Pascarella had acquired during a Peace Corps stint. Eventually some students guess that the rope is actually a slingshot, and of course Pascarella obliges with a demonstration, using a projectile of wadded foil so no one gets hurt. Other items remain puzzling. Most of the students have never seen a gourd—they're city kids, after all—and the challenge of dealing with their lack of prior knowledge is evident. Pascarella has a lot of teaching ahead of him for the year. Nevertheless, this is their first vivid lesson in the challenge of interpreting historical facts.

Now the students must apply their nascent inquiry skills for the first time in the year, choosing ancient cultures to research in teams (a learning strategy most have experienced all too infrequently in school). The projects culminate in posters and presentations, with a debate on which culture the students consider the most "advanced." This is the big question the projects have been leading to. Of course, this generates much discussion about what we mean when we say a culture is "advanced." These first projects don't have the kind of depth that the students will achieve later in the year, but it's important for them to start developing their skills at inquiring and researching and interpreting information right away.

It's instructive to listen to what the students say about this work. We asked them why anyone should study these long-lost civilizations.

Samantha A.:   Some descendants are probably still here today.

Luis Z.:   So they're never forgotten. And I like their art—the calendars.

David G.:   I'm interested in their games, like the one where the losing team gets scarred or killed. I also like that they preserved their history.

Jose D: It's our roots.

We wondered whether these students, mostly Mexican American, felt any connection with the old civilizations, so we then asked how many thought that they might actually be descendants of these long-ago peoples. About half the class raised their hands. But a bigger question is how the kids view their own identity and whether that changes over the course of the year. So the following May, Pascarella invited the students to write about this. One theme in their responses emerged sharply: a wide concern about the terms they wanted to use for describing themselves. Were they Latinos and Latinas, Chicanos/Chicanas, Mexican, Mexican American, Hispanic? Most decided on "Hispanic" because, in their view, it identified the language they spoke at home, and language, it turned out, was especially important to them.

Beyond that, their views of themselves had become more complex. "I'm mixed," Samantha A. explained in an interview. "I think of myself as everything my parents are, plus American. I love dancing, and that's from my Mexican father. And I love singing, which comes from my Irish American mother." Samantha muses on how things might have been if history had turned out differently. "What if the Aztecs had won out over the Spaniards? What would our world be

It's important for them to start developing their skills at inquiring and researching and interpreting information right away.

like?" She especially appreciated the documentary film *Guns, Germs, and Steel*, which helped explain why history didn't in fact happen that way.

Samantha returned again and again to the various inquiry projects the students carried out over the year, and the reports they shared in class. "One small fact sparks a twenty-minute discussion," she explained, "and that's when you really learn." Her favorite project was her own individual inquiry on a historic person—Frida Kahlo.

Other students were similarly thoughtful. Explained David G., "Before, I just thought about myself as 'I'm alive.' But now I think more about who I am. I'd fight for America, but my blood line is Mexican. This summer I plan to look up my family history on www.ancestry.com." And Nayelly T. asserted, "I need to do something to support Mexicans in the United States." These students were now thinking about their place in the world—something we'd certainly want for all of our country's maturing young citizens.

Works Cited

Alleman, Janet, and Jere Brophy. 2001–2003 (set of three books). *Social Studies Excursions, K–3*. Portsmouth, NH: Heinemann.

Apple, Michael W., and James A. Beane. 2007. *Democratic Schools* (2nd edition). Portsmouth, NH: Heinemann.

Brady, Charles, and Phil Roden. The DBQ Project. www.dbqproject.com.

California Department of Education. 2001a. *History–Social Science Framework for California Public Schools, Kindergarten Through Grade Twelve*. Sacramento, CA: California Department of Education. Available online at www.cde.ca.gov/ci/cr/cf/documents/histsocsciframe.pdf.

———. 2001b. *History–Social Science Content Standards*. Sacramento, CA: California Department of Education. Available online at www.cde.ca.gov/be/st/ss/documents/histsocscistnd.pdf.

———. 2009. 2003 Through 2008 CST Released Test Questions. Sacramento, CA: California Department of Education. Available online at www.cde.ca.gov/ta/tg/sr/css05rtq.asp.

Harvey, Stephanie. 2011. "Comprehension to What End?" In Harvey Daniels, ed., *Comprehension Going Forward: Where We Are/What's Next*. Portsmouth, NH: Heinemann.

Harvey, Stephanie, and Harvey Daniels 2009. *Comprehension and Collaboration*. Portsmouth, NH: Heinemann.

Levstik, Linda, and Keith Barton. 2010. *Doing History: Investigating with Children in Elementary and Middle Schools* (4th edition). New York: Routledge.

Lindquist, Tarry. 2002. *Seeing the Whole Through Social Studies* (2nd edition). Portsmouth, NH: Heinemann.

National Center for History in the Schools. 1996. *National Standards for History Basic Edition* (revised). Los Angeles: National Center for History in the Schools. (Original edition issued in 1994.)

National Council for the Social Studies. 1994. *Expectations of Excellence: Curriculum Standards for Social Studies.* Washington, DC: National Council for the Social Studies.

———. 2007. *National Standards for Social Studies Teachers.* Washington, DC: National Council for the Social Studies.

———. 2010. *National Curriculum Standards for Social Studies: A Framework for Teaching, Learning, and Assessment.* Washington, DC: National Council for the Social Studies.

———. 2010. Report in *The Social Studies Professional.* March/April, p. 1.

Partnership for 21st Century Skills. www.p21.org.

Pennsylvania Board of Education. Standards Aligned System. www.portal.state.pa.us/portal/server.pt/community/standards_aligned_system/4228/social_studies/44202.

Primary Source, Inc. 2004. *Making Freedom: African Americans in U.S. History.* Portsmouth, NH: Heinemann.

Schmidt, Laurel. 2007. *Social Studies That Sticks: How to Bring Content and Concepts to Life.* Portsmouth, NH: Heinemann.

South Carolina Department of Education. 2005. Social Studies Academic Standards. http://ed.sc.gov/agency/Standards-and-Learning/Academic-Standards/old/cso/standards/ss/.

Technology in Education Laboratory. The History Lab. http://hlab.tielab.org.

Wynne, Harlan, and Heather Malcolm. 1999. *Setting and Streaming: A Research Review* (revised edition). Edinburgh: Scottish Council for Research in Education.

Zemelman, Steven, Patricia Bearden, Yolanda Simmons, and Pete Leki. 2000. *History Comes Home: Family Stories Across the Curriculum.* Portland, ME: Stenhouse.

Suggested Further Readings

Banks, James A. 2007. *An Introduction to Multicultural Education* (5th edition). Boston, MA: Allyn & Bacon.

Cruz, Barbara, and Stephen Thornton. 2008. *Teaching Social Studies to English Language Learners.* New York: Routledge.

Edinger, Monica. 2000. *Seeking History: Teaching with Primary Sources in Grades 4–6.* Portsmouth, NH: Heinemann.

Loewen, James. 2008. *Lies My Teacher Told Me: Everything Your American History Textbook Got Wrong* (revised edition). New York: The New Press.

National Council on Economic Education. 2005. *Choices and Changes: In Life, School, and Work* (four-volume series covering various grade levels). New York: National Council on Economic Education.

Percoco, James. 2001. *Divided We Stand: Teaching About Conflict in U.S. History.* Portsmouth, NH: Heinemann.

Selwyn, Douglas, and Jan Maher. 2003. *History in the Present Tense: Engaging Students Through Inquiry and Action.* Portsmouth, NH: Heinemann.

Zinn, Howard. 2005. *A People's History of the United States, 1492 to Present* (revised). New York: Harper Perennial.

Note: The range of materials available on the web is enormous. Following is a small selection of high-quality sites.

EdTechTeacher Inc. Best of History Websites. Annotated links to over 1,200 history websites and hundreds of history lesson plans and activities. Rather than compile our own list, we refer readers to this powerful web tool.
www.besthistorysites.net/

Library of Congress. Civics and Government Lesson Plans. High-quality interactive lessons (not all such websites are of this caliber).
www.loc.gov/teachers/classroommaterials/themes/civics/lessonplans.html

Mid-continent Research for Education and Learning (McREL). Lesson plans for behavioral/social sciences, civics, economics, geography, and history, at various grade levels.
www.mcrel.org/lesson-plans/index.asp

National Board for Professional Teaching Standards. Information for teachers seeking national certification—the process, benefits, and links to support groups.
www.nbpts.org

National Council on Economic Education. A collection of interactive lessons on economic concepts organized by grade level, concept, and standards.
www.ncee.net/resources/lessons.php

National Council for the Social Studies. News, research bulletins, publications, and conference information.
www.ncss.org

National Endowment for the Humanities. Edsitement History and Social Studies Lesson Plans and Websites. Many history lesson plans at various grade levels. Samples were mostly good quality, interactive.
http://edsitement.neh.gov/lesson-plans

National Geographic Society. Lesson plans on topics like ecology, resources, and wildlife (those we sampled were not highly creative or interactive).
www.nationalgeographic.com/xpeditions/standards/matrix.html

New York Times. The Learning Network. Resources from the *New York Times* on a range of social studies topics. Lesson plans sampled were sketchy.
http://learning.blogs.nytimes.com/

Smithsonian Institution. Materials on a wide variety of social studies topics on archaeology, economics, studies of war, and more. Some include virtual tours of museum exhibits, or articles and links to online copies of primary sources, and detailed lesson plans.
www.si.edu

Verizon Foundation. Thinkfinity Lesson Plans. Large number of lesson plans on a wide range of grade levels and subjects, including social studies. Sampled lessons were of good quality.
www.thinkfinity.org/lesson-plans

Recommendations on Teaching *Social Studies*

▲ INCREASE	▼ DECREASE
In-depth study of topics in each social studies field, in which students make choices about what to study	Cursory coverage of a lockstep curriculum that includes everything but allows no time for deeper understanding of topics
Activities that engage students in inquiry and problem solving about significant human issues	Memorization of isolated facts in textbooks
Student decision making and participation in wider community affairs, to build a sense of responsibility for their school and community	Isolation from the actual exercise of responsible citizenship; emphasis only on reading about such topics
Participation in interactive and cooperative classroom study processes that bring together students of all ability levels	Lecture classes in which students sit passively; classes in which lower-achieving students are deprived of knowledge and opportunities to learn
Integration of social studies with other areas of the curriculum; use of real-world reading	Narrowing social studies activity to include only textbook reading and test taking
Richer content in elementary grades, using children's prior knowledge. Even at a young age they've had experience that relates to psychology, sociology, economics, and political science, as well as history and geography; as well as to social institutions and problems of everyday living	Assumption that students are ignorant about or uninterested in issues raised in social studies Postponement of significant curriculum until secondary grades
Students' sense of connection with American and global history, diverse social groups, and the environment that surrounds them	Use of curriculum restricted to only one dominant cultural heritage
Inquiry about students' cultural groups and others in their school and community, thus building ownership in the curriculum	Use of curriculum that leaves students disconnected from and unexcited about social studies topics
Use of evaluation that encourages further learning and that promotes responsible citizenship and open expression of ideas	Assessments only at the end of a unit or grading period; assessments that test only factual knowledge or memorization

What School Leaders Can Do

*I*n highly effective Best Practice schools, there are many leaders: classroom teachers, special educators, tutors, coaches, parents, and, of course, students who take important leadership roles. But there are also some people, like building principals and assistant principals, curriculum specialists, librarians, and even superintendents, whose jobs make them especially critical. We've seen great *teaching* in all kinds of schools; we have very rarely seen great *schools* without passionate and effective building-level and district leaders. So take your cue from what we have seen great leaders doing:

▶ Be a visible thinker, reader, and writer. Visit classrooms and read aloud or discuss books with children. Try the math problems, dissect a frog. Write and share your writing in the school community. Learn every student's name if you possibly can.

▶ Be an audience for students. Read kids' work on the walls and in classrooms. Attend as many learning performances as you can. Let the creators know you've appreciated their words, their art, their songs. Have a principal's mailbox, and enter into active correspondence with kids.

▶ Work your budget to make sure classrooms have all the supplies and materials needed to create a true workshop atmosphere; above all, this means books and materials that go beyond textbooks. Don't make teachers have to beg for these supplies.

▶ Celebrate learning in your school. Incorporate reading, writing, math, science, history, and research into special school events and programs. Create space and occasions for sharing student work noncompetitively. Everyone needs an audience, not a contest with few winners and many losers. Our aim is for all to achieve.

▶ Help teachers communicate with parents *proactively* by letting the parents know how the different subjects are being taught and why the school has embraced the Best Practice model of education, and *reactively* by stepping in and supporting the teachers when uninformed or skeptical parents question their pedagogy, book choices, or activities.

▶ Use your role as instructional leader, supervisor, and evaluator. Let teachers know it's good to take kids outside to study insects, do algebra with chocolate, use language arts time for book clubs, or adopt other promising practices. In your classroom visitations, evaluate congruently: if teachers are using a Best Practice approach, you'll see nonpresentational, highly individualized, student-centered workshop activities in which the teacher often takes a facilitator/coach role.

- Work at the district level to align the curriculum guide, textbook adoptions, and the standardized testing program with good instruction. It may be necessary to work for the *dis*adoption of test-prep, skill-and-drill workbooks, or other materials that undermine a challenging, balanced curriculum and don't really contribute to higher test scores anyway.

- Ask teachers what kind of professional development activities they would value and then provide them. If you already have Professional Learning Communities (PLCs) in your school, give them your support. If not, adapt the model, making sure your PLCs are truly teacher-led inquiry and application groups, and not just test-prep skull sessions.

- If teachers want it, bring in genuinely facilitative consultants to help faculty members explore the research, standards, and classroom practices of good instruction. After the initial workshop or demonstrations, make sure there is support to help teachers "install" new practices in their classrooms. Professional development sessions are only one part of a broader development effort.

- Nurture continuing growth and emerging peer leadership by sending volunteer teachers to workshops, courses, summer institutes, or teachers-training-teachers events. Starting a "teacher book club" that meets once or twice a month (at school or at different colleagues' homes) has been a powerful change strategy in many schools.

- Even though you don't have time, read the research, scan the journals, and pass along ideas and articles to your teachers. Linda Darling-Hammond has written two books that are vital for school leaders to know: *The Flat World and Education* and *Powerful Learning*. Order books that your teachers request for their own growth—from Heinemann, Stenhouse, NCTE, IRA, Teachers College Press, Brooks, Jossey-Bass, Scholastic, Corwin, and others. Pay for journal subscriptions delivered to school. Above all, help teachers find *time* to talk about teaching together, exchange ideas, work on joint projects, and think and grow as a faculty.

Chapter *8*

How *to* Achieve

Best Practice
Schoolwide

Entering McAuliffe Elementary School in Chicago, you immediately step into an airy three-story atrium. This relatively new and bright building in the middle of a predominantly Hispanic neighborhood on the near northwest side of Chicago serves 850 children. Principal David Pino and Assistant Principal Serena Peterson arrived there in 2004. And while both are very strong and caring leaders, this is a not story about saviors charging in to sweep away all the problems; rather, it is about learning and growth for *all* the adults in the school—so perhaps it can help us see how powerful instruction can develop in many settings.

At first teachers were excited about their new leadership team, and test scores started to rise. But as Pino and Peterson introduced new curricular initiatives and started asking why some classes weren't improving, some teachers grew defensive. One vocal faculty member began lobbying the local school council not to renew Pino's contract (almost every Chicago school has a parent/community council that hires the principal and decides on renewing the contract every four years). She was joined by a small, disgruntled group of teachers, and the atmosphere grew negative. Most of the staff liked their new leaders but felt too intimidated to speak up.

Meanwhile, however, some supportive outside relationships began to develop. In the summer of 2005, the school served as the site for the Illinois Writing Project (IWP) summer leadership institute, and several McAuliffe teachers participated, followed by additional IWP workshop sessions for all the staff. Then in 2006 McAuliffe joined the Chicago Schools Alliance (now called the Partnership for Instructional Leadership), a network of city schools that shared information on school improvement projects and discussed their challenges. (Co-author Steve Zemelman helped create the Alliance with Kim Zalent, director of the Public Education Program at Business and Professional People in the Public Interest, a Chicago nonprofit organization.) In addition, McAuliffe gained two reading coaches, increasing the staff available to work on instructional improvements.

As the atmosphere grew more tense at McAuliffe, Alliance leader Kim Zalent and consultant Harry Ross brought teachers together for several meetings to establish a "teacher voice" and enable the more positive people to speak out. Key to the success of these meetings was the administrators' agreement to absent themselves, and participants were assured of confidentiality. As a result, most teachers felt safe voicing their support for the principal, and the few negative teachers realized they were isolated. Developing trust was essential to this process. Peterson explained to us that Zalent and Ross seemed impartial and focused on careful planning rather than responding emotionally to the situation. And the extensive planning time they invested convinced her and others that they cared about the school. Pino's contract was renewed, and the school was now on a more collaborative footing.

At about the same time, the Chicago Schools Alliance facilitators realized that a structure was needed to help Alliance members make improvement efforts more effective, and invited them to form instructional leadership teams made up of both teachers and administrators. Consultant Jeff Nelsen trained McAuliffe teachers and leaders (along with colleagues from eight other Chicago schools) to work as planning teams on the following steps and strategies to advance learning across their building:

- Identify a targeted area of learning especially in need of improvement.
- Consult regularly with all the teachers to build commitment.
- Research and choose a promising practice to develop this learning across the school.
- Decide on professional development strategies and readings to prepare teachers to apply the new practice.
- Arrange cross-classroom visits for teachers to observe and support one another.

- Gather information of various kinds to determine whether the strategy is advancing kids' learning.
- Decide on successive rounds of the process based on how the work is proceeding.

McAuliffe teachers chose writers workshop as the strategy to implement. And they smartly divided the effort into small, doable steps, with a cycle of development for each step. They started simply with teachers arranging their rooms to facilitate a workshop approach in which students could concentrate on individually chosen writing topics. The second round of work focused on effective mini-lessons, an effort that required more time to develop than some of us outside "experts" might have realized. Next came strategies for holding effective individual teacher-student conferences with kids.

As a result, any visitor could see writers workshop just about every morning in every classroom. The amount of student writing grew voluminously, along with extensive teaching of a wide range of writing skills. Teachers ran weekly instructional leadership team meetings with skill and efficiency. Serena Peterson and David Pino were extremely proud of the teachers' commitment and problem-solving ability. Pino explained, "I always wanted more teacher leadership in the school, but this gave me a structure to make it work." Pino and Peterson found that on instructional matters, they could do much more listening than talking or mandating. "The teachers come up with amazing ideas," Pino declared. And the number of students who met or exceeded the state writing test standards went from 47 percent to 61 percent in a single year.

Why Is It So Hard to Get Such Efforts Going—Especially in Schools That Are Struggling?

This is not an easy question to answer. Many good individual teachers in schools everywhere hone their skills, gather new knowledge about teaching and learning, and seek out more effective classroom strategies. But it can be hard for schools or districts to change as a whole. Like many organizations, they aren't really structured to do that. And yet it's crucial to find ways to make this happen. It's crucial for the sake of the kids and their futures. It's crucial for achieving Best Practice instructional improvements that really last and don't just fade when a new principal takes charge or a new pedagogical fad comes along. And it's crucial for advancing Best Practice in general, because only when whole schools achieve great things for students do educators and the public take notice, give this work the credit it deserves, and begin to ask how those effective strategies can spread more widely. We know improvement is possible when, in schools like McAuliffe, we see advances across a whole building in a low-income neighborhood. But to make this happen, we must understand the obstacles clearly—without letting them discourage us. Following are some of the common hurdles.

Overdependence on charisma. In some fortunate schools or districts, a really savvy principal or curriculum coordinator knows how to pull the staff together and get everyone focused on a new effort. But such a school can seem like a special case, a "boutique" achievement. The Education Trust has spotted schools across the country where kids in poverty-laden neighborhoods are achieving at high levels (Chenowith 2007, 2009). And while many of the steps and strategies used involve thinking and planning by everyone in the school, it's most often the principal who initiates the key changes. Unfortunately, when that aggressive administrator moves on, we've seen too many schools revert to a more plodding norm, even with some very good teachers in the building. Or sometimes the school continues to look good, but only because it sits in an affluent neighborhood where literacy and achievement bloom more in the kids' homes than in the school itself. At McAuliffe School, as we've described, the effort doesn't depend on just one inspiring person, so this vulnerability is greatly reduced.

Bureaucracy. Americans love to sneer at it. But bureaucracy represents jobs, so it rarely shrinks, and it usually resists change. In big-city bureaucracies, programs need to be approved at many levels. The system serves politics and entrenched groups more than the needs of teachers and children. District leaders may advocate innovation, but they also, in contradictory fashion, institute monitoring systems focused on uniformity and compliance. Thus charter schools, despite their limited number, seem to some to be one of the few pathways out of the bureaucratic tangle because they operate with more autonomy in exchange for accountability contracts.

Here's one typical way we've seen politics, bureaucracy, and a lack of resources combine to undermine change: as a program is launched, an administrator worries, understandably, that people in one area will raise a ruckus if services are offered elsewhere but not for them. Because funds to serve every location adequately are lacking, one teacher from each building is ordered to a superficial one-day training session and then expected, believe it or not, to change the practice across her building. The program limps along; isolated change agents get discouraged; it fades away.

The discouragement factor. Especially in schools with a history of failure, finding a new footing can be especially hard. American education has repeatedly seen ambitious projects featuring powerful teaching approaches result in precious little ultimate improvement. Too often people blame the kids or their families. More recently pundits and politicians are going after individual "bad teachers." But as Charles Payne explains in *So Much Reform, So Little Change* (2008), what so many projects have lacked is attention to the complex adult social dynamic in schools. A demoralized professional climate in an under-resourced school leads to a host of dysfunctional attitudes and behaviors, compounded by impossible bureaucracies, inflexible educational ideologies, and self-fulfilling prophecies about what "these kids" can't do, all of which Payne catalogues with depressing but incisive alacrity. But again, with a leadership team structure like the one we described at McAuliffe school, this discouragement can be overcome.

One phenomenon that Payne describes, which we've frequently seen, is the "beachhead" effect. A new program is introduced with some professional development, and a few enthusiastic teachers latch on. But others in the building feel threatened or disagree philosophically, and factions harden around people's differences. The positive group closes ranks, but grows isolated. The principal tries to keep everyone happy—or, conversely, tries to enforce the new program, which usually leads doubters to teach it with as little enthusiasm as possible. After a couple of years with little real progress, the program is pushed aside by the next new solution.

Poverty. No one seems to want to talk about it these days, but in a very real sense, as we explained in Chapter 1, America has two school systems: perhaps three-fourths of our kids attend decent schools in middle-class areas, while the other fourth attend schools in high-poverty areas weighted with grievous problems. Rather than averaging together these two separate systems to derive the false and misleading picture that America's main educational problem is mediocrity, we really have something much worse: a country of educational *haves* and *have-nots.*

Let's be clear: we're not about using poverty as an excuse when schools are failing. But analysis from the Chicago Consortium on School Research shows that when a neighborhood lacks social capital (a sociologist's term for resources like community organizations, thriving businesses, social networks, and community norms), effective improvement strategies have a much harder time succeeding (Sebring et al. 2006, 39–43).

Student mobility. This is a condition that can strongly affect the stability and progress in a school. The 2010 report on Rhode Island student mobility (Rhode Island Kids Count 2010) provides one example; it showed that "between 2006

*W*ith a leadership team structure like the one we described at McAuliffe school, discouragement can be overcome.

and 2008 . . . 26% of Rhode Islanders over age one living below the poverty line moved, compared with 10% of higher income residents . . . High mobility rates in schools can have a negative impact on all students because teachers must slow curriculum progress, repeat lessons and adjust to changing classroom dynamics and student needs. Within-year moves are particularly disruptive for students, teachers and schools."

Safety. Outside of school, family instability and neighborhood violence pressure children tragically. In several schools where we've worked, large numbers of children have witnessed shootings and deaths. Younger kids—in grades one to four or five—remain quite open to schooling, although some become withdrawn or overly needy of attention because of threats in the neighborhood, or are untrained in self-discipline and social cooperation. Alex Kotlowitz' moving chronicle *There Are No Children Here* (1991) describes how the brutality of neighborhood violence can leave a child unable to concentrate in school. But it's the older students who are increasingly preoccupied with the magnetism and danger of the streets, especially when they experience repeated failure in school.

Even more heartbreaking is the amount of anger and hostility we sometimes see in poverty-area schools. The kids can seem undisciplined, and teachers yell and label them harshly to their faces to maintain basic control. Some teachers assert quite openly that "these kids" lack discipline in their homes or are accustomed only to such tactics. Some education writers and theorists have argued that only a skills-and-worksheets approach will succeed with some children because of their cultural backgrounds. Complicating the discipline issue, in many schools nonwhite children, boys especially, are disciplined more frequently and for smaller offenses than other kids. Teachers are often unaware they are doing this, and uncomfortable talking about it. Staffs become divided along racial lines and around various issues, and many school leaders lack the skills to air issues constructively (Lewis 2003).

Cultural differences between students and teachers. There *are* cultural differences among groups, and it's important for teachers to understand them and take them into account, as Lisa Delpit so passionately argues in her classic work on culturally sensitive teaching (2006). Especially because teachers are mostly middle class while many of their inner-city charges are poor, considerable misunderstanding occurs. One research project showed how some urban teachers underestimated parents' willingness to help their kids or support the teacher's policies. The teachers initially failed to contact parents whose children were struggling, or failed to fully enlist the parents' help at home. But when they finally did, late in the year, they were surprised at the cooperation that took place (Goldenberg 1989).

Anthropologist Shirley Brice Heath provides an explanation of the puzzling gap between families and schools in her classic comparison of working-class communities (1983). Heath observed that language use in some cultural groups harmonizes with the patterns of student-teacher communication, while for others it does not. Some children get lots of school-talk practice at home, answering questions about toys and books, or giving factual information. Kids with a different communication style who don't learn this talk quickly fall behind—frustrating their parents, who usually believe strongly in education. When teachers designed learning projects more in tune with their children's cultural language patterns, the kids did far better.

However, without dismissing the need for culturally sensitive teaching, our observation of successes in urban schools like McAuliffe tells us that teachers can learn to overcome these cultural differences. In classrooms using Best Practice strategies in the poorest areas, we've observed that discipline and relationships aren't a problem at all. Teachers can use approaches such as Responsive Classroom (Charney 1992), which builds a strong climate and good communication habits. They can provide student-centered learning activities that keep kids engaged. And they can give students increasing responsibility and choices to expand their intrinsic motivation to learn.

Tests versus resources. Many politicians and policy makers seem to believe that more tests, centralized mandates, and lots of teacher firings will strengthen schools to overcome all the challenges we've listed. But so far this approach has demoralized teachers even further and not created the great leap forward in learning that was hoped for. Studies by the Chicago Consortium on School Research (Sebring et al. 2006) reveal five major supports that *do* make a difference for struggling schools:

- Inclusive leadership focused on instruction.
- Strong parent and community ties.
- Building of professional capacity.
- A student-centered learning climate.
- Ambitious instruction.

Meanwhile, resources for schools have only been shrinking. OK, so just throwing money at a complex set of problems like this won't solve them. On the other hand, without the funds, how would we ever provide the in-depth coaching and planning time for teachers and school leaders to achieve the kinds of reorganization accomplished by McAuliffe?

But enough of this gloomy catalogue. It's not the whole story.

What Schools Can Do to Meet the Challenges

None of the obstacles that we've catalogued is insurmountable. Thoughtful and creative educators have found ways to cope with them or rise above them—and they don't have to depend on superstar teachers or one-in-a-hundred principals. Of course, more resources make a difference, though a lack of funds is no excuse for shortchanging our children. But we don't need to wait. Charles Payne (2008, 94), for example, offers a list of "six characteristics of high-impact instructional programs in urban contexts":

1. Protection of instructional time.
2. Intellectually ambitious instruction.
3. Professional community—teachers collaborate and share a collective sense of responsibility.
4. Academic press combined with social support.
5. Program coherence—i.e., institutional focus; are we all on the same page?
6. Teacher quality/diagnostic ability.

These are based for the most part on studies by the Chicago Consortium on School Research (Sebring et al. 2006 and Lee et al. 1999).

While these are important principles and tell us what a good and improving school should look like, they don't say much about how to get from here to there. How does a school move from demoralized and dysfunctional to active, healing, and moving ahead? How do we help administrators move from defensive to collaborative when they're under so much pressure? How do we help the adults and the kids themselves perceive the children's hidden potential? If the social dynamic is especially important for effecting change, how can we work with it to improve learning across a school?

Follow us one more step in thinking this through. Perhaps education researcher Richard Elmore's analysis of schools' internal dynamic can help. In *School Reform from the Inside Out* (2004, 133–199) Elmore identifies three big influences on teachers' classroom efforts:

- Teachers' personal sense of responsibility—for their students, for improving the community, or toward other major purposes.
- Expectations—that is, the understandings and attitudes shared by the educators in the school about how they view their work, their goals, their students.
- Accountability—that is, giving *"an account* of their actions to someone in a position of authority inside or outside the school."

Clearly, each of these can affect change efforts in various ways. In schools where teachers are fairly unified about their educational beliefs and philosophies—that is, similar *expectations* are widely shared—*responsibility* and a shared sense of *accountability to each other* will be easier to achieve. But in buildings where people work in relative isolation or in sharply divided factions, actions will be governed mainly by individual rather than collective responsibility—which may or may not support a particular program that has been introduced. So, no matter how intense the external pressure—"performance management" reviews, tests, rewards, punishments, "restructuring"—the effect depends mainly on how these three factors, responsibility, expectations, and accountability, play out within the whole-school context.

However, if we were able to help teachers in a school bring these elements more into alignment with each other, a school could begin to work productively on some of the elements listed by Payne (2008) or Sebring (2006). In fact, in our own school change efforts, what we've found is exactly that, as we've experienced it again and again in workshops and consulting roles in schools over the years:

> When a faculty is helped to develop *mutual* accountability—a commitment to one another and to the students to work together to improve some aspect of learning—and has an effective process for carrying out this improvement, then meaningful change begins to happen not only in a few classrooms but throughout the school.

A new set of studies by the Ontario Institute for the Study of Education and the University of Minnesota Center for Applied Research and Educational Improvement (Louis et al. 2010) strongly confirms this idea. The studies look at the effect of various leadership roles and strategies on student achievement. And what stands out as the single most effective strategy is the development of professional community—that is, the structures, practices, and relationships among teachers themselves. The report defines professional community to include the following:

> Supportive interaction among teachers in school-wide professional communities [to] enable them to assume various roles with one another as mentor, mentee, coach, specialist, advisor, facilitator, and so on. However, professional community amounts to more than just support; it also includes shared values, a common focus on student learning, collaboration in the development of curriculum and instruction, and the purposeful sharing of practices. (42)

To improve student learning, the single most effective strategy is the development of professional community.

▶ Programs That Focus on Professional Community and Whole-School Change

A number of ideas and programs have developed around the country in recent years to help schools or districts build structures that support professional community. Some examples:

- Professional Learning Communities (PLCs), promoted by Richard DuFour and his colleagues, are groups of teachers who collaborate not just to study a new strategy or concept, but to apply it in their classrooms and observe the effects on student learning (DuFour et al. 2010). PLCs can lead to significant long-range advancement, but we do worry that DuFour and company's approach sometimes focuses more on data points than on teachers' new learning. However, smart educators needn't let that happen.

- The National Equity Project (formerly BayCES, the Bay Area Coalition for Equitable Schools) coaches schools and school leaders to develop professional learning communities. As their website explains, a key part of their work is to create "teams that demonstrate high degrees of relational trust, collaborate effectively toward shared goals, develop and facilitate agendas that advance productivity and results, and foster distributed leadership" (www.nationalequityproject.org).

- In Chicago and a number of other sites, the program titled Schoolrise has employed a three-year process "centered on a developmental model and focused on fidelity to a process of change, rather than a set program" (www .schoolriseusa.com/SRPublic/research.html; also see Au 2009 and Raphael 2010). The program starts with an assessment of the school's level of development as an organization. Teachers work together to develop a vision for the particular aspect of learning they will focus on. And then, grade by grade, they develop benchmarks, elements of student learning they are aiming to achieve. The teachers create these themselves, so that they own the results and develop leadership skills and professional community in the process.

- Instructional leadership teams (ILTs) for whole-school change have been trained by Jeff Nelsen of Targeted Leadership Consulting. Steve learned about these as they were developed in two networks of Chicago schools, the Network for College Success (focused on high schools), and the Partnership for Instructional Leadership (elementary schools). The key steps in the work are outlined in our story about McAuliffe School at the start of this chapter. Some essential principles for making ILTs work:

  - Team members are representative of the faculty, and communication flows both to and from the team, so everyone gets heard as well as informed.

  - The effort focuses on just one improvement area and strategy at a time, so teachers aren't pulled in many directions at once, and maximum energy focuses on the effort.

- Campaigning to make the change schoolwide sends a powerful signal to students about what truly matters. When all teachers are on board, expectations are shared by all.

- Team members develop a range of leadership skills—working together, managing conflicts constructively, making sure tasks get done, communicating with the rest of the faculty, creating buy-in especially with those who are hesitant, breaking down the new strategy into manageable steps, analyzing various kinds of information to decide what's needed next.

- Teachers' learning about new ideas is not limited to traditional workshops. The team determines, based on knowledge of colleagues and the chosen strategy, the modes of adult learning that are appropriate, such as professional book groups, attendance at conferences, or visits to other schools.

▲ ▲ ▲

Whatever their differences, these programs all focus on developing professional community. They are not touchy-feely initiatives that focus only on "process." They all address instructional improvements and use information on student learning to guide their work and confirm their success. And they promote the kind of shared, mutual accountability that Richard Elmore pinpoints as essential to real and lasting school improvement. As with our McAuliffe School example, outside coaches may be needed for training and for bringing an outside perspective to help the teachers reflect on their effort. The particular content of the work, however, is chosen and planned by each school rather than mandated from above.

Yes, but . . . is "professional community" really about working together and learning new ideas about teaching and learning? Or is it just a way to make us teachers use last spring's state test scores to pressure colleagues who seem not to measure up?

So much talk—and action—in the education world these days centers on "data-driven instruction." And in too many cases this appears to be about singling out strong and weak teachers, and punishing (or firing) the latter. But meaningful information about students' learning is an important part of this effort so that teachers can see if their new efforts are bearing fruit. However, it should be just one integral part of a bigger process.

An effective professional learning community or teacher leadership team looks at various kinds of information to determine students' needs. The teachers study books and articles that address those needs and identify an effective instructional approach to try. They compare and troubleshoot their efforts and look at student work together to see how their new strategies impact learning. They seek resources for supporting the professional development that may be needed, and plan for sharing their learning more widely in the school.

In this setting, data is not about being monitored to make sure you are complying with a mandate. It's about working together on some improvement and then seeing if all the hard work makes a difference for the kids. If it does, we can celebrate and move on to the next step. If it doesn't, we can analyze the situation together and adjust our efforts. The teachers have to own and control this process for it to be meaningful—though of course the ultimate focus is on students and their learning.

What Individual Teachers Can Do

Obviously, one teacher acting alone is unlikely to initiate a professional community across a whole school. Teachers can easily feel that large-scale improvements in their school are beyond their control. The district hands down mandates. The principal makes decisions based on his or her style and philosophy. Not everyone on the faculty necessarily sees things the same way, so they might not agree on a direction even if consulted.

But there *are* things a teacher can do, steps that can help a school become more of a professional community of educators who work collaboratively together. Acting on these will also build teachers' leadership capacity. Here's a starter list:

- Start a professional study group with some fellow teachers. Read books and articles together on educational concerns that you share. Apply the ideas back in the classrooms and compile results among the group to see if the strategies make a difference in students' learning.

- Conduct a classroom research project—again, with some colleagues—and share results with others in the school. There are many important issues that can be investigated—students' learning styles, their challenges outside school, the effects of particular instructional strategies, kids' reading habits. This will help everyone better understand students' needs and strengths and thus make more well-informed decisions about the focus of school improvement.

- Meet informally with other teachers in the school one-on-one—particularly people you *don't* normally connect with, or may not see eye-to-eye with. Don't try to advance any special agenda. The aim is to get to know and understand each other better professionally, to build a basis of trust. This is essential for collaboration on any efforts down the line. Community organizers consider it their most important tool for making change happen.

- Talk with the principal about student learning needs that you and he or she observe. Don't wait for a crisis or major request to get started; rather, try for regular, if brief, check-ins so that when a more pressing need arises, each of you knows what to expect from the other and some trust has been established.

- If you perceive a major need for improving student learning in your school and wish to take action (such as finding an improved math curriculum), plan strategically and consult with influential teachers and key administrators. You'll want to get them on board and uncover and address any concerns they may have. You'll also need to develop strategies for getting everyone behind the effort.

- Constructively advocate for clear, focused, supportive leadership that nurtures a positive school culture. Significant change requires collaborative, social experiences and extensive, open discussion of issues. The principal will not be able to achieve things alone.

- Advocate for common planning time and quality professional development beyond the traditional professional development workshop—experiential activities built around common challenges and needs. And choose a strategy for your own development—professional learning communities; online study and inquiry; job-embedded learning such as analyzing student data, case studies, peer observation, action research, lesson study, professional readings, book studies, on coaching; and courses and workshops, of course.

In fact, everyone in a school (or any organization, for that matter) leads in some way.

Particular leadership skills are needed to make these kinds of efforts successful. Teachers can learn how to conduct good classroom-based research, handle conflicts constructively, lead effective meetings, plan a change process strategically, and maintain focus on a project over time. We often haven't learned these skills with intentionality in our own education and work as educators. We understandably focus on the needs of our students, our first priority of course. And we tend to define leadership in terms of the position that someone holds, rather than the actions they take. But in fact, everyone in a school (or any organization, for that matter) leads in some way, whether in an active role or by more passively lending assent to actions taken by someone else. And we all know respected teachers in our schools who influence decisions and can make or break a new project—people who wield relational power without ever holding a formal position.

We can learn these skills, just as we learn to handle the complex dynamics of thirty kids in a classroom. One resource we recommend (and from which the above ideas are drawn) is *13 Steps to Teacher Empowerment: Taking a More Active Role in Your School Community*, by Steve with colleague Harry Ross (2009).

We've seen it over and over. What excites us about a school like McAuliffe is that it's a school in a high-poverty area that *has* advanced from a struggling building with an unhappy staff to one where the existing faculty and school leaders are making real strides. We know dozens of schools in Chicago and around the country that have achieved great learning for children from struggling neighborhoods and families. And their progress is not all because of some charismatic leader who will be gone in a few years. The teachers may have to work hard, but the kids are industrious and upbeat, the teachers calm and collaborative. We know it's possible, because we've observed so many inner-city classrooms (some of which are described in this book) where kids of all colors and backgrounds thrive on self-directed and collaborative tasks. Here are some of our favorites in Chicago, where we've worked most intensely (and of course there are many others around the country that we don't get to see):

- Burley School—www.burley.cps.k12.il.us
- Spry Community School—www.spry.cps.k12.il.us
- Telpochcalli Small School—www.telpochcalli.cps.k12.il.us
- Namaste Charter School, Chicago—www.namastecharterschool.com
- North Kenwood/Oakland Charter School—www.uei-schools.org/nko/site/default.asp

The reader should visit the websites as well as the schools themselves to see what success looks like. Each of these schools has outstanding innovative programs as well as a vibrant professional community that ensures their programs continue to thrive and adapt to the needs of the children. And collaborative school improvement programs like the ones described earlier are bringing more schools onto this list.

We cannot delude ourselves that a single institution like the public schools can, without key social services and stronger economic conditions, overcome all the problems facing struggling families and kids. And yet we must not allow naysayers to deny that intensive, well-executed efforts in urban schools do pay off. We've seen it happen again and again.

An Eleven-Year Schoolwide Change Effort

INDIAN LAKE SCHOOL, Lewistown, Ohio

In the previous edition of this book we chronicled the development of Best Practice reading instruction at Huntsville School in rural Huntsville, in west-central Ohio, to show how a school can increase student learning. Then, five years later, we learned that in 2009 Huntsville and Lakeview, the two elementary schools in the Indian Lake District, had merged in one new building. We were delighted to find that even with this consolidation plus changes in leadership, the improvement effort had only grown stronger. So we wanted to learn what the students and teachers were now doing, and also to understand the conditions that accounted for such a long trajectory of growth.

First let's recap the story. In 1999, a group of Huntsville teachers approached their new principal, Diane Gillespie, with concerns about kids' learning. Gillespie's twenty years as a teacher and administrator in the district helped them to trust her. In spite of their hard work, state test scores in their 335-student K–4 building were mediocre, hovering at 45 percent passing in reading, and they knew the children were not getting the skills they needed.

So first-grade teachers Becky Grandstaff, Suzanne Headley, and Kris Harper headed to Toledo with Gillespie to hear about Patricia Cunningham's "Four Blocks" approach to teaching reading—focused on guided reading, self-selected reading, writing, and working with words (Cunningham and Hall 1996). Ohio-based consultant Marsha Spears was invited to work with the teachers over the year. The faculty began calling the fourth-grade state test the "K–4 test" to stress everyone's responsibility. Fourth-grade students began writing and reading every day, and a $60,000 grant helped stock classroom libraries and fund more professional development.

Spring test results were astounding—84 percent passed in reading, the second-highest year-to-year jump in the state, and the school received a $25,000 award. "We weren't yet executing many specific new strategies," Gillespie observed, "but our children were doing a lot more reading and writing—there were just more books around. And there was a lot of talk going on, informally, every day. We began to believe in what we were doing." Some key factors:

- Lots of listening to teachers by the administration districtwide.
- Strong staff desire to continue professional growth and development.

- Expressions of confidence in the teachers and encouragement that they see themselves as professionals—and plenty of trust as a result.
- Willingness of staff to pull together and tackle whatever issues they faced.

In the spring of 2000, teachers Suzanne Headley and Kris Harper attended a conference led by reading expert Regie Routman, who was then contracted for a full week of professional development the next September. She started with demonstration lessons, talking with observing teachers before and after each one, and then shifted to coteaching. Finally teachers took over, with coaching. Each day ended with a Q&A after school. "It took a few days to bond," Gillespie explains, "but by Friday, we were all hugging her and no one wanted to let her go."

Regie returned in March and made clear that a weekly "support group," organized by a teacher, was needed to discuss their work and professional readings. Linda Benedict, then a twenty-eight-year veteran second-grade teacher, volunteered. The group started with Richard Allington's *What Really Matters for Struggling Readers* (2001). The Wednesday before-school meetings became essential. Principal Gillespie: "If I had to name the one thing besides staff development that made the difference, it is the support group"—and teachers agreed. "It makes us feel like a team. And now we're a model for other schools to follow," said third-grade teacher Deb Hanson.

While Gillespie greatly appreciated the staff's efforts, they in turn pointed to her leadership in:

- Obtaining information whenever requested and researching topics on the Internet.
- Taking notes during conversations, to be clear on the teachers' needs.
- Updating and personalizing the library (she and her husband even built a loft for it).
- Encouraging teachers to be creative with their room schemes.
- Putting out goodies on the lunch table—often chocolate.
- Creating an extra reading teacher position.
- Promoting wellness among staff.
- Finding money to send teachers to conferences.
- Never missing an opportunity to show appreciation—praise in the weekly staff newsletter, thank-you notes in mailboxes—and whenever good news came in, Gillespie would break out champagne glasses and bottles of sparkling cider.

Throughout, the school maintained a consistent focus. "It's all connected," Gillespie observed. There's no attraction to passing fads. "And no one-shot staff development sessions, either." Reading scores dipped to 77 percent in the second year of the work (not unusual as changes begin at a school)—and then soared back into the 80s and 90s.

The faculty are veteran educators who have embraced profound and thoughtful change. Most have put in more than twenty years at the school. "I'm blessed to have such a caring, child-focused staff," said Gillespie. "Every single thing that has happened here is due to the fact that we believe in 'whatever it takes.'" Grade-level teams meet during the summer whether they are paid for the time or not. Teacher Linda Benedict: "Instead of one person moaning, 'What can I do?' we now ask, 'What can *we* do?' Before I felt isolated. Now we're a team."

A 2011 Update. Much has changed for Indian Lake Schools, but the effort has only grown stronger. In so many cases, school improvements have dissipated, and we've seen one great program after another evaporate when new personnel or programs make their appearance. Indeed, Gillespie had left for a period to head the district's middle school. But the selection team in charge of identifying her replacement appreciated the achievements the school had made, and chose a district middle school teacher who shared that appreciation but also brought to the school his expertise in math instruction, which was just coming into focus. This ensured a healthy combination of continuity for the literacy work with a new effort on math.

Meanwhile, changes were under way at the other elementary building, Lakeview School, as well. A survey showed that many Lakeview teachers didn't believe their low-income students were capable of learning. Principal Deborah Johnson, another strong leader, initiated a faculty book study on the challenges of poverty for student learning. The discussions led to a more positive outlook, and that school adopted the Four Block reading approach that had been successful at Huntsville. When Lakeview reading scores rose to rival Huntsville's, the Lakeview teachers became truly enthusiastic about their new perspective.

Then in the fall of 2009 the two elementary schools in the district merged within a new building. Naturally everyone was nervous about this. However, the achievements at Lakeview helped avoid a "them-versus-us" mentality. And Diane Gillespie returned to head the combined school. To ease the way, curriculum coordinator Jo Cook held meetings of the two staffs together during construction. A key attitude was crucial: the work was about what mattered for kids, no room for egos.

The final change as of this writing is that the superintendent, Bill McLaughlin, who had so strongly supported all of the hard—and expensive—work of school improvement in the Indian Lake district, has retired. Teachers and administrators felt some anxiety about what approach a new leader might take. Fortunately, Patrick O'Donnell, the new boss, has fully appreciated the high distinction in which these schools are now held in the state, so Diane Gillespie and her team are confident about the future. Budget cuts in state funding and new limitations on the teachers unions are unsettling. Some rules, like longer service required to qualify for benefits, may encourage burned-out teachers to stay on too long. But Diane's school will weather these challenges.

The key factors. Let's review the elements that have enabled Huntsville School, now Indian Lake, to make big changes in instruction and improve student achievement for more than ten years:

- Professional community—faculty who work together within the school with a focus on student learning, and who share ideas across schools as well.

- Trust—strong professional relationships, including a positive principal who listens to teachers, responds to their concerns, and celebrates their achievements.

- Leadership stability plus carefully managed leadership and school transitions.

- Professional development that supports the teacher community, develops structures through which that community takes responsibility, and maintains continuity over time.

- Good communication between schools, so that ideas are shared and jealousies minimized.

The community served by Indian Lake School is rural and not wealthy. The median income in the county is near the national average, but just 3.9 percent of the adults have a bachelor's degree or above. Eleven years ago, student achievement was not inspiring. Now it's a school we can all learn from. And what we learn is not just about good classrooms, vital as those are, but also how a thoughtful, caring community of educators can organize for change and make it last.

Works Cited

Allington, Richard. 2001. *What Really Matters for Struggling Readers.* New York: Longman.

Au, Kathryn. 2009. "Real Schools, Real Success: A Roadmap for Change." Paper presented at the 2009 Conference of the New Zealand Reading Association.

Charney, Ruth. 1992. *Teaching Children to Care: Management in the Responsive Classroom.* Turners Falls, MA: Northeast Foundation for Children.

Chenowith, Karin. 2007. *It's Being Done: Academic Success in Unexpected Schools.* Cambridge, MA: Harvard Education Press.

———. 2009. *How It's Being Done: Urgent Lessons from Unexpected Schools.* Cambridge, MA: Harvard Education Press.

Cunningham, Patricia, and D. P. Hall. 1996. *The Four Blocks: A Framework for Reading and Writing in Classrooms That Work.* Clemmons, NC: Windward Productions.

Delpit, Lisa. 2006. *Other People's Children: Cultural Conflict in the Classroom.* New York: The New Press.

DuFour, Richard, Rebecca DuFour, Robert Eaker, and Thomas Many. 2010. *Learning by Doing: A Handbook of Professional Learning Communities at Work* (2nd edition). Bloomington, IN: Solution Tree Press.

Elmore, Richard. 2004. *School Reform from the Inside Out: Policy, Practice, and Performance.* Cambridge, MA: Harvard Education Press.

Goldenberg, Claude. 1989. "Making Success a More Common Occurrence for Children at Risk for Failure: Lessons from Hispanic First Graders Learning to Read," in *Risk Makers Risk Takers Risk Breakers: Reducing the Risks for Young Literacy Learners,* Jo BethAllen and Jana Mason, eds., pp. 48–79. Portsmouth, NH: Heinemann.

Hargreaves, Andy, and Dean Fink. 2006. *Sustainable Leadership.* San Francisco, CA: Jossey Bass.

Heath, Shirley Brice. 1983. *Ways with Words: Language, Life, and Work in Communities and Classrooms.* New York: Cambridge University Press.

Kotlowitz, Alex. 1991. *There Are No Children Here: The Story of Two Boys Growing Up in the Other America.* New York: Doubleday.

Lee, Valerie, et al. 1999. *Social Support, Academic Press, and Student Achievement: A View from the Middle Grades in Chicago.* Chicago: Chicago Consortium on School Research.

Lewis, Amanda. 2003. *Race in the Schoolyard: Negotiating the Color Line in Classrooms and Communities.* Piscataway, NJ: Rutgers University Press.

Louis, Karen S., Kenneth Leithwood, Kyla Wahlstrom, and Stephen Anderson. 2010. *Investigating the Links to Improved Student Learning.* Minneapolis and Toronto: University of Minnesota and Ontario Institute for Studies in Education.

National Equity Project. http://nationalequityproject.org.

Payne, Charles. 2008. *So Much Reform, So Little Change.* Cambridge, MA: Harvard Education Press.

Raphael, Taffy. 2010. Defying Gravity: Literacy Reform in Urban Schools. In *National Reading Conference Yearbook, 2010.* Oak Creek, WI: National Reading Conference.

Rhode Island Kids Count. 2010. *2010 Rhode Island Kids Count Factbook.* Providence, RI: Rhode Island Kids Count. www.rikidscount.org/matriarch/documents/10_Factbook_Indicator_54.pdf.

Schoolrise. www.schoolriseusa.com.

Sebring, Penny, et al. 2006. *The Essential Supports for School Improvement.* Chicago: Chicago Consortium on School Research.

Zemelman, Steven, and Harry Ross. 2009. *13 Steps to Teacher Empowerment: Taking a More Active Role in Your School Community.* Portsmouth, NH: Heinemann.

Chapter 9

Proof *and the* Pendulum—
Assessing Best Practice

I t's easy to become cynical and view new (or revitalized) ideas as mere fads, the latest swing of the never-ending pendulum of reform strategies pushed by the politicians and pundits who have their own ideas about education. But as we've shown throughout this book, Best Practice is far more than that. It represents a broad consensus across the subject areas about how teaching and learning can work effectively. Best Practice draws on a long history of inquiry into the psychology and dynamics of learning. It's confirmed by research and testing that show greater student achievement and learning as a result of Best Practice strategies. And it reflects the concrete everyday experience of talented teachers across the country.

At the same time, identifying and reconfirming Best Practice approaches— as well as understanding how they apply in particular schools and with particular kids—require that we collect the best data possible at every level. So we need a steady flow of reliable information—research on the effectiveness of approaches we are trying and then data about students and whole schools, so we know whether and how our efforts are working. In classrooms where authentic, collaborative, challenging experiences are the norm, do students learn well? Do they understand and remember the content of the curriculum? Can they perform tasks that show us what they know and are able to do? Can they meet the Common Core Standards?

Yet each child and each school embodies a fresh human experience. No educational theory or plan or curriculum, however strong the research, is automatically a success. It's a tool in the hands of thinking people who must figure out how to set high standards for teaching and learning and make them work with *these* children in *this* particular culture and setting.

So as we conclude this book, we remind ourselves that the research—embedded throughout all preceding chapters—confirms the effectiveness of Best Practice teaching and learning, but we reflect on ways to provide ourselves with the best information on how Best Practice works with particular kids and schools. The context, here, is that teachers, administrators, parents, officials, community members feel *accountable* for doing the best for our kids. This means that what needs to be evaluated is not only what teaching and learning strategies work, but also how people work with them. Therefore, once we've looked at the research, we'll try briefly to place it in the larger accountability context.

Research on Best Practice Approaches

We've continually referred to the research that supports Best Practice. Peppered throughout and listed at the end of each chapter are references to the long line of educators and researchers from whom we derive the foundations of Best Practice. Here, we want to round out the picture by recalling the long history of such research, covering a wide range of Best Practice strategies. Now, those of us who work with the research understand that all of it is limited because so many variables are beyond control in any classrooms studied, and we don't have much faith in many of the measures for determining the resultant student learning. Moreover, advocates of every approach to education can produce research supporting their ideas. By testing or measuring different aspects of learning—letter-sound decoding as opposed to inferring the big ideas in a story or historical biography, for example—a researcher can get statistical results that prove his or her point. Nevertheless, dozens of research studies done and repeated over many years have confirmed over and over the positive outcomes for a wide range of progressive teaching strategies compared to more conventional ones.

Collaborative activities, for example (see Chapter 2), have had well-documented success. Researchers have published studies confirming significant achievement gains in a wide range of content areas when classrooms include ample cooperative activity—one of the fundamental components of the Best Practice paradigm (Johnson, Johnson, and Holubec 1998). A second example: in the teaching of writing, a meta-analysis of numerous statistical studies by George Hillocks (1986) showed decades ago that while activities for engaging students with material and ideas for writing have a strong effect on writing quality, lecture presentations and grammar drills are of little use, or even bring down writing scores. Thus the qualities of Best Practice for teaching composition that we've outlined.

Reading is the most heavily researched area of the curriculum, and while it's the most contested, the support for the Best Practice qualities that we've listed is wide and deep. Early on, Michael Tunnell and James Jacobs, surveying several dozen studies from 1968 to 1989, found that kids became stronger readers when reading real literature as opposed to basal readers. The research on literature-based reading programs ever since has repeatedly shown standardized achievement score gains for students in such programs, not just in regular classes but among students with ESL, special education, or disadvantaged backgrounds. So rather than wade through the results of specific studies, we'll briefly list the books and articles that have repeatedly reviewed this vast literature.

Alan Farstrup and Jay Samuels' thorough guide, W*hat Research Has to Say About Reading Instruction* (2002), presents a range of experts who explain the implications of research for teaching reading. Michael Pressley's chapter, for example, examines the importance of above-the-word-level comprehension strategies for good reading. Constance Weaver's *Reading Process and Practice* (2002) is encyclopedic in its review of the extensive research, all supporting the Best Practice approaches to reading described in this book.

Daniels and Zemelman's *Subjects Matter: Every Teacher's Guide to Content-Area Reading* (2004) contains a summary of research implications for reading in the secondary grades. The Carnegie Corporation's study, *Reading Next* (Biancarosa and Snow 2004), reviews the research on adolescent reading and once again confirms the Best Practice approaches we've described. Jane Braunger and Jan Lewis provide a well-organized account of strategies for teaching reading that are supported by research from the 1970s to 2005. The studies covered in their book, *Building a Knowledge Base in Reading* (2005), show that reading is a constructive process that involves complex thinking. More recently, Richard Allington's

Dozens of research studies over many years have confirmed over and over the positive outcomes for a wide range of progressive teaching strategies compared to more conventional ones.

What Really Matters for Struggling Readers (2011) marshals the research on what works, and puts it simply and clearly:

- Kids need to read a lot.
- Kids need books they *can* read.
- Kids need to learn to read fluently.
- Kids need to develop thoughtful literacy.

More broadly, Linda Darling-Hammond of Stanford University and a variety of collaborating researchers have shared studies that offer the most recent evidence of the effectiveness of Best Practice instruction. In her 2008 book, *Powerful Learning: What We Know About Teaching for Understanding*, Darling-Hammond and her coauthors report that:

- Students learn more deeply when they can apply classroom-gathered knowledge to real-world problems, and when they take part in projects that require sustained engagement and collaboration.
- Active-learning practices have a more significant impact on student performance than any other variable, including student background and prior achievement.
- Cooperative small-group learning—that is, students working together in a group small enough that everyone can participate on a collective task—has been the subject of hundreds of studies. All the research arrives at the same conclusion: there are significant benefits for students who work together on learning activities.
- Students are most successful when they are taught how to learn as well as what to learn. (Darling-Hammond, et al., www.edutopia.org/inquiry-project-learning-research. See also Darling-Hammond, et al., 2008)

In her following volume, *The Flat World and Education* (2011, pp. 163–193), Darling-Hammond takes a look at American schools and those around the world to see what practices best support teaching and learning. Among the key findings:

- In high-ranking Singapore, education officials are committed to more "project work, and higher order questions to encourage creativity, independent, and interdependent learning."
- Finland, often called the most literate country in the world, and now the top-scoring nation on math, science, and reading PISA tests, made a commitment in the 1990s to "creative problem-solving and innovative cross curricular projects and teaching methods." Now, inquiry is the main style of teaching in Finnish schools, set in workshop-style classrooms where teachers take the role of coach and mentor, while students work alone and in groups to conduct investigations. Darling-Hammond reports: "The cultivation of independence and active learning allows students to develop metacognitive skills that help them to frame, tackle, and solve problems;

evaluate and improve their own work; and guide their learning processes in productive ways."

- South Korea has made astonishing educational gains. As recently as 1953, it was a mostly illiterate nation with few school buildings, and now its students score at the very top of PISA assessments in all subjects. Among the highlights of current curriculum reforms are "increasing opportunities for in-depth study, the proportion of optional activities in school that encourage students' self-directed learning, students' independent study skills, and other creative activities."

Across the years, then, from Hillocks in 1986 to Darling-Hammond in 2011, the weight of evidence supports Best Practice.

Assessing Best Practice in the Real World

So now we come to the understandable question from teachers, parents, and everyone else—whether and how this research applies to their classrooms and their schools. "So that's what the research says, but will it work—or is it working—with *our* kids?" And now everything gets more complicated. Is a new strategy—say, classroom writing workshop—being applied effectively in every classroom throughout the school? Has there been sufficient support for teachers to learn and implement it? In what ways might it need to be adjusted for English language learners? Do the tests used to measure student achievement align with the skills and understandings that students are learning in the writing workshop, and that they actually need for success in college or later in life? And if something is not working, what do we do—help teachers use it more effectively, or abandon it?

The coin of the realm nowadays for answering such questions is the state-mandated standardized test. Schools that do well on it or improve markedly are praised and their practices are deemed worthy. Those that don't are threatened with sanctions or even state takeover (though as some states have discovered, this is like the dog that finally catches the neighbor's car he's been chasing for years—now what does he do with it?). We've discussed throughout this book the research that unequivocally shows how Best Practice teaching strategies improve student performance on such tests. But that doesn't mean the tests are particularly accurate, meaningful, or useful for "driving" real improvement. Over and over, even when communities and news reporters are confronted with studies showing that standardized tests are inaccurate, discriminate against minorities, and reward memorization instead of thinking, school districts opt to retain them anyway. Better, more complex tests are too expensive, they tell us, and these are the best we've got right now, even if they're not perfect. Now, several coalitions of states have begun developing new standardized tests keyed to the new Common Core Standards. However, even if they are better designed and less discriminatory, they will still embody many limitations. For example, they'll still deliver results no more than twice a year, which is of very limited help to teachers or kids as they strive to improve during the course of their year together.

In any case, performance on the tests, whatever their design, may not be about the effectiveness of particular teaching strategies at all. Many teachers will testify that their district introduced a new initiative, worked on it for one or two years, and then simply jumped onto another new bandwagon—even if the initiative *was* working. Others may tell about the boxes of materials that were delivered to the school, introduced briefly, and then simply left for the teachers to puzzle out how to make use of them. Or administrators may say, "That's a great approach, but we just don't have the resources to get everyone trained for it," or "There will be just too much resistance from parents." Considering the complexity of the change process we described in Chapter 8, we know that there are always many factors at work in a school besides the teaching strategy itself. We must therefore temper our thinking about the questions, "Does it work?" and "Is it working?" with some broader thinking about the "accountability" concern that these questions really represent.

So think about it: tests, measurement, research, are meant to tell us *whether* a school or an educational strategy is succeeding or failing. But the ultimate goal of accountability is to actually *achieve* success for our children, not just to chide us if we haven't. The tests are supposed to not only measure success but also to "drive" instruction. And they certainly pressure schools to focus on reading and math, often to the detriment of other essential subjects for educating responsible, competent citizens. Yet most everyone agrees that the past decade of No Child Left Behind has produced only very limited improvement, and in many cases none for the schools where test scores have been lowest (Neill 2010).

Now, if we are to approach evaluation and accountability more constructively, how are we to do it? Here's a first step toward a better way that brings accountability down to the level of the individual child and makes it useful in the classroom. Back in their preservice educational psychology courses, teachers learned the distinction between formative and summative evaluation—the former a tool to observe interim progress and determine what further work or help is needed; the latter a summing up of what has been achieved at the end of an effort. Recently, formative evaluation has been "rediscovered" and debated as if it's some strange new animal. But good teachers use it every day to understand students' growth and help guide their next steps in learning. Many of the

The ultimate goal of accountability is to actually achieve success for our children, not just to chide us if we haven't.

assessment strategies we described in Chapter 2 are formative ones. Summative evaluation, on the other hand, doesn't aim to nurture learning at all, but merely quantifies what has been learned up to a given point, translating it into a score or symbol that allows students to be ranked against each other. Summative evaluation is understandably needed by communities to help guide larger educational policy. But it isn't really designed to help kids learn or teachers teach; it's mostly a way of reporting periodically to outsiders. Of course, summative evaluation is even less useful when the tests don't connect with Best Practice teaching or the skills that the kids are, in fact, learning.

When teachers and schools move toward Best Practice, they create new, more meaningful forms of assessment, evaluation, grading, and reporting student progress that are indeed more formative. At one school we've worked with, every teacher takes a turn shadowing a student in another class. Then the teachers talk together about the patterns they observed, in order to better understand how learning works in their school. And as these teachers observe other classes, they reflect as much on their own teaching as on the kids themselves. Now accountability is beginning to work at the classroom and school levels.

Many of the schools in the Coalition of Essential Schools (a network of about 600 high schools committed to principles outlined by Theodore Sizer—see www.essentialschools.org) use student presentations and performances of various kinds to have students explain in depth what they've learned. Often these are given to an audience of parents and community members from outside the school, which provides high motivation for kids to do well—and lets the community understand through real content what their kids are learning. So accountability is extending out into the community.

So how do we get to *real* accountability, especially for struggling schools—accountability that leads teachers to employ Best Practice strategies in the most effective ways possible, and that makes sure these are working for their students? As we described in the previous chapter, Richard Elmore (2004) tells us that accountability works most effectively when it lives close to home. When schools are judged by a state test that the teachers see as flawed (as so many policy makers as well as educators agree), it's easy for them to dismiss the data, and often nearly impossible to use it to determine how to improve.

Now the truth is that most teachers strongly see themselves as accountable to students and parents. But for real change, Richard Elmore observes, they need to come together, reach some agreement, and see themselves as responsible to each other as a professional community. In many schools, accountability is mostly individual, with teachers operating essentially as independent hired consultants. Instead, teachers need to hold thoughtful conversations with each other, to coordinate their work (rather than just silently blame previous teachers for not preparing the kids properly) and to collaborate on changes so they aren't isolated, as we described in Chapter 8. This is about strengthening the professional culture of the school and about how that culture is organized so teachers work together. And the research (Louis et al. 2010; Sebring et al. 2006) confirms that this collaboration is exactly the strategy that results in the greatest improvement in student achievement.

Teachers together can examine and interpret data to determine what students need in order to do well. Often a test itself doesn't reveal what might be missing—do the kids lack vocabulary, time to read good books, habits of drawing inferences in their reading, decoding skills or test-taking skills, or has an important concept not yet been taught? After investigating together, teachers are better equipped to try strategies that address specific needs and observe students' work and each other's classrooms to see how the effort is working.

Some may say that an organizational approach like this is just too complex, too hard to initiate, impossible to track or measure. Yet we've certainly seen other organizational developments spread across the whole country to give us the structure of grades, departments, schedules, and such that characterize the schools we have today. And as many readers of this book are aware, more and more schools around the country are instituting professional learning communities for teachers that, when done well, move toward just the kind of shared professional responsibility that Richard Elmore envisions. This is a setting in which Best Practice teaching and learning can thrive and gain in strength over time. And it provides the kind of close-in observing and thinking that enable educators to meaningfully sort out why an instructional effort is working or not, and what to do so that kids continue to learn more deeply.

So, What About the Pendulum Metaphor?

Sometimes teachers wonder: *Isn't Best Practice just another educational fad? And is any of this stuff really new? It sounds just like the open classrooms of the 1960s or whole language in the early 1990s, and those trends died away, didn't they?* What we are calling Best Practice certainly has a very familiar ring to school veterans from the past forty years. It's not surprising that waves of progressive reform are scoffed at by some educators, given the comings and goings of the latest educational efforts. But we think the educational innovations of the late 1960s and early 1990s were important precursors to today's developments, and it's worth understanding what really happened back then, to comprehend our struggles now.

Let's look at one controversial idea from this era to help us revalue our heritage. In the 1970s, some American schools plunged into the "open-classroom" experiment, tearing down walls and offering teachers a one-day inservice at the end of the summer, in which some administrator or outside consultant essentially announced: "OK, next week we want you to throw away the one model of teaching that you were trained for and are experienced in, and instead run your classroom in ten other ways you've never tried and we've never trained you for. Have a nice year." The great open-education movement inevitably collapsed because teachers did not have in their professional repertoire the structures and strategies to run a variety of student-directed, independent, and small-group activities. Nor were their schools organized to help them get there, either through outside professional development or their own thoughtful inquiry. Kids went bananas, and many teachers who were working in huge rooms with hundreds of kids started sneaking in cardboard boxes, shelves, and other large objects to gradually rebuild a classroom-like space inside the trackless waste of the "pod." And so open education disappeared—or did it?

If you were to visit Pat Braun, Laurie Hendrickson, and Kathryn Locigno's team-taught sixth-grade language arts class in River Forest, Illinois, you'd see something that looks very much like an open classroom. Working with a double period totaling eighty-four minutes, the teachers really have opened up the fold-back walls, though only, as Pat explains, because it's more efficient. The resources of three classrooms are shared so there are more materials available for everyone. And both kids and teachers learn to control their voices so work in one area doesn't disturb kids elsewhere. You'll see eleven-year-olds—an age group not usually trusted to take this level of responsibility—working industriously on reading, writing, and research every day. They come into the room, get out their writing folders, and get right to work. One of the teachers may conduct a ten-minute mini-lesson on a writing or research skill, either with the whole combined class of seventy kids or with one-third at a time. Then as kids read or write, teachers hold conferences with them one at a time on their writing, reading, or research project. Big projects occur about once per quarter, with kids working in pairs or teams and choosing topics they are interested in, within a subject-area unit they are studying.

This is an open classroom that works. It works because Pat, Laurie, and Kathryn have set up a structure, norms, a regular schedule, well-practiced procedures, and needed materials so that kids quickly grow into responsible use of this special time and space. And though Pat has retired, the principal, with Pat's help, has found a replacement teacher with the skills and commitment to keep the program going strong. Without sustainability, this would become just another bright but passing moment in the history of the school. This example shows us that there are important links between contemporary Best Practice ideas and past innovations, but it also reminds us that we still have a lot to learn about how to make things really stick this time around. We don't want the pendulum to just swing back to the same place it was in the past.

▲ ▲ ▲

In recent years, it can often seem as if thoughtful Best Practice teaching has been overshadowed by No Child Left Behind testing, narrowed curriculum, programs that leave few professional decisions to teachers, punitive sanctions on schools, and mandated standards written by people who have either never taught in classrooms or have long forgotten what that's like. Lockstep instruction can take the thinking and responsibility out of teaching and learning alike. The pendulum image of progressive versus command-and-control ideas about education might have left us cynical, but now we might begin to fear something even worse: that the pendulum is permanently stuck on one side of our educational grandfather clock.

Progressive ideas evolve through classroom experience, professional writing, and research, and gain strength and coherence.

Yet when we visit good schools, that's not what we see at all. Yes, there are administrators and teachers with a narrower approach who are very comfortable with a mechanical deliver-and-test view of education. However, good teachers and school leaders simply don't let unproductive ideas get in their way. They look at the Common Core Standards and figure out how they can teach the various reading and writing skills within a classroom workshop setting that provides choice and responsibility for the kids. They look at the standardized tests and recognize that wide reading, deep exploration of content, connection of academic material to kids' own lives, and strong thinking skills will ensure that their kids will do just fine. They avoid the easy blaming of teachers and find ways to connect and collaborate with parents and fellow professionals. They don't ignore the standards or the tests, but understand that the Best Practice teaching and learning in their classrooms will enable the kids to do well and learn the skills they'll need as they progress through school and life. And we see this happening in poor inner-city neighborhoods as well as rich suburbs. Perhaps we're not living with a swinging pendulum of educational practice so much as a sea in which waves crisscross each other, headed in different directions, as we and our students paddle like mad to keep our bearings and stay afloat.

Through all this, however, progressive ideas evolve through classroom experience, professional writing, and research, and as they do they gain strength and coherence, exert more influence on schools, and lead to deeper learning for kids. Best Practice, classroom workshop, interdisciplinary studies—if taught in their genuine forms, adaptable to the needs of the students—reflect a set of educational ideas rooted in an ever-deepening understanding of how human beings learn, and so they continue to spread. As a courageous Chicago teacher, Joe Perlstein, once stated and we always remind ourselves:

> It's very difficult to change. It takes a lot out of a person. However, you don't mind if there's a payback, if you feel that the children are growing, that they appreciate what is going on. If you see a light at the end of the tunnel, then you say to yourself, "Don't stop now. Keep pushing, keep pressing." Because it will all be worth it in the end.

Works Cited

Allington, Richard. 2011. *What Really Matters for Struggling Readers: Designing Research-Based Programs* (3rd edition). New York: Addison Wesley.

Biancarosa, Gina, and Catherine Snow. 2004. *Reading Next: A Vision for Action and Research in Middle and High School Literacy* (2nd edition). New York: Carnegie Corporation.

Braunger, Jane, and Jan Lewis. 2005. *Building a Knowledge Base in Reading* (2nd edition). Newark, DE: International Reading Association.

Coalition of Essential Schools. 2011. www.essentialschools.org .

Daniels, Harvey, and Steven Zemelman. 2004. *Subjects Matter: Every Teacher's Guide to Content-Area Reading*. Portsmouth, NH: Heinemann.

Darling-Hammond, Linda. 2011. *The Flat World and Education: How America's Commitment to Equity Will Determine Our Future*. New York: Teachers College Press.

Darling-Hammond, Linda, et al. 2008. *Powerful Learning: What We Know About Teaching for Understanding*. San Francisco, CA: Jossey-Bass.

Elmore, Richard C. 2004. *School Reform from the Inside Out: Policy, Practice, and Performance*. Cambridge MA: Harvard Education Press.

Farstrup, Alan, and Jay Samuels, eds. 2002. *What Research Has to Say About Reading Instruction* (3rd edition). Newark, DE: International Reading Association.

Hillocks, George. 1986. *Research on Written Composition*. Urbana, IL: National Council of Teachers of English.

Johnson, David W., Roger T. Johnson, and Edythe Holubec. 1998. *Cooperation in the Classroom* (7th edition). Edina, MN: Interaction Book Company.

Louis, Karen S., Kenneth Leithwood, Kyla Wahlstrom, and Stephen Anderson. 2010. *Investigating the Links to Improved Student Learning*. Minneapolis and Toronto: University of Minnesota and Ontario Institute for Studies in Education.

Neill, Monty. June 18, 2010. A Better Way to Assess Students and Evaluate Schools. *Education Week*.

Sebring, Penny, Elaine Allensworth, Anthony Bryk, John Easton, and Stuart Luppescu. 2006. *The Essential Supports for School Improvement*. Chicago: Consortium on Chicago School Research.

Tunnell, Michael, and James Jacobs. March 1989. Using "Real" Books: Research Findings on Literature-Based Reading Instruction. *Reading Teacher*.

Weaver, Constance. 2002. *Reading Process and Practice* (3rd edition). Portsmouth, NH: Heinemann.

Index

Steven Zemelman

Steven Zemelman has worked in many capacities to promote the sustainability of innovative schools in Chicago. For eight years he directed the Center for City Schools at National-Louis University, and he is a founding director of the Illinois Writing Project. He has spearheaded the start of a number of innovative small high schools in the city. His experiences and research in these areas led to his Heinemann book *13 Steps to Teacher Empowerment*, coauthored with Harry Ross. Steve's recent work focuses on meaningful strategies for whole-school change and sustainability of innovative programs, as well as on helping teachers take a wider role in their school communities. He provides talks, workshops, and consulting on these issues across the country.

Steve has been a frequent collaborator with Harvey "Smokey" Daniels. They have coauthored six books and videos with Heinemann. Their books are filled with practical strategies for making writing, reading, the content areas, and, indeed, the life of a school itself into a deeper and richer learning experience for kids. Zemelman and Daniels are known for immediately useful teaching strategies that range from brief, easy-to-use reflections that help students learn right in class to bigger public-writing projects that can make school truly memorable for kids and teachers alike.

Teacher Professional Books

* *13 Steps to Teacher Empowerment: Taking a More Active Role in Your School Community* (Heinemann, 2009)
* *Content-Area Writing: Every Teacher's Guide* (Heinemann, 2007)
* *Subjects Matter: Every Teacher's Guide to Content-Area Reading* (Heinemann, 2004)
* *Rethinking High School: Best Practice in Teaching, Learning, and Leadership* (Heinemann, 2000)
* *Rethinking High School Video: Best Practice in Action* (Heinemann, 1999)
* *History Comes Home: Family Stories Across the Curriculum* (Stenhouse, 1999)
* *A Community of Writers: Teaching Writing in the Junior and Senior High School* (Heinemann, 1988)
* *A Writing Project: Training Teachers of Composition from Kindergarten to College* (Heinemann, 1985)

Harvey "Smokey" Daniels

Harvey "Smokey" Daniels has been a city and suburban classroom teacher and a college professor, and he now works as a national consultant and author on literacy education. In language arts, Smokey is known for his pioneering work on student book clubs, as recounted in *Literature Circles* and *Mini-lessons for Literature Circles*. He is also known for helping teachers across content areas find the clarity and confidence they need to teach literacy in any subject area, and his bestselling titles on the topic include: *Comprehension & Collaboration*, *Subjects Matter*, and *Content-Area Writing*.

Smokey works with elementary and secondary teachers throughout the United States, Canada, and Europe, offering demonstration lessons, workshops, and consulting with a special focus on creating, sustaining, and renewing student-centered inquiries and discussions of all kinds. Smokey shows colleagues how to simultaneously build students' thinking strategies, balance their reading diets, and strengthen the social skills they need to become genuine lifelong readers.

Teacher Professional Books

- *Texts and Lessons for Content-Area Reading: With More Than 75 Articles from The New York Times, Rolling Stone, The Washington Post, Car and Driver, Chicago Tribune, and Many More* (Heinemann, 2011)
- *Comprehension Going Forward: Where We Are and What's Next* (Heinemann, 2011)
- *Comprehension & Collaboration: Inquiry Circles in Action* (Heinemann, 2009)
- *Inquiry Circles in Elementary Classrooms* DVD (Heinemann, 2009)
- *Inquiry Circles in Middle and High School Classrooms* DVD (Heinemann, 2009)
- *Content-Area Writing: Every Teacher's Guide* (Heinemann, 2007)
- *Teaching the Best Practice Way: Methods That Matter, K–12* (Stenhouse, 2005)
- *Subjects Matter: Every Teacher's Guide to Content-Area Reading* (Heinemann, 2004)
- *Mini-Lessons for Literature Circles* (Heinemann, 2004)
- *Literature Circles: Voice and Choice in Book Clubs and Reading Groups* (Stenhouse, 2002/1994)
- *Rethinking High School: Best Practice in Teaching, Learning, and Leadership* (Heinemann, 2000)
- *Rethinking High School Video: Best Practice in Action* (Heinemann, 1999)
- *Methods That Matter: Six Structures for Best Practice Classrooms* (Stenhouse, 1998)
- *A Community of Writers: Teaching Writing in the Junior and Senior High School* (Heinemann, 1988)
- *Language Diversity and Writing Instruction* (NCTE, 1986)
- *A Writing Project: Training Teachers of Composition from Kindergarten to College* (Heinemann, 1985)

Professional Development

Harvey "Smokey" Daniels provides on- and off-site professional development through Heinemann Professional Development Services. Visit heinemann.com/PD for more information.

Arthur Hyde

Arthur Hyde is a professor of mathematics education at National-Louis University, where he received its Excellence in Teaching award. Art holds a doctorate in curriculum and instruction from the University of Pennsylvania, where he later was Associate Director of Teacher Preparation. He is widely known for creating highly engaging instruction, based on principles from cognitive psychology, that gets kids deep into problem solving. He developed these classroom innovations while teaching high school mathematics in Philadelphia. Today he continues to work frequently in elementary and middle school classrooms, conducting extensive professional development programs on mathematics and problem solving in Chicago and its surrounding school districts.

Art has created several graduate programs to develop teacher leaders in mathematics and interdisciplinary "conceptual integration." These teachers and Art have conducted professional development activities for school districts throughout the United States.

Teacher Professional Books

- *Understanding Middle School Math: Cool Problems to Get Students Thinking and Connecting* (Heinemann, 2009)
- *Comprehending Math: Adapting Reading Strategies to Teach Mathematics, K–6* (Heinemann, 2006)
- *Mathwise: Teaching Mathematical Thinking and Problem Solving* (Heinemann, 1991)
- *Thinking in Context: Teaching Cognitive Processes across the Elementary School Curriculum* (Longman, 1989)